1986

AN AFRICAN VICTORIAN FEMINIST

Mrs. Casely Hayford at the time of her marriage

AN
AFRICAN
VICTORIAN
FEMINIST

The Life and Times of
Adelaide Smith Casely Hayford
1868–1960

ADELAIDE M. CROMWELL
Afro-American Studies Program
Boston University

FRANK CASS

First published 1986 in Great Britain by
FRANK CASS & CO. LTD.
Gainsborough House, Gainsborough Road,
London, E11 1RS, England

and in the United States of America by
FRANK CASS & CO. LTD.
c/o Biblio Distribution Centre
81 Adams Drive, P.O. Box 327, Totowa, N.J. 07511

British Library Cataloguing in Publication Data

Cromwell, Adelaide M.
   An African Victorian feminist : the life and
   times of Adelaide Smith Casely Hayford 1868–1960.
   1. Hayford, Adelaide Smith Casely
   2. Feminists — Sierra Leone — Biography
   I. Title
   966'.403'0924   DT516.72.H3

   ISBN 0–7146–3226–0

Printed and bound in Great Britain by A. Wheaton &. Co. Ltd. Exeter.

To two friends,
Yvonne M. Simkins of Washington D.C.,
and
Frances Claudia Wright of Freetown, Sierra Leone,
and to my son, also my friend,
Anthony Cromwell Hill.

TABLE OF CONTENTS

LIST OF ILLUSTRATIONS

Mrs. Casely Hayford at the time of her marriage   *frontispiece*

Between pages 64 and 65

Mr. J.E. Casely Hayford

Anne Spilsbury Smith (Mrs. Casely Hayford's mother)

Wedding Party in Freetown around the turn of the century

One of the Smith sisters in London

Between pages 160 and 161

Mrs. Casely Hayford dressed for her speaking tour in the United States

Kathleen Easmon Simango

Gladys Casely Hayford Hunter – as a young girl

Mrs. Casely Hayford and associates in the Moral Rearmament movement, in Freetown

Pupils and Faculty with Mrs. Casely Hayford

Mrs. Casely Hayford participating in a class in physical education at her school in Freetown

Gladys Casely Hayford Hunter as teacher in her mother's school

Mrs. Casely Hayford in later years

The pictures of Anne Spilsbury Smith and Kathleen Easmon Simango are reproduced by permission of *West Africa* magazine.

PREFACE

This version of the life of Adelaide Smith Casely Hayford is largely autobiographical but, while one can honestly express feelings and describe important events in the course of one's own life time, others can better see the setting in which one lived and how one's life impacted on and was affected by others.

Mrs. Casely Hayford's life was not only long but expansive, affecting many persons and many cultures. Therefore, I am indebted to numerous persons in Sierra Leone and in the United States for the knowledge needed to understand and interpret Mrs. Casely Hayford's own story of her life.

Dr. Arthur Porter and the late Dr. M.C.F. Easmon introduced me to Mrs. Casely Hayford and through their writings to the world from which she came.

Many persons in Freetown have given generously of their time and knowledge, none more consistently and patiently than Miss Frances Claudia Wright who provided access to the contemporary society of Freetown, legal research and cordial hospitality. Others without whose assistance I could not have worked were Mrs. Phyllis Renner George-Coker, Mrs. Olivette Stuart Caulker, Mrs. Constance Cummings-John, Mrs. Agnes Smythe Macaulay, Mr. Samuel Collins Hayford, Mrs. Lena Spilsbury Johnson, the Reverend E.J.Y. Harris, Lady Bankole-Jones, the late Mrs. Jenner Wright and the late Mrs. Elizabeth Clinton Dawson.

The late Mr. Archibald Casely Hayford of Ghana permitted me to read and copy many letters exchanged between Mrs. Casely Hayford and his father, her husband. Mrs. Pearl Jones-Quarty, the sister-in-law of Mrs. Archibald Casely Hayford facilitated this contact.

Kobe (Cobina Sydney) Hunter, her grandson, permitted me to read the unpublished collection of his Mother's poetry and to select for inclusion those poems reflecting her feelings towards Mrs. Casely Hayford.*

Mrs. Mary Hayford Edmondson, her niece-in-law, reminisced about life at the Girls Vocational and Industrial School and provided some of the rare photographs still in existence of the school and its pupils.

Dr. Raymond Sarif Easmon and Dr. Davidson Nicol, who knew

---

*See *Memoirs and Poems by Adelaide Casely Hayford and Gladys Casely Hayford*, ed. Lucilda Hunter (Sierra Leone University Press, 1983).

Mrs. Casely Hayford well, kindly read and criticized the manuscript in its entirety.

Parts of the manuscript were read by Dr. Arthur Porter of Freetown, Professor John Willis of Princeton and Miss Margaret Hickey, Public Affairs Editor of *The Ladies Home Journal.*

Mrs. Gloria Dillsworth of the Freetown Public Library, Mrs. Gretchen Walsh, Librarian of the African section of the Mugar Library of Boston University, Dr. Sylvia Lyons Render, Manuscript Division of the Library of Congress, Mrs. Dorothy Cummings of the Museum at Freetown and Mr. Robert A. Hill, Editor of the Marcus Garvey Papers at the University of California were also most helpful in making material known to me and in following up leads I had.

Mr. Brian Willan of the London School of African and Oriental Studies and Dr. Leon P. Spencer of Talledga College, as young scholars pursuing the activities of other Africans who visited the United States at about the same time as Mrs. Casely Hayford, provided additional useful information, as did the Reverend Mr. Anthony Campbell on Nannie Helen Burroughs, Mrs. Casely Hayford's friend and American role model.

Finally, I am indebted to Mrs. Anna Louise McLaughlin for assisting a second generation of the Cromwell family through the troubled waters of biographical writing, and to Mr. Frank Bonitto for the design of the genealogical chart.

INTRODUCTION

Ghana and the University of Legon were particularly exciting places to be in 1959, but I had promised an old friend, Professor Arthur T. Porter, that I would certainly visit Sierra Leone sometime during my stay on the Coast. So, after overcoming numerous bureaucratic interventions which might have interfered with my re-entry into Ghana, I set forth for Freetown – never realizing the rather arduous trip such a short distance would entail at that time or the opportunity I would have of meeting the subject of this book, Mrs. Adelaide Smith Casely Hayford.

After a plane ride, a long lorry ride, and a boat ride, I was met on the quay at Freetown. As an Afro-American with an interest in Africa, I had some familiarity with the Settler country of Liberia which I had visited on my way down the Coast to Ghana; but I really had no knowledge of Sierra Leone or Freetown, its capital.

From the first, I was fascinated by this former British colony. Of course, I had the rare opportunity of being introduced to the country and to some members of the social and intellectual elite by Professor Arthur Porter, a person who was well known, respected, and knowledgeable. But more than that, to me, from an old Philadelphia and Washington family who by this time had spent more than sixteen years among Boston's black elite, there was a pleasant sense of déjà vu – of meeting and getting to know persons of African descent who were at home in the world of the West and who could, if they so desired, look both ways – to roots in Africa or to historical and kinship ties with Europe and Great Britain, in particular. That this group in Sierra Leone had, to some extent, lost the basis of its early status and power by having been challenged by other blacks, was also a phenomenon familiar to me. In a sense, from the very beginning I felt quite at home and had the privilege of making friends with whom I have maintained the closest ties ever since and without whose encouragement and assistance I could not have met, nor could I have written about Adelaide Smith Casely Hayford. On my initial visit, with Professor Porter's assistance, I was able to crowd within a week what on my own would surely have taken weeks, if not months, to learn.

Soon after my arrival, Professor Porter wanted me to visit the Sierra Leone Museum, located prominently across from the famous Cotton Tree in the middle of Freetown and down from Government House, the official residence of the Governor and to meet its founder, Dr. M.C.F.

Easmon. With an introduction from "cousin" Arthur (as in our own South but not in the northern Afro-American communities in the States, everyone in a certain circle seems in some way to be related, and if not, to use kinship terms to express non-kinship familiarity). Dr. Easmon was extremely helpful – although by nature a shy person and already quite along in years, he seemed most gratified to meet me and to show me around "his" museum. Perhaps because of my obvious interest *and* ignorance, or because of my given name, Dr. Easmon suggest to Arthur that I should definitely meet "Aunt Addie" and that he would make the necessry arrangements.

Within a day or two I remember distinctly entering the side door of a large but rather run-down house on Charlotte Street, climbing some stairs and entering a very modestly furnished and not too well lit room to have tea with Mrs. Casely Hayford. Though she was now near the end of her long life and definitely not as strong and vital as she had been, Mrs. Casely Hayford, from the lounge where she then spent most of her days, was a most gracious hostess. She apologized for the frugality of the fare (tea and some simple cookies) and slowly but warmly began our conversation.

Being totally unaware of just who this alert and gracious old lady actually was, other than "Aunt Addie," it took me longer than it might to learn that she had started a school in Freetown and that she had many friends in America whom she had met on two visits to the States seeking funds for her school.

If I had only known then a small portion of what I have learned in doing research for this book, how much I could have asked her! But even so, when she discovered I came from Boston, her eyes brightened as she recalled her visits to that city and inquired of me as to the whereabouts of various friends who regrettably either had died or whom I had never known. I do remember especially her asking of Maude Cuney Hare, of whom I knew but who had died before I came to Boston, and Meta Warrick Fuller who was then still alive, and whom I knew slightly but who was quite a good friend of my aunt. Otelia Cromwell.[1] In some ways than and now, Mrs. Casely Hayford reminded me of Aunt Otelia, whom I always called Aunt Tee.

Pushing back twenty, even thirty years, she seemed to enjoy very much the rare opportunity of sharing her American experiences with a visitor from America. For no doubt related to the inconvenience of reaching Freetown, as has just been described, or the general lack of familiarity of Afro-Americans with Africa, apart from Liberia or just then Ghana, few Afro-Americans would have been to Freetown – indeed even few Americans other than missionaries or traders had. And as it was largely to the world of Afro-Americans that Mrs. Casely Hayford was exposed on her trips to the States, it was Afro-Americans she remembered. But then rather suddenly, perhaps because of courtesy or maybe fatigue from travelling the road back along memory lane, she asked me why I was in Freetown. Anyone who visits Africa has that question posed, often with annoying frequency. It is as though you *must* have a special reason for coming to *Africa*. But I was happy to respond to her enquiry. I explained how long I had been interested in Africa, that I came from a family with interest in and ties to Africa, especially my grandfather, John W. Cromwell; that I was associated with an African Studies Program at Boston University where I had met "Cousin Arthur" and that now I was in Ghana for a term teaching at the university.[2] Mrs. Casely Hayford seemed most interested, perhaps even a little impressed, but certainly interested. However, after my rather long monologue, she looked at me rather sadly and said, "Don't stay here; don't waste your time here, my dear."

That advice, especially as it was unsolicited, struck me at the time as most odd. But I thanked her for it and the tea and made my way from her little sitting room, down the backstairs to the bright sun of a Freetown afternoon. Dr Easmon was with me, though I do not recall that he commented on "Aunt Addie's" advice. But I remembered it. Some weeks later, browsing in the library at the University of Ghana, I came across several articles in a series published in *The West African Review* in 1953 and 1954 written by Mrs Casely Hayford as *Memoirs* of her life. As I read the articles, I began to understand more the woman. My first thought was to edit these articles and include them, if permission were granted, in a larger volume with recollections of some other African women who, in a sense, knew two worlds – the world of tradition or colonial Africa and the world of the West.

Within a year after my visit, she died, and slowly but surely the magnitude and the importance of her life, the world she knew, the contributions she made and the obstacles she had faced forced me to attempt this book. I felt she needed her own statement, not to be beside the lives of less impressive women, but she needed to have even more said about her than she herself had wished or was permitted to say in those articles. [In the course of my research, I fortunately found an early unpublished version of her *Memoirs* which showed clearly that the editors had deleted in the published version much of what she wanted to say.] So, beginning in the early sixties, I began to uncover the more complete story of Adelaide Smith Casely Hayford and to understand better her advice to me.

This book, however, is truly a joint venture; her words in the *Memoirs* and elsewhere, are used whenever possible and the organization of the book is naturally determined by her experiences and the sequence in which they occurred. Autobiography or biography have their limits for research, however. Therefore, it is hoped that my access to letters, published and unpublished, further archival research, interviews with persons who knew her, and a concerned but more detached interpretation will give the reader a greater appreciation of Adelaide Smith Casely Hayford and the world in which she lived.

I

The Creole World of Sierra Leone

Adelaide Smith Casely Hayford (1868–1960) was a special person, belonging to a special category of a special class of people – the Creole elite of Freetown, Sierra Leone. Throughout her long life covering the period from Queen Victoria to Queen Elizabeth, Mrs. Casely Hayford experienced the stimulation and frustrations of change which affected her as a woman and as an African. Like many of her contemporaries, she knew little of Africa other than her own country, Sierra Leone, or more specifically, her home town, Freetown, but she felt quite at home in England, where she was educated and spent most of her formative years, and in other parts of the world where she spent considerable time; in Germany as a young student of music; in the Gold Coast as the bride and young wife of J.E. Casely Hayford, the distinguished West African barrister, and in the United States as a visitor on two separate occasions of more than a year each, seeking guidance and funds for her school.[1] Perhaps more than any other African of her day, maybe even now, she met and came to know well a large number of outstanding and important Afro-Americans from W.E. Du Bois to Paul Robeson, from Maude Cuney Hare to Nannie H. Burroughs and Mrs. Booker T. Washington.[2]

Circumstances placed Mrs. Casely Hayford on the cutting edge of change in Africa. She was part of a society which, though its ties with the West are manifestly stronger and more complex than any other part of Africa, is, paradoxically, less well known than other parts of English-speaking Africa – except probably the Gambia, before the publication of *Roots*!

Freetown, the capital of Sierra Leone, was settled as the result of humanitarian concerns of Englishmen over the plight of Africans living abroad or recently captured. Sierra Leone covers an area of roughly 27,925 square miles, about the size of South Carolina, and is situated on the Atlantic Coast on the lower part of the big horn of Africa, bordered by Guinea on the north and east and Liberia on the south.

In 1786

the humanity of some gentlemen was excited towards the dis-
tressed Blacks (in London) and a Committee was formed, known
as the 'Committee for the Black Poor' to consider ways and means
to alleviate their suffering ... The Committee accepted the advice
of one Mr. Henry Smeathman (a botanist), who had travelled to
those parts ... and decided to repatriate these Black poor to Africa
and recommended Sierra Leone as the most advantageous place
for the experiment.

Accordingly, in 1786 about 500 or 510 passengers, about 440 male and
female black, and about 60 to 70 white, male and female, embarked in
Portsmouth via Plymouth for Freetown in the transports *Belisarius,
Atlantic,* and *Vernon* – conveyed by HMS *Nautilus.* Enroute some died,
some were discharged, and some ran away, but finally 411 (black and
white, males and females) sailed from Plymouth for West Africa. On
May 9, 1787, the 377 who had survived the voyage arrived in Freetown
harbor.[3]

Granville Sharp was the guiding force behind this venture and the
Committee. A grant of land, twenty miles square, was obtained for the
use of the Settlers from King Tom, a neighboring chief. The harbor was
named St George's Bay and the settlement, Granville Town. Inhospit-
able weather resulting in considerable mortality coupled with the defection of some of the better trained immigrants to seek positions as clerks
for the slave merchants in the adjacent regions reduced considerably the
size of the settlement. Sharp then decided to send more Settlers,
particularly whites, who he mistakenly believed would exhibit more
regularity and industry than the blacks. In 1788 the ship *Myro*, chartered
by Sharp, duly arrived in St George's Bay with 39 passengers, the
majority of whom were white. They, too, in time defected.

In November 1789, a neighboring chief, King Jimmy, attacked and
burned the settlement to the ground. The Settlers, now without homes
or property, spread throughout the area. Meanwhile, back in England in
an effort to put the venture on a sounder footing and to foster an
"honourable trade" with West Africa, the St George's Bay Company
was formed in 1790. Among its Directors were, of course, Granville
Sharp, as well as the well-known British abolitionists William Wilberforce, Thomas Clarkson, and Henry Thornton. In 1791 the Company
was transformed into the financially more secure and therefore more
powerful Sierra Leone Company. The Sierra Leone Company altered
somewhat the nature of the experiment by emphasizing trade more than
humanitarianism as its raison d'être and seeking whites rather than

blacks as possible Settlers. In 1791, thefore, they sent 119 whites to Sierra Leone.

Slavery and the slave trade had repercussions in the New World which ultimately affected the growth and character of the Sierra Leone experiment. Hundreds of slaves, or servants, as they often euphemistically were called, belonging to Loyalist masters, and free black men with Loyalist sympathies had gone to Canada, especially to Nova Scotia, at the time of the American Revolution. The free men fought as soldiers in the Black Pioneer Corps or were buglers and musicians in nearly every Loyalist corps. They were settled as disbanded soldiers in Halifax and other parts of the province.[4] But not surprisingly these Loyalist Blacks, as they were called, soon felt the familiar hand of discrimination. They were not given land as promised, or such land as they were given was inferior, thus forcing them to become farm laborers rather than free and independent farmers.

When word of the Sierra Leone experiment reached the ears of these black Loyalists they sent one of their number, Thomas Peters, to London to protest their position. Peters contacted Sharp and Henry Thornton who offered to settle them in Sierra Leone. "After the Company secured the promise of support from the British government, Peters returned (to Nova Scotia) with plans to organize the expedition to Sierra Leone ... In spite of the minimal cooperation of the Nova Scotia government, almost 1,200 free Negroes left Nova Scotia for Sierra Leone in fifteen vessels on January 1792."[5] Sixty-five died on the voyage and the rest arrived at intervals from February 28 to March 9, 1792.

"The Nova Scotian settlers, as this second important group has been called in subsequent history, founded a new settlement at the site of the original Granville Town, and named it Freetown."

Meanwhile in Jamaica in 1800 about 500 slaves had revolted against their British masters and sought refuge in the beautiful but impregnable Blue Mountains of that island. Representing a continuous threat to the stability of the island, as a slavocracy that is, they were tricked into leaving their mountain hideaways, captured, sent first to Nova Scotia and then to Sierra Leone. These Jamaican blacks were called Maroons, a name of uncertain derivation meaning runaway slaves, originally applied to the slaves of the Spanish, who revolted in 1655 when the English took over the island. About 550 of these Maroons were sent to Sierra Leone.

After the passage in 1807 of the Slave Trade Act in England, a court of adjudicature, the Vice-Admiralty Court, was established in Sierra Leone in 1809 to judge the fate of "all captured slaves brought in as prize."[6] Later, Courts of Mixed Commission were established there for the trial of slavers and the liberation of their slaves. Having been rescued before actually being sent to the New World, these slaves were called Liberated Africans. But the Nova Scotians and Maroons with whom they were in the early days often in conflict, called them 'cruits,' 'nata' or 'Willyfossniggers,' the latter a reminder that *their* freedom had been secured *for* them by the efforts of Wilberforce and not by themselves. 'Cruit' was the lingua franca term for recruit, newcomer, or greenhorn; 'nata' was probably taken from the Portuguese word for cream in reference to the newcomers' creamlike separation from the rest of Sierra Leone society.[7]

From 1791 to 1807 the Sierra Leone Company governed Freetown. In April, 1807 a new company was formed, the African Institution, which had as its purpose to promote the civilization of Africa and to monitor the administration of the colony as an experiment in freedom. The African Institution assisted not only in advising the government – which from January 1, 1808 had officially been the British government and not the Sierra Leone Company – on policy but in the selection of European personnel for service in the administration of the colony.

From its earliest days and differentiating it from almost all of conquered Africa, the goal of the settlement of Sierra Leone was to survive as an example of civilization, westernization, and Christianity – all, at the time, being seen as mutually interrelated. Theoretically, all of the persons associated with the founding and early history of Sierra Leone accepted this goal and these values. For while there were differences in experience and status among the Black Poor, Nova Scotians, and Maroons, they had all been exposed to that version of civilization, westernization, and Christianity espoused by the English and were, in addition, now being settled in a society controlled by Englishmen – supposedly humanitarian Englishmen, at that.

There were, however, from the early 1800s members of Freetown society for whom the values of civilization, westernization, and Christianity were seen less favorably – often rejected but more likely unknown – the Liberated Africans. These Africans prior to their capture and subsequent release had never been exposed to western values. Between 1809 and 1863 about 26,253 were settled in Sierra Leone. They arrived as they were when they were captured – as Ibo, Yoruba, Nupe, etc. – all soon given appropriate designation by other members of the society – Aku for Yoruba, Iboe for other Nigerians, Akan for those from the Congo to the Cameroons, Popo for those from Dahomey, Tagba from Nupe, and Calabar for Kalabari. "These groups tended to live together in the villages choosing their own headmen, whom they then obeyed implicitly, to keep order and settle disputes."[8] And there were, in addition, those Africans indigenous to the area who in the course of striking bargains for sale of land with the representatives of the Sierra Leone Company had in no way agreed as a part of the deal to the acceptance of their values.

That these very diverse groups and others who much later joined them such as Syrians and Lebanese traders – all so different in culture, status and power – learned to live together gives Sierra Leone its unique position as an African society. English power and western values represented by the English themselves were never seriously disputed. But the successful administration of the colony required the acceptance of a cultural modus vivendi between English and African, which, while perhaps more fragile than it appeared, was still sufficiently strong to maintain an on-going society relatively free of conflict or tension.

There were several reasons for this. For small as it was, Sierra Leone had the advantage of two channels of cultural escape or, if necessary, cultural reinforcement. Settlers could visit England periodically or go down the Coast to associate with others like themselves, whether they be Europeanized elite or tribal people. Liberated Africans seemed to seek ties in Nigeria while the Creole elite sought their counterparts in the Gold Coast, the Gambia, as well as in Nigeria.

The society which developed from among these ethnically diverse African inhabitants was called Creole. This term, as Porter suggests, has meant many different things in different societies; even in Freetown its meaning has varied according to circumstances, period of history, the perspective of the speaker and what was, in fact, meant or implied.[9] For our purposes, however, to understand the life and personality of Mrs. Casely Hayford and the environment in which she lived, the term Creole implies a cultural mixture of Settler, English and African and the acceptance of a public life style, at least, which is represented by England and things English. That this was not always possible because of changes in the attitudes of the English toward the Creoles or the search for a true African identity on the part of the Creoles does not alter the basic importance of the English life style to Sierra Leone society and the environment in which Mrs. Casely Hayford lived for most of her life. And as this was a life style so different from that in many other parts of Africa and indeed beyond the imagination of most westerners when they think of Africa, it becomes extremely important to comprehend if one wants to know and understand, at least, the more successful or affluent Creoles.

Should a scholar wish to know Sierra Leone or Freetown historically as seen by Africans, he or she must rely exclusively on Horton, Sibthorpe, Blyden, Easmon, Porter, Cox-George, and others, and such

interesting newspapers as the *Sierra Leone Weekly News* edited by the
May family. Fortunately for this book, the *Sierra Leone Weekly News* gave
some considerable coverage to the activities of Mrs. Casely Hayford,
none of which has ever before been incorporated into a larger view of life
among a particular group of Creoles in Sierra Leone.

Spitzer's volume, *The Creoles of Sierra Leone, Responses to Colonialism,
1870 to 1945* (at times more useful than Porter's *Creoledom, A Study of
Development of Freetown Society,* perhaps because to Spitzer, as an out-
sider, even the ordinary seems unusual) gives the uninformed a feeling
for the life style of the world of Adelaide Casely Hayford. Coincidentally, the period he covers, from 1870 to 1945, is almost identical to
her life span, certainly her active life span. Until the recent publication
of *The Politics of Elite Culture, Explorations in the Dramaturgy of Power in
Modern Africa* by Abner Cohen, Porter's work was the only sociological
analysis of Creole culture, and it is on Porter's analysis and interpretation rather than on the more detailed treatment of Spitzer and especially
of Fyfe that this interpretation of Mrs. Casely Hayford's life is given.
Fyfe's *A History of Sierra Leone,* a veritable encyclopedia, is an unbeliev-
ably rich source of information on people and events in Freetown.
Peterson's *A Province of Freedom, A History of Sierra Leone, 1787–1870*
completes one's research by the inclusion of some valuable photographs
and case histories. Aaron Belisarius Cosmo Sibthorpe wrote one of the
earliest and most intriguing books about Sierra Leone, *The History of
Sierra Leone.* Fyfe described it as remarkable: written initially without
access to official records, Sibthorpe continued his research, brought out
subsequent editions, and died in 1916 "an unrecognized, talented
eccentric whose *History* and *Geography* had shown that in 1868 the
Creoles were an articulate, distinctive people, proud of their achieve-
ments and their country."[10]

As one of the few Africans – the only African woman, so far as I know
to write of her experiences in this society, Mrs. Casely Hayford was of
tremendous importance as an example but also as a source of authentic
information. For I suppose one should not be too surprised to find that
few educated Africans, in fact, are even quoted as sources of information about their own societies and that not once, never – not in Fyfe, not
in Porter, not in Peterson, not in Spitzer, not in Skinner and Harrell-
Bond – nowhere are the words and observations of this remarkable
woman, who lived the life, who knew the people, ever quoted! Fyfe in his
"Introduction" does mention an indebtedness to her for "family
reminiscences"; yet nowhere in the body of the book itself is her name
mentioned nor is credit attributed to her – not even in the Index! That
this must be a glaring omission is verified by the description Sir George

Beresford-Stooke wrote as a foreword to Mrs Casely Hayford's *Memoirs*:

> Apart from her personal charm, her wonderful vitality and vivacity and the aristocracy of her intellect, Adelaide Casely Hayford constitutes in her person a link between not two but several generations from Queen Victoria to Queen Elizabeth and also a link between Europe and Africa, between the best of Africa and the best of European culture...

Freetown was started as an experiment in freedom and equality between the races. The first Settlers expected to be active and equal partners in the administration of the colony. Initially, the colony was supervised by a largely self-administered group which organized itself in the Anglo-Saxon precept hundreths – that is, every hundredth household was represented by one individual who worked with the company on colony affairs. The expectation that the mere common badge of color or even circumstances of desperation under the enlightened rule of persons far away, unfamiliar with the area and in many ways quite unlike the Settlers themselves, could have created then or now, for that matter, out of such culturally diverse groups, a strong and viable society seems extraordinarily naive.

And from the first there were problems. The Nova Scotians, bringing with them not only the experience of freedom but also some organizational expertise, were soon in conflict among themselves and with the remnants of the Settlers who had come from England. Their uneasy association was quickly threatened by the coming of the Maroons and in less than a decade of the Liberated Africans.

After 1 January 1818, the British government assumed official responsibility for the area and Freetown became a Crown colony. From 1818 to 1898, when the area of the Crown was enlarged to include the Protectorate of the "Tribal people," there were attempts at consolidation and evidence of fragmentation between the Settlers and the tribal people and between the varying groups of Africans, Settlers and tribal people alike and the Crown.[11] The situation was exacerbated, according to Porter, by a lack of consistent administrative policy after the coming of the Liberated Africans. From Clarkson in 1792 to Cardew in 1896, there were 65 governors, several serving two, or even three terms, and the policy of governing varied with each new governor. Prior to the establishment of the Protectorate, they seemed to vary considerably in their preferences for involving Europeans, Settlers and Liberated Africans in administrative decisions. After the Protectorate the same was true of Creoles, Protectorate people or Europeans. This vacillation did little to establish stability or to strengthen belief in the integrity of the British.

In spite of the absence of firm and consistent administrative policies, the society continued to facilitate inter-racial contacts, encourage education for its citizens and foster opportunities in trade, all of which were responsible for the emergence of the Creoles as a class. The Creoles, originally, saw themselves as Black Englishmen, preferably but not necessarily Christian (Anglican or Methodist), disdainful of super-stition, abhorrent of slavery, Victorian in their morality, and grateful to British philanthropy for freeing their ancestors from slavery, for educat-ing them and placing them in what they believed to be the vanguard of Black people on the continent of Africa. To them, England was their second home, often in fact, always in feeling.

There seems to have been little contact between the settlers and the Liberated Africans until around 1830, when each group, supported by its own value system, pursued its own means of survival. The pressure to survive and achieve was probably especially great among the Liberated Africans who suddenly found themselves placed in a totally unfamiliar environment. But they were industrious and probably as a result of the discrimination against them by the Nova Scotians and the Maroons, some decided to return to Nigeria on boats they themselves had purchased.[12] This feeling of discrimination was certainly not shared by all of the successful Liberated Africans for most of them acquired the necessities for acceptance into the class of the social elite. They acquired wealth through trade and began to send their children, parti-cularly their sons, to England for an education.

Sibthorpe gives the early 1820s as the Golden Age of the Nova Scotians, but so successful were the Liberated Africans in their pursuit of power and status that by 1840 there was dislike, jealousy and envy on the part of the Nova Scotians for them. By this time, Sibthorpe recorded the growth of a frivolous life style on the part of the Nova Scotians and prophesied that the future of the colony lay with the descendants of these industrious and enterprising Liberated Africans because, he felt, the settlers were in the last stages of decay.[13]

There is little doubt that Creole society or Settler society was indeed strengthened, if not rescued, by the infiltration of the talent and drive of the Liberated Africans. Because of their influence and presence after 1870, it was easy to observe a new life and vitality among the Creoles, and the formation of a real elite. Perhaps for a thirty-year period beginning in the 1860s and continuing until the turn of the century, Freetown could legitimately be called "The Athens of West Africa". The divisions among the various non-indigenous groups had been minimized and there was now one identifiable entity, which Porter calls the Creole social elite, among whom were some extremely successful persons. These men were successful in business and increasingly in the professions, for which they were educated either at Fourah Bay College in Freetown, or in England, or on the continent, or in all three places. Their wives might also have been educated in England or at the secondary level in Freetown.

These men and their families lived within a few blocks of each other in downtown Freetown on streets well laid out in rectangular patterns with such English names as Rawdon, Gloucester, Charlotte and Trelawny in houses described as "built entirely of stone, filled with fine European furniture and financed from their own large mercantile profits."[14] Syble Boyle's house on Trelawny Street, for example, "had pedimented windows, iron-work balconies, a pillared upstairs drawing room with a bust of Queen Victoria and a large gilt mirror over the fireplace."[15] Boyle, incidentally, was an Aku recaptive, a successful merchant and a member of the Legislative Council. Fyfe noted that Dr. Robert Smith, a half brother of Adelaide Casely Hayford, also lived in a home large enough to hold a ball and serve a supper for sixty guests.

Culturally, this Creole elite enjoyed the same activities one would find in Britain – cricket matches, choral and dramatic societies, mutual interest social clubs and even a circulating library. "A Sierra Leone Club was founded, modeled on a London club, with premises in Howe Street, its members drawn from senior officials, business and professional men, Creole and European."[16] Some wealthy Creoles joined the Royal Colonial Institute in London and mixed there on an equal basis with the other members. The Good Templars, an English Temperance Benevolent Association, started a lodge in Freetown in 1876 which continued intermittently over several decades.

Freetown as a place was in some ways quite impressive to the visitor unprepared for the kind of cultural life there. Aside from the government buildings, churches, schools and residences of the affluent citizens, Fourah Bay College, founded in 1827 by the Church Missionary Society, was affiliated after 1896 with Durham University, thereby becoming the first institution in West Africa to offer a complete university education. St. George's Cathedral, built in 1828 as St. George's Church, had its first bishop in 1853 and is described by Fashole-Luke as "that bastion of Creoledom."[17] Wilberforce Memorial Hall, whose foundation was laid in 1864 at the corner of Gloucester and Water streets, after considerable difficulties in amassing the necessary funding, was opened on 29 June, 1887, celebrating both the centenary of the first settlement of the colony and Queen Victoria's Golden Jubilee![18]

Wilberforce Hall served as a center for public activities, balls, dramatic events, lectures and concerts. There were meeting rooms and a reading room with magazines and newspapers to which one could subscribe for 7 shillings, 6 pence per year. Freetown had hotels, such as the West African Hotel and Porter's Royal Hotel, both of which served European cuisine and, though African owned, were under European management.

Not surprisingly, for a colony which put emphasis on education and general literacy, there was a vigorous local press in Freetown. *The New Era* published in 1855 by William Drape, an Afro-West Indian, was the first newspaper owned by a private individual. It was openly critical of the government. *The Sierra Leone Weekly Times and The West African Record* was first published in 1862 by Alexander Corbett Harleston, a customs official of Afro-American and Nova Scotian descent. The paper was edited by the Reverend Edward Jones, an Afro-American, first black graduate of Amherst College, who came to Freetown in 1831 from Charleston, South Carolina as a schoolmaster. Jones had been ordained in the Episcopal Church in the United States, and after the new building for the Fourah Bay Institution was opened in 1848, he became its first principal. There were, in all, twelve well-produced, clearly printed and coherently written newspapers which appeared in Freetown in the 1880s.[19] Harleston's paper was the last stand of the Settlers against the mobility of the Liberated Africans. Only the *Sierra Leone Weekly News*, founded in 1884 by the Reverend Joseph Claudius May assisted by Edward Blyden, survived the decade.[20] It was edited by May's brother, Cornelius, who had learned printing and journalism during a seven-year stay in England.

A further testament to the literary interest of some member of the Creole society of the day was the bookstore started by Moses and Thomas John Sawyerr as a stationer's shop on Rawdon Street in 1856. The Sawyerrs sold school supplies to the missionaries and took orders for English periodicals. Later the shop was moved to Water Street and offered a "wide range of books and sheet music for sale." Among the musical pieces sold were "Long Live the Prince of Wales," "Boosey's Twelve Christmas Carols and Hymns," "Ehren on the Rhine," and "D'You Know (I don't like London)," and such books as Boswell's *Life of Johnson, Ball Room Guide, English Journalism and The Men Who Have Made It, Etiquette or The Perfect Lady, England and the English, The Queen's Necklace,* and *Uncle Remus!*[21]

With the new constitution of 1863, a greater participation in government was again assured the Creoles. The first two unofficial members named to the Legislative Council, elected by the mercantile community,

were John Ezzidio, by then an old man, and Charles Heddle. Ezzidio
was described by Peterson as being the most distinguished of the
Liberated Africans of Nupe descent from Nigeria. Liberated by the
Mixed Commission Court, Ezzidio had been apprenticed to a French
shopkeeper in Freetown and after his death had worked for two other
European concerns. At an early age, however, he opened his own shop
and by 1839 had begun to acquire considerable property. In 1841
Ezzidio bought a house on George Street, opposite the Cathedral,
where he resided and carried on business for the rest of his life.
Unquestionably, he was one of the leading merchants of his day in
Freetown.[22] Charles Heddle was the son of an Arkadian army doctor and
an African mother. Although born in Africa, Heddle, Fyfe believes, may
have been educated in Britain. In any case, he first started business in
the Gambia in 1834, and by 1840 was established in Freetown as
Heddle and Co. He was a pioneer in the groundnut trade and by the
mid-1840s he had a half-a-dozen ships of his own carrying groundnuts
and timber to Freetown where he bought Macaulay and Babington's
premises on Water Street, thus succeeding them as the largest merchant
in the colony. Both Ezzidio and Heddle had been politically active and as
the above facts indicate, both were successful businessmen when they
were appointed to the Council. But it is important to note that both men
traced their ancestry to Liberated Africans, not to Nova Scotians or
Maroons.

Professional men, too, came into their own at this time.[23] Some of the
most prominent, described in *The West African Reporter* as the "Upper
Ten", were the men who had been educated in Britain in the two most
prestigious professions – medicine and law. Francis Smith, a half-
brother of Adelaide Smith, was called to the bar in 1871, becoming the
first African, born in Africa, so qualified to practice law there. In 1821
William Henry Savage became the first African to get legal qualifications, but he was born in England. Savage built up "a practice in the
Court of Recorder and in the Mixed Commission Court." Samuel
Lewis, whose ancestors were also Liberated Africans, was called to the
bar one year after Smith and became the most distinguished barrister of
his day. Christian Cole, grandson of an Ibo recaptive, became the first
African B.A. (Oxon, 1876).

Nova Scotians and Liberated Africans were also among the pioneers
in the medical profession. With the publication in 1858 of the first
Medical Register for the Colonial Service, there were three Sierra
Leoneans: William Broughton Davies, M.D. (St Andrews, 1858), a
Yoruba, born in Wellington and married to Mary Smith, a half-sister of
Adelaide Smith; James Africanus Beale Horton, M.D. (Edinburgh,

1859); and Thomas Hamilton Spilsbury (MRCS Eng. 1865), an uncle of Adelaide Smith[24] and the first African head of a Medical Department in British West Africa. A few years later, Robert Smith (MRCS Eng. 1865; FRCS Edinburgh, 1871) also qualified.

Although there was an established church in the colony and having a Cathedral gave special status to its Creole communicants, religion per se did not seem to be a divisive factor. Many important Creoles were members of denominations other than the Anglican Church – especially Methodists – and some were Roman Catholic. Also while the differences between Christians and Muslims were acknowledged, there seems to have been little overt conflict between these two religious groups within the Creole elite during this period.

As in all societies, marriage and funerals were important social occasions – times for kinship ties and affluent status to be most obviously displayed. There was within this group considerable inter-marriage with Africans of similar taste and life-style down the Coast, as illustrated by the marriage of Adelaide Smith and Joseph Ephraim Casely Hayford. There was also much intermarriage between the previously separated groups of citizens, Nova-Scotian, Maroons and Liberated Africans as well as between families of the European and Creole business communities.[25]

Porter refers to the period of the 1870s as the apogée of Creole ascendancy. But perhaps the most unfortunate consequence of the economic, political and social control we call colonialism, here exercised by the British, was the cultural, psychological, and social dependency it created. Yet evidence suggests that for these Creoles at least until the 1890s there continued to be more or less willing acceptance of British values giving a richness and vibrance to their life and culture which would have gladdened the hearts of the founders. This was their Golden Age, and so it might have continued, if not indefinitely, for some considerable time, perhaps until the First World War, had not some other changes occurred. Both of these changes took place under the administration of Colonel Frederic Cardew, a former soldier in the Zulu Wars who came to the colony in 1894.

Putting the highest priority on transforming the area outside of the colony itself, then ruled technically by sovereign chiefs, into a Protectorate directly under the Crown, Cardew sought tax revenue to cover the cost of administering the Protectorate. This decision, made with little or no consultation, resulted in what is known as the Hut Tax War during which many Europeans (especially missionaries) and Creoles were killed by Africans under the leadership of the famous Bai Bureh, chief of the Kebalai people. Ironically, Cardew felt that the Creoles by inciting the Africans not to pay the tax and by fomenting disloyalty in the press were, in fact, more supportive of the "native peoples" than of the government. Therefore, he set about diminishing the administrative authority of the Creoles. He asked that every European Head of a Department have a European, not a Creole, Assistant.[26] Governor Hennessey had in the early 1870s at the peak of Creole ascendancy and florescence requested just the opposite – that every European Head of Department have a Creole Assistant!

The consequences of Cardew's pronouncement were far reaching. In the first instance, by making a reality of the inclusion of the Protectorate into the government, Cardew began to pay more attention to people from the Protectorate, he gave them more privileges and thus diminished the influence and importance of the Creoles. And by providing more positions for Europeans to fill in the colony, Cardew encouraged the growth again of the European population. Also during this time, British public opinion, fanned by a knowledge of low economic productivity and the rising costs of maintaining so unhealthy a colony, as reported in the press by writers like Richard Burton and Harry Johnson,[26a] began to reassess the wisdom of their policies and reappraised the value to them of the leadership of the Creoles. If the colony were to succeed, so the thinking went, the position of the native people must be elevated above that of the Settlers, and trade and business must be placed in the hands of non-Africans, preferably Europeans – thus weakening the position of the Creoles. Hence, a further reason for the European population to increase.

Anticipated or not, even under the most favorable of colonial settings, the growth of the European population was bound to change the character of race relations within the colony. A larger European community inevitably meant more European wives and sometimes children and the possibility of socializing exclusively among themselves, thus having a social life increasingly segregated by color. For the reasons already explained, this was something that had not until that time occurred in Freetown.

To encourage Europeans to come to Sierra Leone and to stay healthy there, something had to be done to improve the sanitary conditions of the colony. The history of the colony had been marked by the frequent occurence of one deadly epidemic after another, taking its toll on the lives of all the citizens, European and African, from all levels of society. The short tenure of governors and the poor health of their families all reflected these facts. In any case, after a disastrous yellow fever epidemic in 1884 in which twenty Europeans, including the colonial surgeon, had died, and which had been described as due to lack of sanitation, a special investigative team from England indicated that the conditions in the colony for Europeans could only be improved by implementing a policy of sanitary segregation – that is, by settling all the Europeans on a plateau about 750 feet above the town.[27]

Prior to this time, most of the Europeans had lived in close proximity to the Creoles in houses which they usually rented from Creoles. But in 1904, as a result of Cardew's policy toward Europeans and the recommendations of the health report, twenty houses were built for Europeans on a plateau, quite a distance from the town. About the same time, plans were made to lay a railroad from Freetown to this new area, now referred to as Hill Station. While it can be verified that initially there was no racial or segregationalist intent in the setting up of Hill Station (even the Creoles in the beginning saw it as a necessary sanitary precaution), its existence did, in fact, further separate Creoles from the English and perhaps made it easier to do what the changing character and attitudes of the Europeans would have preferred.

The period from the 1880s to the 1890s saw the emergence of racial cleavages that were to mark this society until independence and make people like Mrs Casely Hayford more pessimistic over its future. While life continued to flourish, other changes were evident. Syrians, as potentially keen competitors in the trade previously monopolized by Creoles, began to arrive in the colony in the late 1880s and sparked a feeling of hostility towards them which continued through independence in the 1960s. Increasingly also during this period, educated Creoles felt they were being discriminated against in civil service appointments, promotions and salaries, and especially in such important fields as the medical service. All of these changes were, in a sense, a spin-off of Cardew's administrative policies.

The Creoles did not take these changes passively. Faced with a sense of British rejection (seen by some as a result of their own weaknesses) and with the familiarity some had with Africans outside the colony, some Creoles reacted by seeking an identity different from that of being "Black Englishmen." Edward W. Blyden, the brilliant charismatic intellectual who first came to Freetown in 1865 as the Liberian Secretary of State and again in 1870 as a private citizen, brought an international focus to the Creoles' crisis in identity. Blyden espoused a new and psychologically helpful philosophy for the Creole elite. He stressed the importance of the Negro personality, the need to develop Negro qualities through the church, school, farm, and workshop.[28]

Blyden also stressed the importance of indigenous African institutions – such as Islam – to Africans including Creoles. Influenced by him and the reality around them, some Creoles did, in fact, attempt to cast away any vestiges of British cultural imperialism. In 1881 they started a Dress Reform Society to encourage the wearing of African-style dress; they gave themselves African names; they became interested in African rather than European history, albeit the history of Roman and Egyptian Africa – not West Africa; they developed a greater appreciation for and pride in their own language – Krio. Of course, reaction to British racism as it affected life in the colonies was not always an acceptance of Blyden's philosophy, the search for a new identity. Some Creoles in this period sought an even greater identification with England and things western, including the inevitability of and preference for intermarriage between Africans and Europeans.[29]

In sum, from 1900 on Freetown was a culturally fragmented society – with some of its members looking backwards towards remembered but now lost status and equality; others, more and more affected by the reality of the changes around them, now seeking new values and life styles to bring them closer to Africa and things African. Political representation had increased but it was far from a state of equality; economic power had certainly been eroded and institutions so vibrant and necessary in the past now seemed less and less relevant. Creoles came to realize that the government was becoming utterly estranged from them and they saw a hypocrisy in a government which supposedly encouraged education but spurned the educated. By 1912 a revolution in public service had occurred, for while in 1892 Creoles had 18 of the 40 senior posts, by 1919, of the 92 senior posts, Creoles held only 15, five of which were abolished within the next five years as their holders retired.[30]

At this time, two influential persons whose values and life style had been rallying points for differing models of accommodation died. Sir Samuel Lewis, distinguished barrister, first African to be knighted, died in 1903. Edward Blyden died in 1912. The First World War affected Freetown as it did many other colonial possessions – there was a slowly rising sense of discontent among more than the intellectual few; there was an acceleration in the feelings of hostility towards outsiders, such as the Syrians, whose national allegiances were being questioned, and there were the societal disorders such as the influenza epidemic in 1918 when 1,000 civilians, both African and European, died between 23 August and 18 September. Finally, there was the general state of famine which affected the colony by the middle of 1919.[31] Such was the social and cultural disarray that for some there was no longer any reason to believe in the past and no clear guidelines for the future.

Other colonies along the Coast were undergoing similar difficulties, but none had the problem of an elite class so culturally bound to a European power and so economically and politically weak and culturally

disoriented. The educated and advantaged elite down the Coast reacted
to their changed situation by taking political action, organizing in 1920
The National Congress of British West Africa. At the instigation of two
men from the Gold Coast, T. Hutton Mills and J.E. Casely Hayford, the
first conference of the Congress was convened in 1920 in the Gold
Coast. And early in 1923 a second session met in Freetown with Mr. J.E.
Casely Hayford in the chair (Mrs. Casely Hayford was out of the country
at the time). Two subsequent sessions were held – one in the Gambia
and the other in Lagos. The conference lost its momentum after the
death of Casely Hayford in 1930. But the desire for greater political
freedom in the colonies, including Sierra Leone, continued.

However, compared to the subsequent dramatic political events in the
Gold Coast and Nigeria, the political and social scene in Sierra Leone
was relatively uneventful. There was the rise in 1938 of the West African
Youth League founded by Mr. I.T.A. Wallace Johnson, a journalist who
had studied at the Peoples' University in Moscow.[32] In the 1940s and
1950s other political groups emerged, and by 1951 a new constitution
was introduced which provided for an elected unofficial African majority and party rule. The Sierra Leone Peoples' Party, under the leadership of Milton Margai and composed of people from the interior who
were largely non-Creoles, emerged as the majority party and was duly
invited to form the government.

By this time no doubt many Creoles and others felt that at long last
they were, as Clarkson had stated at the founding of the colony, "men,
and that no distinction [would] be made between them and the whites."
They saw themselves as descendants of the people "better than any
people in the laboring line of life in England ... for strong sense, quick
apprehension, clear reasoning, gratitude, affection for their wives and
children and friendship and good will for their neighbors."[33]

So the days of Dignity Balls, Philosophical and Literary Societies,
prestigious visits to Government House soirées and the prominence of
such outstanding doctors as Smith, Davies and Easmon and lawyers
such as Sir Samuel Lewis and Francis Smith or business men such as
Heddle or Ezzidio, were over. Mrs. Casely Hayford and others of her
generation saw that society was changing. By the time she returned, after
her years abroad, the seeds for change had already been planted.
Nevertheless, she expected, never forgot and continued to hope that
with some modest alterations the Freetown of the 1870s – the life and
values about which her parents must so often have spoken – would be
recreated. Instead, she found on her return a society, perhaps regretfully
but accurately described in the following passage from Graham
Greene's *The Heart of the Matter*:

One old hand speaking to a newcomer, "I hate the place. I hate the people. I hate the bloody niggers. Mustn't call them that you know ... A man's boy's always alright. He's a real nigger, but these, look at 'em, look at that one with a feather boa down there. They aren't even real niggers. Just West Indians and they rule the Coast. Clerks in the stores, city council magistrates, lawyers – my God. It's all right up in the Protectorate. I haven't anything to say against a real nigger. God made our colours. But these – my God! The Government's afraid of them. The police are afraid of them ... Look down there, look at Scobie (the white police chief). ... He loves 'em so much he sleeps with 'em."[34]

Where had the culture and the gentility and the closeness of England all gone? And why? How does the life of Adelaide Smith Casely Hayford reflect these changes?

II

The Education of Girls in Freetown

To appreciate Adelaide Smith as a person and to understand the importance of what she was trying to do in Freetown, one must look more closely at the role of education as it affected the society and the position of girls and women in particular.

Education in any society is a most effective means of exercising social control, of shaping the citizens as the system wishes them to be. To leave education exclusively in the hands of the government may assure a kind of equality, but at the same time prevents originality and innovation. In a colonial society especially, government-sponsored education reflected and reinforced administrative policy. Colonial authorities were only prepared to offer to the colonies the minimum amount of education necessary to develop the kind of subjects who could function in the system. During the period of colonization, it was easy to correlate educational policy with over-all administrative policy – whether the colonized person was to be the worker, the scholar, or the drone more or less outside the system, could be ascertained from a knowledge of the educational system. In most of the English and French-speaking colonies, there had for some time been the opportunity for the exceptional African to escape the strictures of colonial society and seek further education in Europe or England, often at government expense. In addition, there was always the ambitious and industrious African who struck out on his own to seek the kind of education he wanted – either in a part of Africa other than his home, or in England, or France, but increasingly in the United States. From the earliest days, however, education in Sierra Leone was viewed as the key mechanism for mobility and success in the colony – where initially, at least, everyone was to be equal to everyone else. Settlers were to be educated to become like Englishmen and Liberated Africans were to be educated to become like Settlers. Education in Freetown, unlike in England, was to be available to all, boys and girls alike, theoretically at government expense and the curriculum ostensibly was to be no different from that then in vogue in England.[1]

However, certain pedagogical considerations from the first affected the education available in the colony. The teachers in the Settler population were unable to offer more than rote learning, largely of the Bible, so a preference was soon given to the recruitment of teachers from abroad, thus keeping the control and supervision of education in the hands of the British. Secondly, government support of education was soon not sufficient to meet the needs of the populace so the government sought the assistance of the Church Missionary Society in the starting and maintenance of educational institutions. Other mission groups as well as individuals soon began to do their part to meet the growing need and zeal for education. In fact the existence of a private educational system with or without government subsidy characterized the education available to children in the colony as well as later in the Protectorate. Beyond the issue of financial assistance, there was the question of the kind of education available ... literary or vocational? It was difficult, if the Settlers were indeed to be equal to the Europeans, not to offer, in fact to stress, a classical or liberal education for them – whether or not it was really equal to that of Englishmen or really appropriate for Settlers. And endeavours to introduce industrial or agricultural training met with little success in the colony.

Finally, given the obvious fact that all that was viewed as superior in the colony came from Britain, as soon as they could afford it, first Settlers and then Liberated Africans sent their children to Britain to obtain the education that was not available in the colony, such as law or medicine, or simply to obtain what they believed to be a better education. Both boys and girls were given this opportunity by their parents. For example in 1865 a lady had opened a seminary in Kensington, England, for young American women. Many of the wives of prominent Creoles of the mid- to late 19th century had been educated in England. Christine Horton, the wife of Sir Samuel Lewis, was educated at Catholic schools in England, and the daughter of J.H. Thomas, Laura, was just back from finishing school in Hampstead when she married Councillor Christopher Claudius Nicols in 1896.

The problem of education was always seen as affecting both boys and girls – albeit differently. In 1847, Miss Hehlen of the Female Institution wrote, "The female African children are nearly a century behind the males in every respect." Nevertheless, the interest and concern had been there. For in 1816 the Church Missionary Society, having been invited by the government to assist, founded the Christian Institution at Leicester, a short distance from Freetown, for boys and girls who had been rescued from slave vessels and had no one to care for them. Most of the pupils, about 350 in number, were boys and the school was run on the British system under Mrs. Horton and Mrs. During, the wives of two missionaries. The children were supported by benefactors in England whose names they often took. The curriculum included half a day at work and half at play, with girls studying from 9 to 12 in the morning and 2 to 5 in the afternoon. In 1818, Governor McCarthy suggested that the girls be housed with various Liberated African families.

One of the earliest efforts to improve the education of girls was the school started in 1830 for recaptives by Hannah Kilham, an English Quaker. Miss Kilham had developed her own methods of teaching African children in their own language using familiar images and ideas. Unfortunately, her death two years later ended this educational innovation.[2]

Twelve years later the Church Missionary Society (CMS) set up two institutions near Freetown, the Grammar School for Boys and the Female Institution for Girls. The frist principal of the Female Institution was a Miss Morris who left within a short time to marry. Then Mrs. Denton, the wife of a resident missionary, was acting principal until a replacement could be found. Both the CMS and the government felt that it was in the interest of the colony as a community that women be educated sufficiently to become equal partners of educated men.[3]

Later, Sophia Hehlen, who perceived the retardation in girls' education, was employed by the CMS to replace Miss Morris at the Female Institution. The school was located, at that time, in the same building at Charlotte occupied by Miss Kilham's School. A year later, the school moved closer to town, to Kissy Road, at a site known as Kissy Road Cemetery in the CMS House.

In 1849, Miss Sass became principal of the school. Fees for the students were paid by either the parents, the CMS, or friends in England. The purpose of the school was "to produce noble, gracious, and well-educated women who would exercise a strong beneficial influence in the community, a liberal education first and foremost with the utilitarian purpose secondary." By 1854, there were 25 pupils (11 day and 14 boarders) in the school. The boarders usually exceeded the day school students in number, some coming from other parts of Africa, such as the Niger Delta, Fernando Po, Liberia, and the Gold Coast. Miss Sass had to go to Europe for her health in 1853 and did not return until 1855. In the interim, Mrs Dicker, wife of the Reverend Dicker, was in charge, assisted by Miss Wilkerson.

Plans were made to build a special building for the school. Before it was completed, the building collapsed and funds had to be sought to begin work on another building. Mr. and Mrs. Walsh of Wanstead, England contributed £2,500 towards the new building in memory of their daughter, Annie, who died before realizing her dream to go to Africa as a missionary. The school was then appropriately named The Annie Walsh Memorial School and was the only institution for the higher education of girls of any standing on the West Coast until the Roman Catholics started St Joseph's Convent in 1861. The Wesleyan Female Educational Institution was opened on January 2, 1880, thus adding to the facilities for girls.

Miss Sass remained at the helm of Annie Walsh Memorial School for 21 years, retiring in 1869. She was followed by women more or less like herself, whom Sibthorpe described as "the old race of CMS ladies before the newer developments beginning in 1887."[4] He was referring to Miss Bywater who was in charge for four years until she married the Reverand Brierly and then left the school. After her husband's death, she ran for seven years a school for liberated girls and orphans at Charlotte. Miss Illott and Miss Thomas followed her. Mrs. Caiger took charge from 1872 to 1874, followed by Miss Caspari, Miss Shoad, Mrs. Burton, Miss Absell, Miss Bissett (who stayed for thirteen years) and Miss Henderson – all European and all missionaries. Miss Dunkly (later Mrs. Humphrey) took over and the school continued to improve. Between 1893 and 1894, its enrollment increased from 86 to 103 pupils, 59 of whom were boarders. Ten out of eleven passed College Preceptors Examination and gained a first in Religious Knowledge and History.

The curriculum of Annie Walsh remained liberal arts and students were accepted in a preparatory class for infants. Children of agents of the CMS were admitted without tuition and children of native clergy at reduced fees. "Outside" children of Europeans were not admitted because it was felt their parents could afford to sent them to England.[5]

In 1911, as a result of unsanitary conditions at the school, the number of student boarders decreased. Beginning in 1913 a teacher-training class was started. In 1919 typing and shorthand were added to the curriculum as well as lawn tennis.

The Annie Walsh Memorial school stood as a model for the higher education of girls – "to train them to become integrated members of their communities and as real partners to their menfolk." This philosophy and the responsibility for administering it remained in the hands of English women. The first African headmistress was not appointed until 1961.

Sibthorpe noted the lack of African teachers (Mrs. G.C. Nicol, Bishop Crowther's daughter, was the first native teacher), but he goes on to remark that there were always a number of blacks on the staff such as Miss Quaker and Mrs. Boyle, and interestingly too, in speaking of education for women, he urged the women not to forget how to sew, wash, and particularly to cook ... no matter how educated they might be in other ways![6]

Charlotte MacCaulay Smith, a sister-in-law of Mrs. Casely Hayford, had taught at the school for fourteen years, and when she left to marry Dr. Smith there seemed at the time no suitable African replacement, although Mrs. Casely Hayford was in the colony and had been doing volunteer teaching at the school. It would seem obvious that she would have welcomed an opportunity to teach there.

A most revealing note was included in the Minutes of the Annie Walsh Memorial School for 9 March 1897, which offers some evidence of the educational environment:

> Today a letter has been written to the Rev. T. Bayles laying before him and the Committee the approaching changes in the teaching staff of the School and in the event of our not being able to secure efficient native help, asking the Committee kindly to consider the question of sending out a fourth European to the school. Qualifications are : 1. A fully-trained teacher, government or high school or one who has had some years' experience of teaching in a large school though not certified, and able to maintain order and good discipline in a large school room. 2. A knowledge of housework and ability to direct others as to the best methods of doing it; 3. Musical, if possible. 4. A knowledge of French, sufficient to prepare girls for Cambridge junior. 5. A large stock of common sense. This letter has been sent to Mr. Bayles through the Secretary at Fourah Bay College.

The Minutes of 14 April 1897 reported: "Charlotte MacCaulay who had been at the school for 14 years left to be married. No other lady has yet been found to take her place."

At that time, there were only two African teachers at the school: Charlotte MacCaulay and Nancy Coker. There was no mention at all of Adelaide Smith.

Stimulated by the activities of the Annie Walsh Memorial School, "two successful private girls schools were started in the 1870s by Creoles – Mrs. Rose Hughes in Little East Street where her husband, an Aku recaptive, had his shop, and by Mrs. Rosa Farmer in Regent Road."[7] Sibthorpe also reports Mrs. Beale's Female School "overlooking the old burial ground" which did much good but ceased almost immediately with her death in 1860.[8]

Mrs. Casely Hayford, whether she desired it or not, became as a David to the Goliath of colonial educational policy of her time. For she attempted to develop a school for girls which stressed vocational subjects and African arts, which was to be controlled by Africans at a time when there was still the reliance upon classical, academic western-oriented education and when the ultimate control was always in the hands of Europeans. Colonizers were understandably most reluctant to release the control of *any* institutions to the colonized. The church in its various denominations came nearest to achieving a kind of semi-independence from colonial control. But this was often a mirage, and few, if any, churches of any denomination were without some type of outside surveillance.

As the administrative policies towards the colony people began to shift from equality to inequality, educational policies shifted similarly. And as growing political restriction predictably encouraged the move towards political independence, so did the appreciation of the ineffectiveness of the poorly administered archaic educational system encourage a few far-sighted persons, such as Mrs Casely Hayford, to consider alternatives – with or without community or colonial support or approval. It is not possible here to document all the shifts in educational policy which reflected and affected the climate of the day – which determined who was teaching what to whom. To assess this in relation to Mrs. Casely Hayford, a few landmarks will have to suffice.

In January 1880, as has been mentioned, the Wesleyan Female Educational Institution was started as a secondary school by a private group composed largely of Wesleyans and managed by Mr. James Taylor, not by the mission itself. Its first two principals were English, but as they soon died, the leadership reverted to Africans, one of whom had spent considerable time in England. The curriculum included domestic as well as academic studies. And as her *Memoirs* indicate, Mrs. Casely Hayford, a Methodist herself, was welcomed at this school if not at Annie Walsh.

In 1882, the Government introduced a policy of Annual Inspection of elementary schools. The results of this inspection would determine the eligibility of a particular school for government subsidy. Also a Board of Education was appointed composed of the Governor as President, official members of the Council and nominated members. Sir Samuel Lewis, the Reverend James Quaker, principal of the CMS Grammar School, and the Reverend J.C. May, principal of the Wesleyan Boys' High School were the first appointed African members. The following year, 1883, the Reverend M. Sunter, Principal of Fourah Bay College and CMS Secretary was made The Government Inspector of Education of the Schools in Sierra Leone, Lagos, and Sherbro. Mr. M.J. Marke was appointed his assistant. In 1884 the Reverend James May died.

The ferment around educational policy at this time was further illustrated on March 31, 1889 when, because of a decrease in its enrollment and an increase in the enrollment of mission and private schools, the Government Model School on Oxford Street (the only existing government school) was closed. It then became official policy to provide government assistance to those non-governmental schools which successfully passed the Annual Inspection of the Inspector of Education.

In January 1896, the Technical Institute was started in Freetown, "for educating youths of the colony in carpentry and masonry." This endeavor was to receive government support, and it is perhaps not insignificant that it was opened the same year the Protectorate was proclaimed. The following year the *Sierra Leone Weekly News (S.L.W.N.)* in an editorial stressed the importance of having voluntary schools on the assumption presumably that there was more than enough work to be done in the field of education and that the government would welcome voluntary initiative in this area.

Reacting to these new winds blowing, Adelaide Smith Casely Hayford started her first school for girls.[9] This institution, as short lived as it was, was nevertheless the first private enterprise for the secondary education of girls in Sierra Leone.

From the period of the late 1880s on, the field of education reflected the struggle over leadership in the Freetown community – the Creoles were definitely being threatened in their traditional leadership roles by the changes in the attitude of the English colonizers and the reality of the need to extend some type of education to the people of the Protectorate. It was not so easy to determine the kind of education the Protectorate people would want or the kind of education they would need in this next period of colonial control.

Adelaide Smith was absent from Freetown during most of this period of educational turmoil. In 1911, for example, it was again necessary for the *S.L.W.N.* (1/27, p.5) to stress that future awards to schools would be made on the basis of annual inspections – which would include the inspection of all of the activities of the school.

The Annual Report of the Education Department for the Year 1924 provides further insights into the educational climate in which Mrs. Casely Hayford would have to survive upon her return from America. Mr. H. Blackmore, the newly appointed Chief Inspector, reported that there were 32 assisted schools, including primary and secondary industrial schools, in Freetown – all characterized by having poorly kept buildings, inadequate equipment and teachers on deplorably low salaries. Furthermore, he noted, "there was no place where persons desiring to take up the profession of teaching could be suitably trained. As a result the education offered the students was inadequate." He continued,

> it is no uncommon thing to find the pupil able to repeat the reading lessons off by heart ... but little attention has been paid to the real Hand and Eye Work and small effort is put forth to make the school work really attractive to the pupil. Mechanical methods have naturally produced mechanical results. Training in the initiative and imaginative has been neglected and apparently no effort has been made to encourage the pupil to think and do for himself. Handwork is not viewed with too much favor by either the teachers or the scholars.[10]

To correct these and some other flaws in the educational administration, a "New Educational Ordinance and Code of Rules" was prepared by the Education Committee and published to become operative by 1 January 1925. Among the more significant features of the new rules were: the abolition of Elementary and Intermediate Certificate examination, for the reason that they proved an irresistible inducement to cramming; the adoption of a scale of minimum salaries payable to teachers who show themselves worthy of them by submitting to certain tests; the direct encouragement of teacher training; the publication of a detailed syllabus for the elementary schools; the compulsory introduction of some form of handicraft or manual work therein and the introduction of a more elastic scale of capital grants. The passage of such rules should have made it a most auspicious time for Mrs. Casely Hayford to start her school of vocational training for girls – the old educational system was not working and there was spelled out in explicit government policy some indication that innovation was to be welcomed. But, as the facts will reveal, there was to be no welcome for the ideas of a native, over-educated, perhaps overbearing, extremely secure but unprotected woman.

However, Mrs. Casely Hayford was a believer; she tried to carry out what Government said was wanted. She became discouraged, sought support from abroad, from outside the community itself and returned to try again. That educational policy was still, at the time of her return from her second trip to the United States, a matter of dispute is revealed in the passage of the Education Ordinance of 1929. An examination of the specifics of this Ordinance provides an explanation of what had not been accomplished in the intervening years since the passage of the 1924 Ordinance and what was theoretically to be expected from this time forward. Yet even this new Ordinance would not ensure the success of

AVF-B*

someone as independent and as nonparochial as Adelaide Smith Casely Hayford, however compatible her ideas might have been with it.

This Ordinance, which was considered to be of sufficient import to warrant its full publication in the *S.L.W.N.* of 15 June 1929, called for numerous innovations, only some of which would or could directly affect what Mrs. Casely Hayford was trying to accomplish. These were as follows:

(a) An acknowledged need for both Teacher Training Institutes and Industrial Schools. In the Industrial Schools, at least, all the pupils or a certain number would devote not less than two-thirds of their time to (in the case of females) domestic science;

(b) An officially recognized and enlarged Board of Education for the Colony, composed of the Directors of Education, three government officials, and four unofficial persons appointed by the Governor, of whom at least three would be persons representing missionary and educational societies working in the Colony. In the absence of any regular member of the Board, the Governor could appoint anyone temporarily to fill the place; also the Governor could appoint, for purposes of any particular session or sessions, any person in Sierra Leone as an extraordinary member of the Board. Such a person would not be entitled to vote, however;

(c) On the recommendation of the Board, the Governor in Council would make rules for the manner in which and the extent to which schools might be assisted from public funds, and the conditions of such assistance. He might also prevent the opening and carrying on of new schools deemed by the Director to be unnecessary or to be likely to affect prejudicially any existing school, and otherwise to prescribe the conditions under which new schools might be opened and carried on.

(d) Public primary schools, public secondary schools, *industrial* or agricultural schools and *such other schools* as the Governor in Council might from time to time approve, and training institutions, could be assisted from public funds.

(e) No person would be permitted to open or carry on a school which did not satisfy the requirements of the Ordinance.

(f) No person would be permitted to teach in any Government-assisted school, unless registered on the Register of Teachers or unless his name was on the Provisional List. The Director could recognize or not any person as a teacher under this subsection as he in his absolute discretion might think fit.

(g) "On the recommendation of the Director, the Governor in Council may authorize special payments from public funds for the erection of school buildings, their maintenance and for scholarships."

(h) "The manager of a non-assisted school in which fees, emoluments or gratuities of any kind are taken or received shall on or before the 31st day of July, 1929 notify the Director in writing of the existence of such school, and shall furnish all particulars relating to such school and the staff thereof as shall be asked for by him; and thereafter changes in the staff shall be notified to the Director by such persons as they occur."

(i) "Any person contravening any of the above provisions ... shall be guilty of an offense and shall be liable on summary conviction thereof of a fine not exceeding five pounds."[11]

The requirements of the two Educational Ordinances (the 1929 one repealing naturally those of 1924) if followed to the letter immediately suggest the difficulties Mrs. Casely Hayford had. Her major problem was securing funding. Now that public monies were to be made increasingly available to non-public schools, would Girls Vocational, as Mrs. Casely Hayford called her school, be eligible? To secure the necessary funds, Girls Vocational was in obvious competitition with others schools, such as Annie Walsh.

Also related to the question of funds was the problem of gaining access to those persons who had it within their power to determine which schools would get funding – that is, the Governor, and those closest to him (maybe even his wife), the Board of Education and finally the Director of Education.

There was the additional possibility of being appointed to serve in some capacity as a citizen helping to determine the policy of education, to be the person asked to fill a temporary vacancy, or indeed to serve as a regular member of the Board ... Of course, Mrs. Casely Hayford had received none of her education in Freetown and did not have a formal college degree as such and then too her source of support had been mobilized in America not in England – all of these points weakened her eligibility to be recognized in this maze of jealousy and pettiness where there was so much room for reward and punishment.

Mrs. Casely Hayford, especially in her earlier designs for a school, wanted to do just the things that the Ordinance required. She wanted to develop a teacher training component, she wanted to stress domestic science; she wanted to develop African art, to minimize examinations and cramming and reach the student as a person. All of these points she

indicated in her early Prospectus for the school and developed even
more fully in the printed statement of the talk which she was to have
given at the Geneva meeting.[12] But she had one cardinal factor against
her – she wanted to be in control of her own school. As an "unprotected" (without a husband or son or brother), well-trained, autocratic
African woman, that she would dare to assert that kind of leadership and
authority in education was indeed anathema to the British government,
the missionary societies and the male-orientated Creole society of the
time. And, as she reported and her activities indicated, Mrs. Casely
Hayford was actually more comfortable with and more accepted by the
Governor and his set and her own family and intimate circle of Creole
friends from the established families than she ever was with the whites
or lesser Creole government functionaries who carried out educational
policy.

In a society stratified as Freetown was, this type of cross-racial,
intra-class association is predictable. In the following chapters we shall
attempt to describe how Mrs. Casely Hayford survived in such a milieu
and to evaluate from this perspective her final victory, the receipt of the
MBE from the King for her contribution to education in Sierra Leone at
the age of eighty-one.

III

Family and Early Years in England and Germany

Most, if not all, colonial and post-colonial history of Africa has been written with little or no attention given to the personal lives of the people and families of the Africans who made it. Biography of individuals or families is an approach whose time has not yet come to Africa.[1] However, the importance of the family as an institution or as a collection of personalities to an understanding of an African society and culture could never be more vividly illustrated than with the family of Adelaide Smith Casely Hayford. Her relatives, close and remote, represent every major thread from which the fabric of Creole society was woven.

Born in Freetown on 2 June 1868, Adelaide was the second youngest of the seven children born to Anne Spilsbury Smith and William Smith, Jr. Her mother was one of twin daughters, (the other, Elizabeth, died in England) of Hannah Carew Spilsbury and Joseph Green Spilsbury. Hannah was the daughter of Thomas and Betsy Carew. Thomas was a recaptive Bambara butcher; his wife Betsy was a shrewd Hausa trader to whom he left most of the responsibility of running his trading and contracting business. Later, Thomas Carew went into real estate. Betsy was apparently most successful in trade, but, according to Fyfe, the Carews lost later in life what they had amassed in their prime. If this is true, it suggests that any money Ann inherited must have come from the Spilsbury not the Carew side.[2] In their affluent days, however, the Carews, though illiterate themselves, sent their children to school in England and, while there, Hannah was placed with a "splendid Quaker family which had a high class business premise on Regent Street which was patronized by Queen Victoria." As a wedding gift, Thomas and Betsy Carew gave Hannah and Joseph a spacious home on prestigious Rawdon Street that had cost them nearly £300.

Mrs. Casely Hayford describes her great-grandmother, Betsy Carew (whom she does not call by name), as "an absolutely illiterate Mandingo trader" and she describes her great-grandfather on the Spilsbury side as having been "a patent medicine dealer from London." Yet a Betsy

Carew, "a pioneer woman trader," is listed as among the original Settlers from Nova Scotia.[3] Mrs. Casely Hayford makes no reference at all to her maternal great-grandfather, Thomas Carew, and, if Fyfe is to be believed, she is somewhat in error about the Spilsbury line. Joseph, her grandfather, was the son of a Maroon mother and a former Colonial Surgeon, Dr. George Spilsbury, who would be Mrs. Casely Hayford's great-grandfather. However, Dr. George Spilsbury was indeed the son of a "well-known London patent medicine maker" who would be Mrs. Casely Hayford's great-great-grandfather.[4]

In any case, Hannah's marriage to Joseph Spilsbury, who at the time of his death in 1853 was noted as one of the nineteen biggest land and home owners in Freetown, brought the necessary combination of Settler status and financial security to place her, the daughter of recaptives, firmly within the evolving Creole elite. Funds from her grandfather's estate were most important, as will be discussed later, in making it possible for Anne and William Smith to take their family to England. However, Joseph Spilsbury, as was the custom of the time, had "outside" children whom he recognized and whom he remembered in his will, thus creating unanticipated financial problems for the family at Anne's death. Joseph Green Spilsbury's will, which was filed on 31 May 1853, just twenty-eight days after his death, provides much information about the family and the society of the day beyond his obvious wealth. Furthermore, the existence of such a document about a family in Africa well over one hundred years ago would certainly surprise all but the most informed westerners.

Spilsbury left money both to his mother, Elizabeth Fowler, and to his grandmother, Sally Fowler; he remembered, in addition, by gifts of land or money or both, a half-sister, Sarah Gray, an uncle, Alexander Fowler, a half-brother, William Gray, an aunt, Mary Bicknor, a godmother, Lydia O'Connor, a godson, Joseph Carew, his mother-in-law, Elizabeth Carew, three cousins – Anne Davis, John Sweeney, Elizabeth ..... (illegible), two friends – Nancy Hughes and Robert Dongan, Jr., his grandfather-in-law, David Bucknor – and of course, his wife, Hannah, his daughter, Anne and *two* sons, Thomas and Henry, who were initially left a similar amount of £200 each but considerably less than Anne who had a trust fund set up in her name and property. This property after her death was to go first to Thomas, then to Henry, then to Sarah Gray, and then to the "heirs of my said children." Furthermore, any surplus after all legacies had been paid were to be divided equally between "my grandchildren." Anne was certainly well provided for with the trust fund for her education and practically all her father's real estate – but only throughout her life time.

Anne was the second wife of William Smith, Jr., Registrar of the
Mixed Commission Court. Smith's father was a Yorkshireman who
came to the West Coast – to the Gold Coast – about 1820 to work with
the African Company. His status and salary made him the equal of the
European officials and missionaries and apparently he helped bridge the
gap between them and the rest of the community.[5] Later William Smith,
Sr. was appointed the first Registrar and then Commissary Judge for the
Mixed Courts in Freetown. He retired in 1835 and died about 1875.[6]
Smith had two sons – William Jr., by a Fanti woman when he was in the
Gold Coast and Frederick by an English woman to whom he was
supposedly married.

Smith was certainly a man of importance and wealth in Freetown.
When he came from the Gold Coast to Sierra Leone, he purchased the
farm owned consecutively by Governor MacCarthy and Kenneth
Macaulay. Macaulay later became William Smith, Jr.'s first father-in-
law. Smith also purchased a house on the northeast corner of Wilberforce and Cross streets from Eli Akim, a prosperous settler of Nova
Scotian origin.

Both sons of Judge Smith worked in his court – Frederick, the
English son, as a junior clerk and William Jr., the African son, first as a
young clerk in 1841 and then from 1850 until he retired, as Registrar.
William Smith, Jr. was also recruited as a lay preacher by the Wesleyans
to increase the dwindling number of their missionaries. It should not be
overlooked that in Freetown at this time the elder Smith son who was
legitimate and European had less status than his half brother, who was
African and illegitimate.

William Smith, Jr. married Charlotte Macaulay, the daughter of
Governor Kenneth Macaulay, brother of Governor Zachary Macaulay
and relative of the distinguished English historian, Thomas Babington
Macaulay. Charlotte's mother was one of two recaptives brought up as
his own children by Governor Macaulay. When she died at the age of 36,
Charlotte and William Smith, Jr. had seven children. All but one of the
children, Francis, were older than Anne, Adelaide's mother, at the time
of her marriage to Smith in 1858.

Anne Spilsbury Smith and William Smith, Jr. also had seven children.
To trace the activities of each of the fourteen Smith children, or the
twelve who reached adulthood – where and in what field they were
educated, whom they married, where they spent most of the lives, when
they died (Mrs. Casely Hayford survived them all) – would be a colonial
history of Sierra Leone as well as, in some ways, of the Gambia, the Gold
Coast and Nigeria. This would be a formidable task, beyond the scope of
this book. Nevertheless, the prominence of these Smiths is extraordin-

ary and some knowledge of their lives gives greater insight into the people and changes of the time and, of course, to the world of Adelaide Smith Casely Hayford.

The seven children of William Smith, Jr. and Charlotte Macaulay were William Henry (1836–1871), Robert (1840–1887), twins – Philippa (1843–1909) and Mary (1843–1884), John Frederick (1845–1848), Francis (1847–   ), and Charlotte (1851–1857). The brothers, Francis and Robert and the twin girls, Philippa and Mary had the most unusual lives – a bit beyond even the most successful Creole elite. Both the boys were sent to Queen Elizabeth's Grammar School, Wakefield. Robert then went into medicine at Birmingham and London and returned to Sierra Leone in 1865 with a Glasgow LFPS[7] to which he added in 1871 an Edinburgh FRCS.[8] He started his government service as Inspector of Health and Shipping and later became Assistant Colonial Surgeon in charge of the Colonial Hospital. Only his death in 1887 prevented Smith from becoming Colonial Surgeon, a post for which he had already been recommended. Dr. Smith married the daughter of Sir Benjamin Chilley Campbell Pine, Queen's Advocate from 1841, Acting Governor of Sierra Leone from April, 1848 to November 1849. Their residence, once owned by his maternal grandfather, Kenneth Macaulay, on Gloucester Street opposite the post office has already been described as being most spacious and commodious.

In 1868 Francis Smith entered the Middle Temple to begin the study of law and was called to the bar in 1871, as the first African so qualified. He returned to practice in Freetown and was appointed a temporary Magistrate in the Gambia. He was later appointed Puisne Judge of the Gold Coast. While Smith was in the Gambia, he married a European woman by whom he had one daughter. When he left his wife and daughter and moved to the Gold Coast – to Cape Coast – he had another daughter, Charlotte, and two sons, William and Robert, by Elizabeth Blankson, the daughter of Charlotte Hutton. When Elizabeth died, Judge Smith brought his two children, William and Charlotte (Robert had died in infancy in the Gold Coast) to Freetown to stay with his half-sister, Elizabeth Smith Awoonor Renner (Bea to Adelaide). Charlotte was enrolled in St. Joseph's Convent and William in the Grammar School. Later, with Dr. Renner giving her away, Charlotte married Joseph Peter Brown-Pobee, a barrister, and moved with him back to Cape Coast in the Gold Coast. Mr. Pobee died in 1914 and about the same time so did Charlotte's grandmother, Charlotte Hutton, so she wrote her half-sister, Eva Lumpkin Wright of her situation. Eva Wright was herself another outside child of Judge Francis Smith, from his early Sierra Leone days. Her mother was Emma Wilkinson Lumpkin, wife of

Joseph Lumpkin. Eva had married Claude Wright, the distinguished barrister, who with his brother, Dr. Jenner Wright were the two outside children of their father Mr. Claudius Wright and an English woman, Sophie Slocombe. It was to Claude Wright, Sr. that Adelaide and her sister (see later letters) hoped to rent or sublet their apartment. Charlotte returned to Freetown with the surviving of her two children, a daughter, Josephine; her son had died in infancy. Within a year after her return to Freetown, Charlotte married Dr. Jenner Wright, her half-sister's brother-in-law. They had three children: Sophie, Margaret, and Grace (also a son, Emile?).[9]

The twins, Philippa and Mary Smith, by their marriages to outstanding Sierra Leonians, further enhanced the status of the family of William Smith, Jr. and broadened their network to important people in Freetown and down the Coast. Mary married William Broughton Davies.[10] Philippa married Thomas Spilsbury.

To repeat a bit of Davies' biography, Davies was born of Yoruba parentage at Wellington and was selected by the Church Missionary Society as one of three young men (the other two were James Horton and Samuel Campbell) then at Fourah Bay College to go to England to study medicine. Davies received his MD in 1858 at St. Andrews and with Horton, who also had an MD but from Edinburgh, entered the army in 1859 with the rank of Staff Assistant Surgeon. On returning to Freetown in 1881 with the rank of Surgeon, Davies practiced privately in his offices on George Street until his death in 1904.

Mary's twin, Philippa, married the "outside" son of Joseph Green Spilsbury, Thomas Hamilton Spilsbury. Thomas was educated at Rochester, became a Customs Clerk and in 1859 resigned from Government service to study medicine. He qualified in 1865. Dr. Spilsbury served in Bathhurst in the Gambia from 1872 until his death in 1890. He was the first African to be made the Head of a Medical Department in the British West African colonies.[11] Spilsbury's marriage to Philippa Smith was a further example of kinship interlock when it is recalled that William Smith, Jr. married, as his second wife, Ann, Spilsbury's half-sister, who became the mother of Mrs. Casely Hayford, and that Smith's first wife had been the half-sister of Mrs. Casely Hayford herself. These kinds of interkinship ties, as have also been illustrated above, have probably accounted for the years of law suits brought by Spilsbury's grandchildren over the ownership of the former Mixed Commission building.[12]

There is no record of what happened to the eldest son of William Smith, Jr., William Henry Smith (1838–1871); the younger son John Frederick (1845–1848) died when he was still an infant.

The children of William Smith, Jr. and Anne Spilsbury were as outstanding as the children Smith had by his first wife, Charlotte, but their experiences as a family were considerably different. In 1871, William Smith, Jr. retired from Government Service and the following year he decided to follow what his daughter, Adelaide, described as "a most unique path," by taking his entire second family to Europe for their education. Sending children on their own to England, as has already been indicated, was not really unusual for Creole elite families but to move one's entire family abroad was. No doubt the security of knowing there were funds from his father-in-law for his wife and his own pension of 666 pounds gave Smith reason to feel he could afford to move. Mrs. Smith's health had not been good and then as now a move to England was believed to be ameliorative. And so in 1872 when the Smith family set sail from Freetown to England begins the story of the growth and experiences of Adelaide Smith Casely Hayford.

The family settled first in Norwood, a suburb of London, and shortly thereafter, presumably for an even better climate for the ailing Mrs. Smith and in search of larger grounds on which the children might freely play, they moved to St. Helier on the Isle of Jersey. St. Helier (number 13 Queen's Road) was their family home until shortly after Mr. Smith's death in 1895. As planned, all of William and Anne's children were educated abroad and, except for Adelaide, exclusively in England. The eldest, Joseph Spilsbury Smith (1859–   ), was educated at the Wakefield Grammar School, Victoria College, and after what his nephew described in a letter to me as "an extravagant stay in London, qualified as a doctor and was employed by the Gold Coast government and stationed in the mid-90s at Tarkwa where he was both doctor and District Commissioner." Joseph Spilsbury Smith apparently never married, though he did have children, according to an informant.

Thomas (1867–   ) was described by Mrs. Casely Hayford as her "twin in prosperity and adversity, in joy and sorrow a continuing source of worry and anxiety to her," as letters to her husband reveal. He did not have the bent to become either a doctor or a lawyer in the family tradition but studied photography. Later, Thomas became a trader in the Gold Coast, apparently following his sister Adelaide there; he became involved in the Ashanti War over the Golden Stool and escaped death by "the skin of his teeth." Still later, no doubt through family connections, he became Registrar of the Court at Axim in the Gold Coast and spent the last years of his life in Nigeria – where he died. One much younger relative described him as a "playboy and ne'er-do-well."

Emma, the middle child (1864–1928), was remembered by her sister Adelaide as reserved and extremely self-contained, and by a younger relative, as "beautiful and brilliant, a real blue-stocking." In later years, as the maiden aunt, Emma "undertook to carry out with great ability and abnormal self-denial the many behests of her numerous family residing in Africa," her sister Adelaide recalled. It was, therefore, a source of great sorrow to the family that none of them was with her when she died in a nursing home in England.

The other four Smith girls, including Mrs. Casely Hayford, were most unusual for their time – as much because of their marriages as for their personal talents. Elizabeth or Bea as she was called, the eldest (1860–1947), more or less ran the Smith household on Jersey after their mother's death and before their father's third marriage. Bea married Dr. William Jarvis Awoonor Renner, a Sierra Leonian whose family was from the Gold Coast. Dr. Renner, MRCS (England) 1880, LRQCP and LM (Ireland) 1880, and MD (Brux. with distinction 1881), was Assistant Colonial Surgeon from 1882 to 1913. When the West African Service was formed in 1902, he was excluded because of his color and placed in the new category – that of Native Medical Officer – thus automatically making him junior to any European doctor who at that time might just join the regular service. On retirement, he ran a small nursing home in a house situated in Oxford Street in Freetown where the Bata Building now stands. The Renners lived for some time in Jersey, where he is buried.

There were three Renner children from this marriage. The eldest, Roland, trained as a lawyer, became a judge in Nigeria. His first marriage to Theresa Smith was childless, but through his second marriage to a Calabar woman (from a ruling house in that region of Nigeria), Roland had three children: Lelia, Edward and Charles. Edward and Charles became physicians. Lelia married a Nigerian physician, Dr. Culerick, but was childless. Edward, known affectionately as 'Teddy' (d.1955) married Carmela Pitt, a Guyanese who died in England in 1960. Dr. Teddy Renner was awarded an OBE and was Director of Medical Services in Sierra Leone. He and his wife had four children: Noreen, Louis (who married a Canadian), Archie (who married Helen Akiwumi of Ghana) and Elizabeth (who married Egerton Luke, a Sierra Leonean specialist physician).

Hannah Smith (1862–1896), another daughter, married a brother of Elizabeth's husband, Peter Awoonor Renner (d. 1938) who became a leading barrister on the Gold Coast. Interestingly, at one time in their married lives, because of their husbands' occupations, three of the Smith sisters, Adelaide, Hannah, and Nettie, were living on the Gold Coast, which after all was the birthplace of their father. Hannah and Peter Awoonor Renner had four children: Charles, a lawyer who prac-

ticed in Cape Coast, William, also a lawyer, and two other sons, Ernest
and Walter, both of whom died in infancy. William (d. 1943) married
Ada Hebron, the granddaughter of Abraham Hebron, a wealthy rum
merchant of Kissy Road, Freetown and the daughter of Abraham
Spencer Hebron who was called to the bar in 1882 and in 1898 became
an Honorary Member of the Legislative Council in Freetown. William
and Ada had four children: Ernest, Raymond, Walter, and Donald.
Ernest married an American and settled in New York. Walter practiced
medicine in Freetown and was educated at Amherst College and Germany. Raymond, who married Marilyn Jarvis, a writer and educational
specialist from Guyana, was Solicitor General in Freetown, and Donald
married Annie King and settled in England. When Hannah died in
1896, her two children, Charles and William, went to live in Jersey with
their Aunt Bea (Mrs. William Jarvis Awoonor Renner) along with
Hannah's husband's second wife, Beatrice Bernard, who was only a few
years older than her stepsons.

Annette Kathleen, or Nettie, as she was called (1870–1951), the
youngest of the Smith daughters, married Dr. John Farrell Easmon in
Jersey in 1889. Adelaide, who was one of her sister's maids of honor,
described the occasion in her *Memoirs*. Fortunately for our documentation on this family, Dr. M.C.F. Easmon, the son of Nettie and Dr. John
Easmon, wrote a brief family history.[13]

Dr. John Farrell Easmon on his father's side descended from "good
settler stock" (Nova Scotians who came to Sierra Leone in 1792). On
his mother's side, he had Irish ancestry. His father, Walter Richard
Easmon, married three times and Dr. John Easmon was the son of his
second wife, Mary Ann.

> Now Mary Ann McCormack was the daughter of a wild Irishman
> (John McCormack) of a well-known Northern Irish Medical
> Family, being born in Lurgeon near Londonderry in 1794. He
> came out to West Africa ... in 1813 and to Sierra Leone in 1816
> where he started a timber business ... which became the first major
> export from the Crown Colony of Sierra Leone. ... He became a
> member of the Governor's Council, and in 1850 was Police Magis-
> trate ... He also became very religious and was the founder and first
> Pastor of the Church of God (Baptist) in Regent Road. His town
> house was at the corner of Rawdon and Oxford Streets where the
> new building of the Bank of West Africa has been erected. He
> returned to Britain in 1864 and died in London in 1866.

While in West Africa, McCormack had a daughter Mary by a Miss
Cuthbert (Dr. Easmon does not indicate whether he married her). In

any case, the daughter's surname was that of her father, McCormack. Mary McCormack married Walter Richard Easmon and by him had one son, John Farrell Easmon.

Old John McCormack did not forget his grandchildren in Africa and Johnnie inherited about 400 pounds when the estate was settled. He promptly left for England to study medicine in 1876.

He entered University College Hospital, Gower Street and qualified as M.R.C.S. in 1879. Easmon went to Ireland to take the L.M. and L.R.Q.C.P. and over to Brussels where he got the M.D. (Bruy with distinction).[14]

The Irish Branch of the McCormack line comes into the picture again when the famous Surgeon Sir William McCormack, P.R.C.S. (Eng.) (President of the Royal College of Surgeons), Senior Surgeon to St. George's Hospital and Surgeon to Queen Victoria and the most decorated man in Europe at the time, hearing of a distant cousin's success, invited him to come over to St. George's as his House Surgeon leading to becoming his assistant. No other West African had had such an opportunity. But Johnnie turned it down deciding that his place was back in Settler Town with his people. ...

He returned to Freetown early in 1880 and put up his plate at No.2 East Street.

He later went to the Gold Coast, which offered a better salary, entered their service in 1881 as an Assistant Colonial Surgeon. "His first station was Lagos, Nigeria; the next year or so he was at Quitah." In 1889, he was married to Miss Nettie Smith and "in due course he rose to the rank of Chief Medical Officer of the Gold Coast in 1893 at the early age of 37 after 12 years of service." After a most distinguished medical career, Dr. Easmon died in Cape Coast on June 9, 1900, just three weeks before his 44th birthday.

To pick up now the threads of Adelaide's life from the *Memoirs*, the Smith family left for England in 1872. She was only four. Her earliest memories begin with the excitement of the voyage itself and the settling in their new home. She remembered vividly the four weeks' voyage, spending her fourth birthday on board ship and a growing awareness of the illness of her mother requiring that the three younger children including Adelaide be supervised by nurses.

Once ashore on a pouring wet afternoon "the family with all the girls dressed alike in stiff plaid dresses with removable sleeves and scarlet cashmere shawls crossed over the chest and tied in a bunch at the back" made their way to the Langham Hotel. Soon afterwards they moved to

Norwood, a London suburb. It is of Norwood that she gives the first description of a home abroad: "we had a semi-detached house with a large garden and I remember rebelling furiously, when we children were sent to bed at seven in the long summer evenings. Surreptitiously, we watched the grownups playing croquet on the lawn."

Hers was a glorious childhood, initially in rather affluent circumstances because of the combined income from her father's pension and from rents on the property which Mrs. Smith inherited from her father. They were, she recalled, always entertaining, especially visitors from afar – such as the first Afro-American choir to visit England, some of whose members stayed with them (probably the Fisk Jubilee Singers) – Minnie Tate's solo rendition of "Go Down Moses" left a permanent impression on her.[15] "Life went on at a joyful pace with my home life being augmented by the presence of the grandchildren of Mr. Smith's first marriage. So many young people could be most independent, neither seeking nor needing companions beyond the family." That this would produce a cohesion is obvious, but less anticipated is its utility in helping a different family to survive in an alien land.

The only dark blot on Adelaide's early childhood was the death of her mother at the early age of 36, "just after my seventh birthday." Mrs. Smith's health must have affected very radically those early years, for beginning with the voyage from Freetown to London, Mrs. Casely Hayford had no recollection of her mother "ever playing with her children or ever taking part in any of (our) frolics; she spent her days more or less on a luxurious sofa, roomy enough at any time to fondle her kiddies."

After a while the English climate seems to have been too severe for Mrs. Smith so the family moved to the Isle of Jersey, to "a big rambling old-fashioned house with a large garden behind which was allocated to the children." This move to 13 Queen Road, St. Helier, was futile, for shortly thereafter, on June 26, 1876, just about three years after the family came to England, Mrs. Smith died. Though she was only seven, Mrs. Casely Hayford remembered the day of her mother's death:

> we three younger ones were sent out to make daisy chains in a nearby meadow, but at the back of my mind I had an ominous foreboding that something sinister was happening at home ... after the funeral she came to me one night speaking words of comfort, consolation and telling me I must not forget that she would never be far away from her beloved offspring. I had cause to remember this when in after years I found myself in imminent danger, and she appeared as a guardian angel on my right hand, my father taking up

a similar position on my left. He was a darling. As Mother died in
my early childhood, I really owe my upbringing to him, fulfilling as
he did, the dual role of Father and Mother.

Although Adelaide did not sense a direct influence of her Mother upon
her life – in her formative years, she felt her more as an absence than as a
presence – there seems to have been a psychological tie between them of
which she was only vaguely aware – which was the result of the color of
their skin.

Color as a distinguishing characteristic does not appear to have been
overtly important in the Creole society of Sierra Leone at that time.
Position seems to have been based exclusively on origin, money and
education or occupation. And as persons of any shade could have the
requisite amount of each of these and through intermarriage or mis-
cegenation many colors were found in the same immediate family, there
was, in fact, no separate mulatto status – a position accorded one in some
countries merely by virtue of the color of one's skin. The color lines, to
the extent that they existed, or were acknowledged, were between
English and African. To be Creole did not mean to be mulatto. Of
course to be mulatto probably did mean one was Creole, but not
necessarily elite Creole. Therefore, the appreciation of color within a
family depended very much on outside influences. But leaving Africa
placed Adelaide in a setting where her complexion, not black but darker
than that of her father and sisters, was frequently for her the source of
great insecurity. Adelaide resembled her mother, whom she described
as "dark – a real Sambo – and my father was exceptionally fair. Consequently, the children varied in complexion. I was a Hamite, so was very
much left out in the cold, but shared the leftovers with my precious
off-white youngest sister, Nettie, who was only four when Mother
died." Mrs. Casely Hayford's feeling of difference because of her
darker color shows again in Germany and in her relation to her step-
mother who was English, and even in the Jersey College for Women
which she adored – "as a teen-ager, I was terribly shy – probably
because I was too race-conscious. In a white country I felt so conspi-
cuous that I always wanted to hide my diminished head."

This feeling allied her, in a very special way, with her Mother, the
granddaughter of the "Mandingo trader," who, even when she is introduced to the reader of the *Memoirs*, is presented as being "without
aristocracy."

After Mrs. Smith's death, the family stayed on in Jersey with "sister
Bea taking the overall responsibility for the children augmented in her
task by a Governess and the necessary maids." Their mother's death

and the loss of income to the family from the mother's estate inevitably affected the life style of the family. Although they continued to live in the same house, the number of children having considerably increased by the advent of seven nieces and nephews from Africa (offspring of the children from Mr. Smith's first marriage), an economy in expenditures was required.

> Clothes were strictly rationed and reduced to a minimum of two dresses a year – one for summer and one for winter ... last year's wardrobe evolving into a second best for weekdays. If, however, they had not survived the wear and tear of twelve solid months [the] elder sisters' clothes were generally allocated [to the younger], after being turned, washed and pressed to make them look like new, even if they did not feel that way. It became a red-letter day when brand new material was actually brought to make ... brand new clothes. Shoes were taboo, only boots made to order ... either laced or buttoned magnanimous boots, reaching far away up the leg, encasing calves like a vice and leaving our ankles far behind!

The Smith family lacked money but "integrity and honesty took pride of place in their general make-up." Their childhood, Mrs. Casely Hayford reminisced, did not depend

> upon lovely toys, elegant clothes, and choice delectable tit-bits. There was much we could and did enjoy that did not require money. In spring the Sports Field was divided up into beds and the children competed with each other as to who could produce most riotous variegated covers which also were generally lavishingly interspersed with weeds. In winter, we resorted to other forms of inexpensive recreation, the principal one being to produce plays to which grown-up friends and school chums were invited.

On one occasion they acted "Beauty and the Beast" in which Adelaide made, she recalls,

> a most realistic Beast but on kneeling down to offer my hand and ... heart to my Beauty, in a split second my borrowed breeches tore, disclosing that part of my anatomy which should always be discreetly veiled. The uproarious laughter which greeted the episode brought me quickly to my feet and with the proposal still hanging in the balance I rushed out to hide my diminished head behind the door. When I finally emerged as the Prince, magnanimously decorated with silver paper I carved for myself the sobriquint of "Daddie Spangles" or monosyllabic "Dad" [which] has stuck to me ever

since [with] Adelaide or Addie being solely reserved for moments
of strained relationships or wounded vanity.

In her surviving correspondence to sisters and her husband she is either
Addie or Adelaide Casely Hayford.[16] I have only one letter where Dad is
used and it in a reference to her by a niece-in-law.

Mrs. Casely Hayford well remembered these years of pinching and
scraping, of untold self-denial on her father's part whose income as a
pensioner, now without any help from her Mother, was barely enough.

Yet her older sister Bea, who was only sixteen when her Mother died,
shouldered the household management. As Adelaide recalled, this
"entailed endless discipline, foresight, method, planning and economy
to a point"; she felt that they were overmanaged. For instance, food was
of the simplest so that she and her nephew Chilley (son of her half
brother Robert) formed a deputation to wait upon her father in his
private sanctuary, at the top of the house, to enquire whether jam was
not sometimes permissible at tea. They got jam, with some spicy currant
buns thrown in. "Slowly and with faltering steps our education progressed. The three elder girls were sent to finishing school from which they
emerged, armed with the accomplishments considered necessary for
young ladies of 'gentle' birth. As the novelettes of the time would have
said." Since their real education was somewhat meager, as the youngsters had been allowed to run wild, Mr. Smith installed a governess, the
daughter of an Anglo-Indian colonel. "Her activities were confined
principally to the older girls, and as her geographical speciality was the
British Isles, the rest of the world was entirely off the map." Mrs. Casely
Hayford never remembered being taught to read but did recall "my
habit of getting hold of the Dictation Book and memorizing the words of
the portion I knew would be assigned by the 'slow-witted teacher'."
After this rather casual, informal and very impersonal education, she
recalled how excited she was when soon after her 12th birthday (1881?),
"my father announced that he had joined the committee of an up-to-
date college which [the children] were to attend as foundation pupils. So
the seven of us – 'the young section' of the family – enrolled." (These
would be the young children of Anne and William Smith, Jr.) The Jersey
Ladies College, as the school to which they were sent was called, had,
according to Mrs. Casely Hayford, a very high academic standard
permitting some of the brighter girls to take their B.A. London degree,
without attending a university. After two years she received her Junior
Certificate (age fourteen).[17]

Adelaide remembered the years at Jersey College with considerable
pleasure but also with some pain. In her first year her school activities

were interrupted by a sharp attack of typhoid fever from which she suffered for six weeks. As a result of her illness "my fingers became so bent that I could not stretch an octave properly, thus handicapping my future musical career." However, this illness did not stop her from enjoying life at the school which she described as "a gorgeous memory" because "there color rather than being a handicap was the basis for our receiving extra tidbits of love, kindness and good will." As an illustration, Mrs. Casely Hayford described one incident:

> At fifteen, a batch of us from the Jersey Ladies College where I was one of the foundation pupils were invited to a lecture by George Macdonald, who though one of the minor poets, was very renowned in his day. "Alice," I said to my companion, "When the lecture is over I am going to shake hands with him." Alice gasped in astonishment, "You, Adelaide, with no more spunk than a mouse, I don't believe you." "Wait and see!" "Knowing you as I do," was the rejoiner, "I am prepared to bet you will never do it!" "Bet what?" "A bar of chocolate." "Right oh!" Like a shy little mouse, I approached the great man from behind, and gave a rather wheezing cough. He turned around, and was quite taken aback to see a little black teenager standing there. I seized my opportunity. "Please may I shake hands with you?" "Why certainly!" And he gave me a grip. I won my bet.

During this period shy Adelaide Smith was most attached to the Principal of the College, Miss Eliza Roberts. "As a graduate of Girton College, Miss Eliza combined high academic attainments with the culture, poise and large-hearted humanity for which the leaders of her race are famous." Quite possibly Miss Eliza Roberts and her sister Frances who was the school matron and "stood out in my memory as the finest type of women England can produce" were the models after whom Mrs. Casely Hayford fashioned herself – at least until she came to the United States and met Nannie Helen Burroughs.

In 1883, on June 16, Adelaide received a great shock; her father married for the third time. "The third Mrs. Smith," as Adelaide always described her, was Elizabeth Jewell of Yorkshire whom Mr. Smith met at the Methodist Church he and his family attended when she was spending the winter in Jersey.

Why Mr. Smith chose to marry seven years after the death of her mother was never clear to Adelaide. In her published *Memoirs* she stated that Bea married after her father's third marriage, implying that she felt her presence was no longer needed in the home, but in her unpublished manuscript, Adelaide said she felt her father's marriage was because

"Bea the super-manageress" was leaving as the wife of Dr. Awooner Renner to return to Africa, and her father felt "he could not cope with such a brood of unruly children without adult help."

In any case, Mrs. Casely Hayford remembered her father's endeavors to explain to her his reasons for remarrying – "that my own mother was dead and that he was so lonely without any grown-up companion." She assured her father "that it would be all right – it would mean one more person in my household to love."

Elizabeth Jewell Smith was described by her step-daughter as

> elderly, plump and tall enough not to be dumpy. Her great beauty was her hair, a mass of black greying lovely hair which was braided, not plaited, in an intricate bi-weekly performance. In the summer her back view, with its basket of braids surmounted by a flowery bonnet, looked like a corner of a florist's window. She dressed handsomely and becomingly in rich silks, with good old-fashioned jewelry and delicate lace collars.

In character, according to Adelaide, she was "a woman of extremes, if she liked you, nothing was too good, but if she didn't, well – that's that! She was, it was true, a pre-eminently good woman whose humanity was somewhat swamped by her rigid religion." Nettie, Adelaide's youngest sister, the apple of Mrs. Smith's eye and, to a certain extent, the glory of the home, departed when she married Dr. Farrell Easmon – but this did not occur until after Adelaide's return from Germany.

From the first, Adelaide felt "my step-mother took a dislike for me for she showered presents upon my sisters and granted them privileges which were denied me." At one point her feeling against Mrs. Smith was so strong that she told her father she would leave should anything happen to him. Adelaide felt her father noticed this display of discrimination on Mrs. Smith's part. Many years later Mrs. Casely Hayford was to confide in Miss Graves that Mrs. Smith's lack of sympathy with her was due to the fact that she was much darker than her sisters.[18] However, in her *Memoirs*, Mrs. Casely Hayford is ready to assume her share of the blame. "It was unreasonable to expect that a lady so rigidly religious, and devoid of humor could put up with an impulsive harum-scarum teenager who never thought before she spoke, and who consequently was definitely lacking in tact." Of course, her own experience in the intervening years as stepmother to Archie Casely Hayford no doubt softened her assessment of "the third Mrs. Smith."

The growing crisis between Adelaide and her step-mother was solved when about two years after Mrs. Smith "took over the reins of management," Adelaide Smith left Jersey College for Germany. In her con-

versations with Miss Graves, she stated that this was her father's solution to the conflict with her step-mother. But in her published *Memoirs*,
Mrs. Casely Hayford makes no connection between her feelings
towards "the third Mrs. Smith" and her going to Germany. In the
twilight of her life, Mrs. Casely Hayford recalled that the opportunity to
go to Germany was the suggestion of her teacher, Fräulein Matilda
Bazlen. But one senses the influence and direction of her father and of
Miss Eliza Roberts, the Principal of Jersey College, who "were the
principal factors in shaping my life."

Although Adelaide clearly adored her father, who was old enough to
be her grandfather, she found it hard to come to terms with his remar-
riage. In the course of her reminiscing about this dilemma (in the
unpublished *Memoirs*) we learn a bit more of Mr. Smith and their
English environment.

> Father had two or three distinct hobbies. He liked good, solid,
> handsome well-made furniture. So the house was richly adorned
> with splendid old furniture, cumbersome beds, wardrobes, dining
> tables and chairs galore, and settees, tall boys and bookcases. He
> would also go round to second-hand dealers and pick up very
> handsome valuable old-fashioned trinkets which we all got in turn
> ... Then he went in for clocks of all descriptions – elegant gold-gilt
> French time pieces, more ornamental than useful, sedate, sombre,
> utilitarian clocks and three very handsome inlaid mahogony grand-
> father clocks. It was his habit to go round once a week to wind them,
> and as we crossed over the border, every one of them stopped dead.

As a person, according to his daughter,

> Mr. Smith was, without being in the least sanctimonious or goody-
> goody, deeply religious and always insisted on putting first things
> first. His yea was yea, his nay, nay. If on rare occasions we ventured
> to disobey, we got it all right – good measure, pressed down and
> running over to such an extent that any further repetitions were
> vigorously banned. There was no compromise and a very wide line
> of demarcation between what was right and what was wrong ...
> Family worship, instead of being mere routine was more like a
> Devotional, in which we youngsters all participated, reading the
> Scriptures in turn. Only an earthquake or a snow storm prevented
> us from attending services, twice a day, and as the Methodist
> Church was a mile away, it meant tramping four miles there and
> back – and for me six – when I became a Sunday school teacher.

Through her father, Adelaide Smith learned about the Salvation Army.

In those initial days it achieved its aims as it does today, by catering for the outcasts of society, so we unmitigated little snobs strongly disapproved of my father, a very highly respected member of the community, sneaking out to enjoy a little 'knee-drill'. If he managed to emerge unnoticed, he was invariably caught on his return, and treated to large doses of cold shoulder. That did not detract from his enjoyment, nor prevent him from subscribing to the *War Cry*, and if our welcome to the vendors was somewhat stand-offish and patronizing, they came all the same. One day they invited us to attend a meeting to be conducted by the great General himself, who was combining business with pleasure by taking a holiday in lovely little Jersey. He was a magnetic personality, with his hawk-like features and uncompromising jaw. When he turned his penetrating black eyes on you, it was like an X-ray searching the hidden precincts of your soul.

I was very young at the time, and possible passed quite unnoticed, but in later years I realized that the colossal success of this amazing movement was largely due to the amazing faith and indomitable grit of its founder.

Adelaide Smith also believed that the idea of her going to Germany was really as a result of her teacher's appreciation that she would need a firmer grasp of German if she intended to be examined in it for the London matriculation. It was agreed that this might be facilitated if she spent the long summer vacation in Germany. So off she went with her teacher Fräulein Bazlen and two friends. She was just seventeen and was not to return to England for three years.

From an African perspective and more particularly from the perspective of an Afro-American, the idea of taking this trip would, at that time, have seemed almost unthinkable for a young girl of seventeen. However, one of the consequences of being colonized was to be a part of the steady stream of promising young subjects from the colony to the metropolis in an effort to expand their knowledge by a visit or attendance at school. True, the visits were usually to the country of which the individual was a subject, but as the careers of the medical men, above described, indicate, there was also some movement from one European country to another – from England to France or Belgium or vice versa. In these early years, for obvious reasons, the United States was rarely if ever included in this circuit. In the case of the Smith family, Adelaide was not at that time alone in Germany for two of her half nieces were boarders at Catharinenstift, "an extremly exclusive school in Stuttgart under the direct patronage of the Queen of Württemberg."[19]

So the little group from Jersey went to Germany. Oehringen Württemberg, the home of the Bazlens, was their ultimate destination. They went via Granville in Brittany and then to Paris. Only Adelaide and her teacher continued beyond Paris, first to Baden Baden where they spent a couple of days with Fräulein Bazlen's uncle. There Adelaide was most impressed by the beauty of the Schwarzwald and the scent of the forest pine.

Her German experience made a great impact on Adelaide Smith who was acquiring a sense of purpose, determination and identity that she would need in her long and varied life. She wrote: "After 66 years, memories of my welcome in Germany are as warm as ever."

At first she lived with Fräulein's parents in "their roomy flat above the station." Herr Bazlen was a Railway Inspector. Almost immediately upon their arrival, Fräulein Matilda left for another post at Biberach, thus "catapulting [Adelaide] into a family not a single member of which could speak a word of English."

The cultural isolation she experienced and the separation from her family took their toll on the young woman who became increasingly downhearted and depressed. Mr. Bazlen helped to some extent by bringing her two half nieces from Catharinenstift for a surprise visit. How pleased she was to see them and to hear all about their school which had about 600 pupils, only thirty of whom were boarders.

Shortly, Fräulein Bazlen returned to Oehringen Württemberg to marry and Adelaide, who was then at Stuttgart, was asked to be one of her bridesmaids. Fräulein Bazlen wrote to her: "I am getting married in a week's time, and you must come to the wedding. I simply won't get married without you." Adelaide had to decline the invitation for lack of suitable clothing. A telegram arrived: "Come as you are," to which she replied, "I am not coming."

Imagine my consternation, [wrote Adelaide] when my fosterfather, Herr Bazlen, marched in a day or two after, with instructions from his daughter to bring me by force. And how nice they all were! Nobody seemed to notice either my colour or my morning dress. As I had no groom attendant, Matilda's brother-in-law shepherded two of us, one on each arm, and I was by no means left out in the cold – an act I shall never forget.

At the Polter Abend – the night before the wedding, which is devoted to feasting, orations and many expressions of felicity – somebody read out a poem, about "the little stranger within their gates," whose presence had added so much to their enjoyment. I

was overwhelmed with embarrassment and simply had to hide my
head. What a Germany it was in those days!

For reasons that Mrs. Casely Hayford does not offer, she decided
after the first summer was over, before the wedding apparently, to stay
on in Germany. So she took up residence in a pension in Suttgart run by
Fräulein von Riecke, the daughter of a deceased physician at the Court
of Würtemberg, "thus giving me entry into Stuttgart society." Fräulein
von Riecke was a chaperone at Catharinenstift. Through her, Adelaide
was introduced to a German lady teaching Fräulein Margarerita von
Palm, the daughter of the King's Chamberlain. The two ladies agreed
each to teach the other her own language.

Frau von Palm, "a haughty, dignified Prussian lady," heard of Adelaide and employed her as a "sub-teacher" to read English books with
her daughter Ghita, "a charming girl of the same age as myself." This
experience not only afforded her much needed money but the opportunity to be introduced to upper-class turn of the century German life.
She remembered how formal the children were with their parents. "The
only son, Philip, age 14, never left the room without going to kiss his
mother's hand and then facing her all the time backing out, giving her a
courteous bow before disappearing."

Adelaide was also invited by Baron and Baronin von Palm to spend a
few days at their country residence. But the major part of her time was
taken up with her musical activities as she had enrolled in a branch of the
Stuttgart Conservatory to concentrate on music. The piano was her
principal instrument, but she also did singing and practiced upon the
violin. Adelaide "did enjoy Germany and had I had the funds, I would
have accomplished something worthwhile." But "financial stringency
compelled me to return to England after a wonderful, happy experience
of Germany and its people ... Just a year before my younger sister's
Nettie's wedding to Dr. John Farrell Easmon."

Her stay in Germany did many things for Adelaide Smith, not the
least of which was to force her to face even more her color difference.
"There were times, however," she wrote,

> when in spite of the great kindness, I felt horribly homesick.
> Germany had only just begun to acquire colonies, so I was the first
> little negress they had seen and instantly became Curio No.1. I
> suffered from acute self-consciousness not so much because I was
> black but because I was so conspicuous. I could never withdraw and
> was always in the limelight. I remember once going into a shop to
> buy something and everyone of the assistants fled, leaving me

monarch of all I surveyed. Fortunately, my sense of humor came to
the rescue, and I was able to make a big joke over it, but it did hurt.
Now, I realise that was because I was not sufficiently sensible to see
things in their right light. I know that God never makes any
mistakes, and that my black skin was part of the equipment with
which he endowed me to make good in life. So, I 'took Fate by the
throat,' and decided to turn this liability into an asset, by facing up
to life and carrying on my career. This decision, as I can now see,
was the right one ... the only one.

With this new maturity, Adelaide Smith returned to England, better
educated, more sophisticated and more sure of who and what she was
and could become.

IV

England, Africa and Return

Adelaide Smith returned to the family home in Jersey in 1888 to find "the third Mrs. Smith" still in charge and her younger sister Nettie excited about the prospect of marrying within the year Dr. John Farrell Easmon, who subsequently became Principal Medical Officer of the Gold Coast. Their wedding in 1889 in the Wesleyan Church at St. Helier was a charming affair, but far less formal than Fräulein Brazlen's. Nettie only had two bridesmaids – two of her sisters, Adelaide and Emm. Nettie's departure for Africa so soon after Adelaide's return and no doubt her own sense of now being different and no longer the child she was when she left for Germany, made Adelaide restless. Although she busied herself by giving tangible assistance in the household duties the place was not the same to her after Nettie's departure.

So, more in search of her family than of herself, Adelaide left Jersey for Freetown in 1892 "to try my hand at teaching as a prelude to earning a living." It was certainly clear to her that with her father's increasing age and no additional sources of money and the departure of her two sisters Bea and Nettie she too must be prepared to stand on her own. On her arrival, she stayed with her older sister Bea, Mrs. William Awooner Renner. This visit to Freetown gave Adelaide a glimpse into the educational facilities in Africa of the day. She took a "part-time teaching position at the Methodist School, known then as the Female Institution, which was carried on in one of my mother's houses, now known as The City Hotel."[1] The Wesleyan Female Institution, as mentioned above, was started in 1880 by a group of Wesleyans, not by the mission itself. It was managed by James Taylor but in its earliest stages had European headmistresses.

> Taylor was a prominent trader in Freetown, whose capacity for business entirely eclipsed his capacity for training girls. The highlight of the day's program was when the girls marched past for [the headmistress's] benefit, led by 'Langa-foot' Taylor with his enormous feet protruding in front, all shouting at the top of their voices:

We all go to our places
with clean hands and faces,
And pay great attention
To what we are told;
Or else we will never
Be happy or clever
For learning is better
Than silver and gold.

It was not very inspiring, but to judge from the many suppressed giggles, it was highly entertaining. ...

In my leisure hours, I taught at the Annie Walsh Memorial School, under the Principalship of Miss Dunkley (1893–95), who specialized in character training and married Mr. Humphrey, a missionary who was subsequently killed in the Bai Bureh Uprising (1882–1896). My spare moments were filled in by taking music lessons.

As an attractive woman, fresh from study in England and Germany and a member of a well-known and distinguished family, Adelaide Smith must have caused quite a stir in Freetown. How she felt about this first return to Freetown is not recorded, but what she does say about her next trip suggests that there was at that time more distance than cordiality between her and her peers. By the 1890s there had been a definite shift in the relationship between the Creoles and the British. The Creoles were no longer the favored community. Furthermore, it is curious that Adelaide Smith was not offered a teaching post at Annie Walsh. Undoubtedly, she would have wanted such a position for by volunteering her services there she must have been trying to call attention to her presence and her talents. There is no mention at all of her in the available minutes of the school during this period. But Adelaide Smith through this slight was gaining yet another lesson in race relations – perhaps she was too educated, too secure to be seen as a real or genuine African by the European Board of the school. She was perhaps, in their view, neither a real European nor a real African. And, of course, her manner was probably far from subservient; she had not been socialized to behave as a colonial – not even as an educated colonial. For the disbeliever, one can point to DuBois' difficulties in adjusting to or being accepting by Wilberforce University, the all-Black Methodist school in Ohio, when he had just returned from Germany and had a Ph.D. from Harvard, or DuBois' inability to secure a full-fledged teaching position at the University of Pennsylvania when he was appointed researcher on the

Philadelphia Negro. The road of the exceptional Black is often hard. An example from a family story told later to me by an aunt, Otelia Cromwell, is a further illustration.[2]

In his recorded autobiography, DuBois recalls,

> I was asked to come to the University of Pennsylvania to make a study of the Negro population of the 7th Ward of Philadelphia ... Of course I couldn't be an instructor, I couldn't be a scholar because I already had my Ph.D from Harvard so they made me an assistant-instructor. Which meant that I didn't do any instruction but that I did make this study and I made it on my own plan.[3]

While Adelaide Smith did get some needed experience in teaching while she was in Freetown, she was probably not sorry to leave when in April, 1894 she was called back to England because of the sudden death of her step-mother. "The third Mrs. Smith's" death, following a heart attack, came as a great blow to Mr. Smith who began to age rapidly. He suddenly developed a roaming spirit and was never satisfied to remain at home. Accompanied by another old crony, the Reverend Robert Dillon, who had married his first wife's [Charlotte's] twin sister, Margaret, he set off for Buxton Spa spending weeks on end there.

Then he thought it would be nice to visit the Isle of Wight. At that time Adelaide and Emma accompanied him to Ryde, and he seemed to take on a new lease of life.

> It did not last long, however, because about May, 1895 we noticed he was getting terribly yellow.
>
> Dr. Dunlop, our family doctor, said his liver was entirely out of order, but if we cared to get an expert opinion, we could do so. Emma and Bea, who had come home for a holiday with her son Roland, took him to London to consult Sir William Broadbent, the Queen's physician, a benign old gentleman who gave him a thorough examination. "Mr. Smith," he said gently, "we physicians cannot always effect cure. Sometimes we can only alleviate suffering. I advise you to return home immediately."
>
> The passengers had all landed when father was hoisted gently up in a chair and taken to the waiting landau. His face proclaimed his dying condition.
>
> There were so many grandchildren visiting Jersey that summer, that we packed them off to La Roque where we had taken a charming cottage by the sea, so that father could be kept as quiet as possible. We four daughters – Bea, Emma, Nettie and myself taking turn to nurse him.

He was very calm and peaceful but one thing seemed to weigh upon his mind – the fact that he was leaving us, his two unmarried daughters, so badly off. "My dears, "he would say, "you will have to subsist on eggs for your principal meal when I am gone." We assured him that that was not any hardship at all, and nothing whatever to worry about. His worry was so acute that he even insisted that they were not to bedeck his dead body with gold studs or links. In his feeble voice, he kept on calling for our mother – not the first or the third, but the second Mrs. Smith, "Anne, dear, I am coming." At 10:00., August 5, 1895, he breathed his last, and life was never the same to me afterwards.

This beloved father of ours left a goodly heritage as an example of a steadfast, serene, utterly selfless, upright life, and an unshakable faith in God.

According to the terms of his will, filed 16 September 1896, William Smith, Jr, named William Broughton Davies, Mary's husband, and William (Jarvis Awooner) Renner, Bea's husband, as co-executors. Mr. Smith advised that all of his real estate in Sierra Leone be sold at the discretion of the co-executors and that they would be reimbursed for any cost involved. The sale could be either at public auction or through private contract. Emma and Adelaide, if unmarried at the time, were to share equally in the sale of the real estate. (If one had married, the other would get the results of the sale in total.) He further advised that his personal effects in Jersey (one would assume this meant his home there also) would be apportioned as follows: two-thirds to go to Adelaide and Emma, but if one had married, the entire amount to the single daughter; the remaining one-third to be divided between all the children in equal amounts, and the heirs of any of his children who might have predeceased him. If Adelaide and Emma should have married at the time of these settlements, then all the children would share equally in the sale of his effects on Jersey.

Shortly after his father's death, but before his will was filed, Thomas Smith, his son, drew up a will in 1895 in which he left all he had to be shared equally between Emma and Adelaide. As there is little evidence that Tom, then or for most of his life, ever had any property, one must assume this was merely a legal act relinquishing any shares he might have had in William Smith, Jr.'s estate to his two sisters, Emma and Adelaide.

After Mr. Smith's death, the family had to decide how to survive.

It was our father's dying wish that we should return [to Africa] to be near our own immediate relatives. But Africa at the time did not attract us because we were more or less strangers and although our parents did a wonderful thing by giving us chances for an excellent European training for such a lenghty period, it turned us out as black white women. Our friends did not want us to leave Jersey and it was terrible wrench after 21 years. But with aching hearts we sold most of our furniture, retaining only necessities for our future sojourn in Africa.

Africa Again, But Briefly

"One Sunday morning in November, 1897, we two forlorn orphans [Addie and Emm] landed in Freetown and were met by brother Tom" who apparently left Jersey shortly after executing his will. Tom, it appears, "had not anticipated such an early arrival and gave us a Mother Hubbard reception." Fortunately, the Commissioner for Native Affairs, James C.E. Parkes and his wife came to their rescue and took Adelaide and Emm into their home.[1]

Soon after their return, the sisters sought other quarters because they had decided to start a school. Their nephew, Chilley Smith, son of their half brother, Dr. Robert Smith, offered them the family house opposite the one he had inherited from his father. They gratefully moved in immediately.

It is during this settling in period that Adelaide Smith first begins to know and to feel Freetown. On her previous visit, with her father still alive in the family home in England, both she and the members of her social set in Freetown had probably viewed her stay there as temporary – as just a rather long visit. But now, with Mr. Smith dead and all her ties to Jersey severed, the last of the Smith sisters would seem to have returned permanently to Freetown – and without husbands. One can easily imagine the reactions and thoughts of their contemporaries – male and female – towards these two young, but not so young, attractive, single, sophisticated women attempting to re-enter Freetown society without, it would also appear, any real family auspices. The Renners, with whom Adelaide had stayed on her previous visit, were apparently not in Freetown; the Easmons were definitely in the Gold Coast and Tom, "the ne'er-do-well," had no real status. Adelaide and Emma were left on their own but not as unknowns.

Mrs. Casely Hayford speaks very frankly about this early period and the adjustment it required.

> Most of the educated Africans were definitely hostile. They shunned us, snubbed us, ostracized us ... At a Ball at Government House a few weeks after our arrival, we met a gentleman who had

lived in the same boarding house with us in London. I asked him whether his wife was present, because I would very much like to know her. He came back and told me that his wife did not wish to know me. Such was Freetown's attitude towards us, and this is what invariably happens to those brought up exclusively "on the other side!" ... But in six months we lived down all this black prejudice.

It is not surprising that the idea of starting a school would have occurred to the sisters, especially to Adelaide. Education for what and by whom was being much discussed at the time. Governor Cardew had stimulated an editorial in the *Sierra Leone Weekly News* on the importance of voluntary schools in the colony.[2] There was no novelty in thinking about the importance of girls' education for, in Freetown, some girls had always received excellent education either in the colony or abroad. Also, while some persons ignored or shunned the Smith sisters, there were undoubtedly others who admired them and perhaps envied them. According to Mrs. Casely Hayford, when she first opened the school there was only one pupil but six months later, after the ice had been broken, the enrollment went up. There is some difference of opinion as to the starting date of the school. According to Mrs. Casely Hayford as noted by Robinka Mason, a student at the University of Sierra Leone, in her work, *The Development of Girls' Secondary Education in Sierra Leone,* the school started in 1897.[3] But an official government report gives the starting date as January, 1898.[4]

It is quite possible that both are correct – that not until the 1898 date was there what one might actually call a school in operation though the Smiths had, in fact, tried to start one in 1897. By January, they had received the necessary community support from the Rev. Charles (?) Marke and some other leading Methodists. So the school was opened in the Smith home for adult African girls, as the first private enterprise to establish girls' secondary education in Sierra Leone.[5] There were twelve girls, 15 years and upward at first, but the number quickly grew to fifty.[6] Mrs. Casely Hayford herself was modest in her recollection of the early days of the school. "Looking back," she told Miss Mason, "one can hardly call it a school except that the tuition was confined more or less to the Three Rs, with physical culture and music thrown in." She said the enrollment never exceeded forty pupils.

During this period, Adelaide Smith was simultaneously being introduced to the two Africas, which impinged upon Creole life of the period – the traditional or native life, and the colonial life style. Shortly after the New Year and the starting of the school, her health "became uncertain

... apart from malaria and its attendant inertia I suffered terribly from
ear ache. I tried all the scientific doctors in town, but their remedies
were not effective in stopping the constant flow of matter, accompanied
by excruciating pain." Then, she reports, "I had a brain wave! This is
some climatic trouble: why not try a native doctor – not a medicine man,
but some educated African who understands herbal remedies!" (It is not
clear how she made this distinction for there were native doctors who
used herbs and probably no educated African who did.)

> I sent for one. He examined my ears and then said at once, "I can
> cure you but I shall have to go to bush to find a little insect water
> from which I will dry up the matter. It will take some time, but I
> shall be back here in a week."
>
> I was lying on my couch in the sitting room when he returned. He
> dropped something into my ear and then plugged it up with some-
> thing that looked like cooked spinach. That evening we were all at
> the dining table, when I said to Tom and Emma: "Don't shout."
> They answered: "We are not shouting!" I began to dance around
> the room. Oh, I said, I can hear and my ears are not paining me
> anymore. Thank God!

As a result of being in Freetown at the time of the Bai Bureh Uprising,
Adelaide Smith had another exposure to traditional Africa. And she
spoke vividly about it.

> The introduction of the hut tax had caused a great deal of unrest in
> the Mende country, and the Chief, Bai Bureh, staunchly backed by
> his people,[7] determined to kill the white people and all black people
> as well. I remember how concerned we were about our relative
> Chilley Smith who was practically white in appearance. We wanted
> to darken his skin, but he laughed all our fears away. Fortunately,
> the rising was put down before it reached Freetown, but many
> Africans were plunged into mourning through it.

But colonial Africa was also very much there and Adelaide Smith was
exposed to it. While she was in Freetown, the Sierra Leone Railway was
opened by His Excellency, Sir Matthew Nathan, who chartered a train
and took a great many passengers to lunch with him at the terminus –
Waterloo. Adelaide Smith was among those whom "he managed to give
such a variety of excellent 'chop' right there in the bus ... For every mile
of track laid, one European succumbed, which shows how appropriate
[the appellation] 'The White Man's Grave' was at the time."

Adelaide Smith's obviously positive reaction to the railroad and the
colonial festivities associated with its opening were at variance with

those reported by Spitzer who quoted the description by the editor of the *Sierra Leone Times* of the racial segregation which took place at the inauguration of the track.[8] The railway, it seems, made two inaugural trips: one especially for Europeans – the Segregation Party – on which, according to the editor, Mr. Fitz-John, "there was nothing tawney [sic] to come between the wind and the divinity of anyone of the party – not even the Mayor who at this time was Claudius E. Wright, a Creole; the other trip was 'exclusively for natives.'" If this account is true, Adelaide Smith seemingly saw nothing wrong in this discrimination – at least she did not note it in her *Memoirs*, but then she was riding with cousin Claude, a distinguished barrister, not just those other ordinary European civil servants. One gets the impression that Adelaide Smith was slowly getting to know Freetown, its people and its ways. But it is still difficult to measure with any degree of accuracy her comfort there or her acceptance by the people.

The Smith family was shattered by the sudden death in the Gold Coast on 9 June 1900 of their brother-in-law, John Farrell Easmon, at the age of 44, leaving their sister Nettie a widow at 28 with two small children, Charles and Kathleen to support.

> The Easmon family lived on such a standard that there was hardly any money left. We [the sisters] immediately offered her a home which she accepted, but of course, conditions were different and she wanted to give the children better educational advantages. This coupled with my poor state of health made us decide to return to England. So after closing the school and selling bits of housing furniture, together with all our lares and penates, there was still need for money to cover five passages: mine, Nettie's, the two children's and Emma's.

(Tom apparently did not return to England). Showing her drive and persistence, Adelaide wrote to Sir Alfred-Jones, the founder of the Elder Dempster Line, asking him to give the children free passages – which he did with "a grace I have never forgotten."

Their first residence in England was "a mediocre little dwelling at Shepherd's Bush," 5 Melrose Terrace, chosen

> because of its proximity to Collett Court, The Preparatory School for St. Paul's which Charlie attended. We soon found the need to take in paying guests to supplement our meagre income. We catered to batchelors only. They were not so exacting and were out for most of the day. Then an African lady [Mrs. Victoria Davies] came to stay with us. She was really Queen Victoria's protégée and

god-daughter, having as a girl spent most of her holidays at Buck-
ingham Palace.

According to a letter to me (9/21/71) from Dr. Easmon,

> Mrs. Davies was a native of Nigeria who as a small child was
> captured as a slave and sent to America. On the way, the slave boat
> was [intercepted] by a British Cruiser and the captain brought the
> little slave girl to England and presented her to Queen Victoria.
> She was more or less adopted by the Queen as Sarah Bonetta
> Forbes and brought up with the Royal children including the one
> who became King Edward VII. Queen Victoria, as she grew older,
> thought she would be better off in Africa and sent her back to Sierra
> Leone to be a boarder at the Annie Walsh School in Freetown ...
> She stayed on in Freetown and married Captain Davies. For the
> wedding, Queen Victoria sent out a fine wedding present. Her
> husband had his own ships trading with Lagos. They had a daugh-
> ter who was sent to the Queen in England and brought up with the
> Royal children. This daughter married Dr. John Randall practicing
> in Lagos, a Nigerian but born in Regent near Freetown. The
> Randalls had a son and a daughter both of whom died early.

(Dr. Randall, before qualifying, had gone to Lagos from Sierra Leone as
Dr. Davies' Chief Dispenser.)
  Fyfe's account differs slightly from that of Dr. Easmon.

> In 1851 two Grammar School boys, brothers of Aku parentage,
> James and Samuel Davies, were taken on board the HMS Volcano
> to learn seamanship. Too old to qualify as naval officers, they
> became merchant captains ... James gave up the sea and settled in
> business in Lagos. He married, as his second wife, Sally Forbes-
> Bonetta, a girl brought to England from Dahomey by Captain
> Forbes of *HMS Bonetta*, and adopted by Queen Victoria, who sent
> her to school with the CMS in Freetown. The Queen stood
> godmother to their eldest daughter Victoria, sent her a gold plate,
> and when she grew up used to invite her to Windsor.[9]
> Victoria Davies married Dr. John Randall from Regent who
> qualified as a doctor at St. Andrews and went to practice in Lagos.

There seems to be some confusion in the two stories or maybe merely a
printer's error, for there was no Mrs. Victoria Davies or Mrs. Sally
Davies. In any case, this distinguished lady with Freetown connections
came to live, for a time, at the boarding house run by Adelaide, Nettie

and Emm. No doubt the sisters needed the assistance of a person as well known as Miss Davies for they really knew little of London. Miss Davies was indeed most helpful, introducing them to the Coleridge-Taylors, "who were fast beginning to climb from obscurity to the giddy heights of fame and eminence."

In the best of Creole tradition, the families of the Smiths and Coleridge-Taylors were not at all unknown to each other. Coleridge-Taylor's father, Daniel Peter Hughes Taylor, son of an Aku trader, went from Grammar School in Freetown to Wesley College, Taunton, and Kings College, London. In 1874, he was admitted MRCS; first he worked for the government in Bonthe for a year, then he practiced privately, chiefly in the Gambia, until his death in 1904. His son, Samuel Coleridge, was born to an English mother while Daniel was still in England. Neither the mother nor the son ever visited Africa.[10] Coleridge's mother was a lady companion in the home of one of Dr. Taylor's patients.

Samuel Coleridge-Taylor and his English wife, the former Jessie Walmsley, the daughter of a British Army colonel whom he first met when they were both students at the Royal Conservatory of Music,

> invited the Smith sisters to tea at their home at Selhurst (Croydon) ... Contact with them is an unforgettable memory. It seems only yesterday – but is more than fifty years since we were privileged to share their box at the Albert Hall for an early performance of the complete *Hiawatha Trilogy*, conducted by Sir Frederick Bridge. It was an inspiring evening. The Hall was packed, and Coleridge, who was small of stature, was hiding at the back of the box like a recalcitrant schoolboy anticipating a thrashing. When the shouts of "Composer, composer!" reverberated throughout that immense building he shrank more than ever into his corner until at last Sir Frederick Bridge himself banged the door open and literally dragged him onto the platform, amidst roars of applause from the audience.

> Some time afterwards, we were again privileged to accompany him to the People's Palace in the the East End to listen to his immortal work under the baton of Mr. Allen Gill. It was a superb performance and during the interval Mrs. Gill came to enquire whether her husband might announce the fact that the composer was in the audience. I have never seen Coleridge so angry, "If you do such a thing," he declared, "I shall never come to the East End again" ... Such was the modest, retiring character of the man who was pre-eminently great. His generosity knew no bounds. I never

once saw him pass a poor street musician without dipping his hand
in his pocket.

Coleridge was the most distinguished guest at my wedding and
stood sponsor for my little daughter, Gladys. Never wealthy, he
bitterly regretted selling his copyright of *Hiawatha* to the music
publishers for 300 pounds. He said "If they would only give me a
penny on each copy they sell, I could keep my motorcar," which in
those days was a great luxury. His publishers may be rolling in
wealth, but Coleridge has left the world an immortal memory.

The name of Samuel Coleridge-Taylor was and is well known to any
Afro-American familiar with the history of the music of his people. It has
been said that Coleridge-Taylor "chronicled a new day for the Negro in
music." "Prior to his composition," wrote Theodore De Witt Phillips,
his biographer, "the Negroes' contributions to music were of the communal variety. There had been no native individual voices to speak
commandingly and representatively until the utterances of Samuel
Coleridge-Taylor impressed themselves upon the world."[11]

Whether or not this evaluation of Coleridge-Taylor's contribution
would be universally accepted, there is no doubt that he combined in his
work in an almost unique fashion the talents and influences of Africa
and the West. The overture to *Hiawatha's Departure*, supposedly American Indian in inspiration, was, in fact, one of his first efforts to incorporate African themes in his music and was taken from the Negro spiritual,
"Nobody Knows the Trouble I've Seen." According to St. Laurent,

> [the] most important aspect of the entire body of Coleridge-
> Taylor's music was what critics sometimes misunderstandingly
> called its "wild" and uncouth strain. But critics all agreed on what
> they called "the barbaric" strain in his music, all of it dominated by
> strange rhythms – his African heritage – which provided a breath of
> fresh air to the dreary clichés which prevailed in English composi-
> tion at the time.[12]

Beginning with his admission to the Royal College of Music in 1890
at the age of 15, up until his early death from tuberculosis at the age of 37
on 1 September, 1919, Samuel Coleridge-Taylor was recognized as a
musical genius. On his first appearance, "few men received so much
public attention as the result of one comparatively short work" – the
Ballade in A Minor composed for the Three Choirs Festival.

Three was certainly a tie between Coleridge-Taylor's work and that
of the new world black music, for as he himself said, "as the result of
inner persuasions the idea of doing for Negro music what Brahms has

done for Hungarian folk music and Grieg for the Norwegian, came early to my mind." Living near London and hearing the Fisk Jubilee Singers and meeting their leader, Frederick J. Loudin, led Coleridge-Taylor from then on to the frequent use of Negro Americans themselves in his works, first in his *African Suite* and then in *Bamboula.* An even more important influence in strengthening the connection and improving the understanding of the new world blacks was his friendship and collaboration with Paul Lawrence Dunbar. "The two men collaborated on a series of African romances, notably, 'At Candle Lighting Time' and 'Danse Negre'."

Coleridge-Taylor's works were performed at the Albert Hall, the Crystal Palace and other famous London concert halls. His energy was matched by his versatility. From 1900 to 1906 he was closely associated with Sir Beerbohm Tree, perhaps the greatest of England's theatrical producers, at His Majesty's Theatre, London.

At the height of his fame, in spite of some discouragement from Dunbar, Coleridge-Taylor made two trips to the United States – the first in 1904 and the second in 1907. His first concert was in Washington, D.C. on 16 November 1904, with a chorus of 200 Negro voices.

> He was the first black man to give a concert in New York's Mendelssohn Hall and in the New England Conservatory of Music in Boston. Clearly, his success in the United States was phenomenal – including a meeting with President Theodore Roosevelt and giving concerts in the major cultural areas of the country – Baltimore, Chicago, Philadelphia, New York, and Boston.

The opportunity of knowing well such a distinguished African, comfortable and accepted in England, must have made a tremendous impression on Adelaide Smith. For here was a person, a peer, a fellow Sierra Leoneon, whose training and competence were lauded in England and the United States, who had not been forced to return to Sierra Leone to accept the crumbs from the table of an increasingly racist society but had stood his ground and been acknowledged as a genius in England itself! What is more, his skill and talent had been measured against that of the English. Though the content and spirit of his music were more often African or Afro-American, his method of executing it was purely western. Coleridge-Taylor must have acknowledged to Adelaide Smith this indebtedness to Africa and perhaps through him she too felt the influence and knew the talents of men like Dunbar. She was in a position most likely to understand – being of Africa but so long out of it. Also she must have been influenced by her knowledge of the royal treatment Coleridge-Taylor received on his two trips to the United States – appreciation by both whites and blacks.

It was practically unknown, at that time, for other than impoverished students, hoping to secure an education, albeit inferior to that available in England (it was believed), to come to the United States. Certainly no distinguished Africans would feel the need to do so. It was to England and France that one was supposed to look at that time for qualifying credentials – not to the relatively untutored, rough and racist society of America. It is true that Afro-Americans like Du Bois, Alain Locke and Dunbar or Loudin, or even in the earlier days Frederick Douglass, had come to London and met Africans there, but the thought of Africans coming to the United States for acknowledgment, support or empathy had just not surfaced.

Mrs. Casely Hayford's determination later to come to the States for just those reasons, and to be the first African woman to do so, must have been prompted, to some extent at least, by her knowledge of what the experience and feelings of Coleridge-Taylor had been. Even so distinguished a personage and Pan-Africanist as her husband, J.E. Casely Hayford, never visited the United States.

There could be some dispute as to who was the first African woman to come to the United States. Mrs. Casely Hayford was probably the first to come on a lecture tour but at least two women had preceded her. Sarah Kinson from Sierra Leone, a Mende recaptive of the Amistad Mutiny fame, attended Oberlin College in Ohio for the academic year 1848–49. Charlotte Mange (later Maxeke), who was born in the Cape Province of South Africa in 1874, graduated from Wilberforce University, also in Ohio, in 1901. As a young girl Charlotte went with her parents to Kimberly. There she first made her mark in the field of music with her lovely singing. Her voice brought her the opportunity of going overseas as a member of an African choir which toured Europe and America. When the tour was over and the members of the choir returned home, Charlotte remained in the United States to continue her education.

At Wilberforce she met her future husband and fellow South African, Marshall Maxeke. When Marshall Maxeke completed his theological studies for the AME ministry they married and returned together to South Africa where they started a school, named Wilberforce Institution, in the Transvaal.

Dr. Z.K. Matthews, to whom I am indebted for this information about the Maxekes described Mrs. Maxeke as an eloquent speaker and a fearless campaigner against the disabilities under which her people labored. She was active in the political organizations of the day and encouraged women to enter politics. She herself was for many years the President of the Women's League – the women's section of the African National Congress. Mrs. Z.K. Matthews who knew Mrs. Maxeke when she herself was young remembered "her touring our land urging our women to better themselves and be aware of the dangers threatening their rights" (5/4/64).[13]

Adelaide Smith and Joseph Ephraim Casely Hayford

Surprising as it may seem, there had never been any lack of suitors in my life and four years earlier, I had had the crowning glory of my life by loving a man who had developed tuberculosis. God took him at the early age of thirty.[1] From that experience, I knew I could only offer a second best affection to any suitor who might come along.

But on 31 July 1903, Adelaide Smith received a letter, return address 13 Upper Bedford Place, Russell Square, from a Gold Coast lawyer who was spending some months in England.

It was a very short letter and the orthography a bit doubtful, but it voiced the request that he might be allowed to meet me. He had tried through several mutual friends to bring this about unsuccessfully so he was taking the bull by the horns, and wanting to know whether he would be permitted to call. So, at the age of 35, I wrote to the Gold Coast lawyer, Joseph Ephraim Casely-Hayford inviting him to tea in our unpretentious little home.

One informant said: "because Mrs. Casely Hayford became the image of British aristocracy in thoughts, words and deeds, she turned down many African [Creole] suitors because she felt they had not the finesse of English gentlemen."[2] The same informant said: "Adelaide Smith saw Casely-Hayford was a gentleman, a perfect gentleman, so within a few weeks they were engaged and married."

Casely Hayford (1866–1930) was born 3 September 1866, as the third son of Reverend John de Graft Hayford and Mary (Awuraba) Brew. Both parents were from Anomabu, Gold Coast, a very important center along with Cape Coast, for trading and later the intellectual life of the time. Mr. Casely Hayford had two brothers; Dr. Ernest J. Hayford (1858–1913) and the Reverend Mark C. Hayford (1864–1935) whose daughter, Mrs. Mary Edmondson of Freetown, described him as "the only Hayford who reasonably stuck by women; though even he was

Mr. J.E. Casely Hayford

Anne Spilsbury Smith (Mrs. Casely Hayford's mother)

Wedding Party in Freetown around the turn of the century

One of the Smith sisters in London

married three times – always to Europeans – English, German, and Irish women."

Casely Hayford was educated at the Wesleyan Boys High School at Cape Coast, now Mfantisipim School, and at Fourah Bay College. When he returned from Sierra Leone, Casely Hayford became a teacher and was eventually appointed principal of Accra Wesley High School. Later, he served as articled clerk to a European lawyer in Cape Coast, after which he went to England to join the Inner Temple and to study at Peterhouse, Cambridge. On 17 November, 1896 he was called to the bar. Upon his return to the Gold Coast, Casely Hayford became active in the Aborigines' Rights Protection Society which had been organized on 9 March 1897, and became its head after the death in 1910 of John Mensah Sarbah. In 1916, he was nominated member of the Gold Coast Legislative Council and became an elected member of the Council in 1927, remaining a member until his death in 1930. In 1920, with T. Hutton Mills, he was a founder of the National Congress of British West Africa (NCBWA), the major West African political movement in the first quarter of the twentieth century. He was its president from 1923 until his death, after which the movement itself faded from the scene.

Casely Hayford was a man of parts: lawyer, activist, editor, public servant, author, philosopher, and of strong religious convictions. Though educated in England, he remained a true African.

Through his mother, Casely Hayford was related to a most interesting family, the descendants of Richard Brew (1725–176?) an Irish trader who made a fortune in slaves and other items on the Coast. Margaret Priestly has given a most informative account of the history and impact of the descendants of this man.[3] She concluded that the family's survival rested on incorporating in a most unique way values from their European ancestor as well as incorporating, as appropriate, values and customs from Akan society. Many of its members were outstanding persons of the day in business and in law. James Hutton Brew, Casely Hayford's uncle, was one of the more notable of his family and had, apparently, quite an influence on his nephew. Casely Hayford was, as was Adelaide Casely Hayford, an African who looked both ways:

> Writing to his kinfolk in 1929 shortly before his death, Casely Hayford referred to their family unity and their notable ancestry with his late grandfather [Samuel Collins, great grandson of Richard] in mind. When visiting England, he began to trace Brew origins on the European side, a matter in which his uncle, James Hutton Brew, is also said to have shown interest.[4]

His first book, *Gold Coast Native Institutions*, dedicated to his recently deceased first wife Beatrice Madeline Pynoch, mother of his son Archie, was to some degree a lawyer's book inspired by the opposition to the Crown Lands Bill and reflecting this growing emphasis on the African way of life.[5] The thesis of his third book, *The Truth About the West African Land Question* was even more protective of African values, for to him the land tenure system developed by Africans must be preserved if Africans were to withstand the assault upon their values by colonialism.[6]

But is is to the second book, *Ethiopia Unbound*, dedicated "To The Sons of Ethiopia The World Wide Over," that one must turn to know Casely Hayford, the philosopher, the man as African.[7] Written largely in the form of a dialogue between Kwamanku (himself) and Whitely (the Englishman, his friend), the book is obviously influenced by the style and concerns of W.E.B. Du Bois' *The Souls of Black Folk*.[8] Casely Hayford's book is more clearly autobiographical than Du Bois', yet, as does Du Bois, he explores a range of issues and concepts important to black people everywhere.

The sub-title of the book, "Studies in Racial Emancipation," is so subtle as to be misleading, but intriguing to the reader is his insertion, under his western name, of his African name – Ekra Agiman. As Du Bois eulogized Alexander Crummell in *Souls of Black Folk*, Casely Hayford eulogized Edward Blyden and the ideas for which Blyden stood: The Cross vs. the Crescent, polygyny, and African nationality, and a national university for Africa. Casely Hayford felt that the double consciousness so important in Du Bois' analysis of the personality of the Afro-Americans was not a characteristic of the Africans who could remain firmly rooted in their own culture.

From *Ethiopia Unbound*, it is also possible to get some idea of how Casely Hayford saw his wife, Adelaide, his admitted second choice. Kwamankra falls in love with Miss Mansa. In an early conversation between them, Kwamankra says, "So you deserted us for the continent without a moment's notice. It was really bad of you, and I hope you have made up your mind now to make full amends." She replies, "Yes, I didn't like life here. Somehow it didn't suit me." Kwamankra: "You must have found Stuttgart congenial to judge from the length of time you have been away ... Now that reminds me, by a stroke of ill luck, I arrived at your hotel the day you left for the continent half an hour too late, to find the bird had flown."

For the next few weeks, Mansa and Kwamankra saw a good deal of one another. From the first, there was a congeniality between the two which went to make all intercourse natural, pleasant and spontaneous. It was as if they had known one another all their lives and it seemed the most natural thing that henceforth their joint lives should run in the same tenor.

As the days passed the twain grew in mutual understanding, the true basis of all happy unions ...

Summer was waning into autumn, and the chrysanthemum and sweet mignonette were in bloom when the lovers decided upon marriage before returning to Africa where Kwamankra was to start a practice. It was to be a simple affair, at which there were to be no bride's maids, groom's men, and only the nearest friends were to be asked. Mansa appeared in church on the wedding day in a simple African costume of her own design, tastefully got up, and when someone asked her the reason for her choice, she said she knew it would please her husband!

From here on the narrative seems to incorporate more of the experiences of Mr. Casely Hayford's first marriage to Beatrice. Mansa and Kwamankra do return to Africa, a son is born and the wife dies later in childbirth, this time a girl baby also dies, leaving both father and son "with a twice two-fold bond of love between their souls and the souls of those that had gone before."[9]

In a section on "Love and Death" in this work, Kwamankra goes off in a dream to another world where he is reunited with his dearly beloved departed Mansa and their girl baby – Katsina. After much discussion of love, courage and trust, Mansa is to stay in heaven and Kwamankra is to return to earth. Perhaps as a way of expressing the love and feeling he has for his daughter, Gladys, Kwamankra's daughter is to come to earth to be with him.

"'Father, mother says I am to come back to thee in the other world. I wonder if you will know me when I come?' Kwamankra's eyes filled with tears. 'Yes, I will darling,' he simply said."[10]

Unfortunately, a biography has not yet been written on this outstanding West African leader, therefore it is difficult to relate his total life to that of his wife. Indeed, even those who speak of Casely Hayford often forget Adelaide Smith as his second wife. In a recent brief profile of him, the only reference to his marital life was the statement that "late in life he strengthened his Sierra Leone links by marrying as his second wife, the sister of the Sierra Leone judge Francis Smith."[11]

Casely Hayford was a religious man. Haliburton in his treatment of Prophet Harris says that Casely Hayford was a Methodist, and it was rumored at Axim that he was baptized by Prophet Harris in 1914. Furthermore, it was alleged that he was active in reconciling the Methodists to the acceptance of Harris.[12]

Also, Casely Hayford was a man well accustomed to the ways of the West. The photograph with his son included in the above-mentioned article reveals a most distinguished gentleman, dressed in accordance with the best European style of the day – pin stripe pants, high collar, cuffs showing, glasses, sitting, with legs crossed, and right arm on the shoulder of little Archie who was wearing a proper English suit. The picture was probably taken at the time Casely Hayford and Adelaide Smith were getting to know one another and at the time he was tracing his distinguished European ancestors. In the article, it is ironically placed beside a quote which seemingly contradicts it: "Unfashionably, he was particularly critical of Africans wearing European dress and thought there should be a special uniform for African students."

Apparently, Mr. Casely Hayford did impress Adelaide Smith, as my informant suggested.

> Meeting my correspondent for the first time I was very much impressed with Joseph Ephraim Casely Hayford's quiet, unassuming, straightforward demeanor. He told me plainly that his first wife, whom he adored, had died two years previously, and that he too had nothing but a second-best affection to offer me. I honoured him for his frank avowal, and accepted his offer in the right spirit ... So we started our marriage, on the solid foundation of mutual understanding, comradeship, tolerance and good will not expecting too much from each other, but both feeling we could make a much finer thing together, especially as my husband's little five-year-old son, Archie, needed mothering badly.
>
> On 10 September 1903, we were married at an Anglican Church in Shepherd's Bush, much to the chagrin of the Methodist parson of the West Kensington Park Chapel, where we worshipped. He practically denounced us from the pulpit, stating that as a member of his church I should have been married there. He was right, but he was ignorant of the circumstances, and I was forgetful enough not to have informed him beforehand. In any case, my husband was Anglican.

This does not seem to square with all other available information, especially since Casely Hayford was joint editor of the *Wesleyan Methodist Times* and Methodism was strong in his family; yet Mrs. Casely Hayford could hardly have been in error on this point. Perhaps his first wife was Anglican and he merely accepted that. However, he had written to the clergyman who had officiated at his first wedding, asking him to travel all the way from Wales to marry him for the second time.

The wedding was a quiet affair, although all Shepherd's Bush turned out to see a little black bride, and as we drove through the street to the Holborn Restaurant, where the luncheon was to be held, we received many kindly smiles from admiring groups. Before we sat down to lunch, however, my husband took me to an ante-room where a solicitor was waiting for us to sign a document pertaining, I believe, to that portion of the service stating, "with all my earthly goods, etc." Such was the dear man's precision and method.

Mrs. Elizabeth Clinton Dawson at age 86 reminisced in 1972 about the wedding. Mrs. Dawson lived with the Smiths in London at the time of the wedding and she and Kathleen Easmon, dressed in white dresses with straw hats, were the bride's maids at the wedding. Mrs. Dawson, who was four years older than Charles Easmon and five years older than Kathleen, had a vivid recollection of the Smith sisters as personalities. Nettie was sweet and homelike; Emma was the strict disciplinarian who complained about everything African, especially Freetown and its patois. Mrs. Casely Hayford, she recalled, was "sweeter than her sister Emma, but not so nice as Nettie! She was also very musical."

After the wedding, the couple went to Stratford-on-Avon for their honeymoon.

We put up at the Shakespeare Hotel, where every bedroom was christened after one of Shakespeare's plays. Ours was the Anthony and Cleopatra room, and we spent a lovely week there which was marred by my having a severe attack of rheumatism, which however the doctor put right.

The few weeks ... the only weeks which I ever enjoyed with my husband in England – passed only too swiftly, and sometime in November we set sail for Axim on the Gold Coast, where he had a lucrative practice. It was a rather stormy passage, but very enjoyable after we passed the Islands, and in due course, I was being carried from surf boat to beach by stalwart Kroo boys, who picked me up as if I had been a feather.

I received a very warm welcome from my new relatives, especially my mother-in-law, who occupied the ground floor of the spacious residence which had a nine foot verandah all round which was my new home.

Although her own account and other documents refute some aspects of this story, it is certainly probably true that Mrs. Casely Hayford had some adjusting to do. In addition, Margaret Priestly, in describing the social life of the time in the circle of the Brews in Axim, Cape Coast and Anamabu, indicates that there was a mixture of European and African values which permitted many members of the elite to have numerous wives by native custom, some of whom were even domestics, and one wife, the true "Mrs.", by Christian ceremony.[13]

We sat down to our first meal and my only complaint was being asked to eat sweet bread with ham and eggs. Indeed, all the bread in Axim seemed to be sweet. But one can get accustomed to anything, and this was a mere detail.

Thus began my new life on the Gold Coast. In spite of the fact that my own father was a Gold Coaster, everything seemed very strange to me, and the language loomed up as a formidable barrier, but my husband, who was a Cambridge scholar, interpreted everything so that it was only in his absence that it weighed down.

With my parents' example before me, I had always looked upon marriage as the consummation of human experience and happiness. Single blessedness, however consecrated, however selfless and useful, is still incomplete.

We were very happy for the first three years – in fact, with the exception of one frightening experience, I had nothing to wish for. The one fly in the ointment was lack of finances which necessitated my husband migrating to pick up practice. I was pregnant and was lying one afternoon on our verandah, all alone, half dozing, when suddenly I looked up to see a big chimpanzee a few yards away. I rushed with a shriek into the bedroom, and very nearly had a miscarriage. I am quite sure that this fright affected the delicate mechanism of my little unborn child's brain, and was largely responsible for the eccentricity which developed in later years.[14]

But undoubtedly we were happy. When my husband went away in search of business, so keen were we to be in the foreground of each other's thoughts that we indulged in a six-penny telegram every day with our own little private code: "Flowers blooming," "Flowers fading," which spoke for themselves.

There is an existing letter which perhaps conveys their feelings at this period. It was written in August, 1904, shortly after Gladys' birth.[15]

Interestingly, so many of their thoughts echo again and again in their correspondence: Mrs. Casely Hayford's health, Gladys and concern for and about her, financial difficulties, the family – his and hers, a bit about

Archie and lastly the sense of loss at being separated from one another. This is the only letter which suggests that the couple might have considered a move from Axim and that either Mr. Casely Hayford's practice was not as lucrative, as her *Memoirs* indicate she thought was the case, or that her adjustment to life in the Gold Coast was not easy, and that both he and she were willing to consider an alternative location.

[Mrs. Dawson felt that people in the Gold Coast were worse than in Freetown. "They don't take much with strangers!" she told me.]

August 18, 1904

My own darling husband,

I am writing this in bed but you need not be alarmed because I felt so much better today. Yesterday, I had a nasty attack of malaria and was in for a good dose of fever but I managed to nip it in the bud by taking 10 grms. of quinine and now I am simply lying in bed because I feel so weak. Baby has been good as gold and I have consented to her being carried on the back and it seems to soothe her wonderfully.[16] You can't think what a boon it is especially for now that I am not up to the mark for her to sleep for two or three hours at a stretch. And then it gives my nipples a chance. I don't think it is a good position for her to be in but when I can't take her, I think everything is better rather than to let her cry all the time.

I received your telegram with mixed feelings. It is not a bit of use disguising the fact that my heart sank to my boots, although I am more than delighted to know that you have made another good contact. Tom came up yesterday and told me that you had a case on the 24th which he was quite sure the judge would not adjourn as he is in such a tremendous hurry to get to the other side and he was afraid you would have to pay the costs if you didn't turn up in time. Oh, I do hope with all my heart that you will be here before then, it will be a long time before I allow you to go away again. It is *simply* awful.

I had a letter from the girls and I am so pleased to be able to state the operation is by no means a dangerous one. In fact according to the doctor it is an everyday occurrence. She is going to have one of her ovaries removed and she is sure to get over it all right.

Now that you are not returning soon, I am becoming very short of money. The *Fantee* is not in yet, but I am sure you will write and tell me what I had better do. I have opened both letters from Ernest and Mark and forwarded them herewith for your perusal.[17] They, neither of them, seem to think we ought to go to Sierra Leone and

think Cape Coast would be very much better for us. I am afraid I
don't echo those sentiments.[18]

The weather has been very dull and dreary, and this morning we
had a proper downpour of rain. I do hope you are looking after
yourself all right because it seems to be terribly unhealthy just now.

Dear little Archie is keeping as well as possible and came in
delighted having another play fellow in the shape of Helen's
friend's grandson.[19]

Returning to her activities during this time, Mrs. Casely Hayford
wrote, "There was no Anglican Church in Axim at the time, so twice a
month our drawing room was converted into a little chapel at which my
husband officiated and I played the hymns, and the mutual collaboration
made us so happy.[20]

Of course in a family as close as the Smiths had been, every effort was
made to maintain contact. This next letter, the earliest one extant from
Emma who kept the home fires burning in England, is illustrative of
these family ties, life in London at the turn of the century for Creole
ladies and Addie's life style on the Gold Coast. Emma was definitely the
manager of the family – aristocratic but not without humor.

5 Melrose Terrace, London
Jan. 8, 1904

Dearest Addie,

Another year has arrived since I last wrote you. May it be the
harbinger of all that is bright and fair for you and yours.

Your last letter was very welcome and as you can easily imagine
was devoured by both Nettie and myself. I'm sure you looked
awfully nice at the concert and held your own against everyone
there.

We are longing to know if all that tapestry and cretonne ... is
useful for decoration in your home. You might wax eloquent on the
arrangements and description of such rooms in your lovely home
and give untold pleasure by telling us where this, that, and the other
are to be found ... as I am penning this the wire has just arrived
from Sariter asking if we will put her up till Sunday. Of course we
replied in the affirmative and are feeling quite excited about it. Poor
old Sariter.

With respect to my will, everything I have goes to Nettie for her
life and at her death the shares of Alkerli and Borax go to Kathleen

and my shares in Gloucester House to Charlie and my share in ...
to Kathleen.

We have neither seen nor heard from Mjock since he called. You
must therefore possess your souls in patience a little longer. Apro-
pos of business, I have deducted one pound fifteen and 9 pence (of
the account you mentioned) from your share of the dividend from
the Alkerli (?). The whole amount was 14 pounds 6sh 3 pence half
of which is 7pds, three sh and 3 pence out of which one pd, 15sh
was deducted and 5 pds, 7sh 6 pence placed to your account. I
thought this was the quickest and cheapest to do. I enclose the list
of items. Nettie cut out the gowns and Mrs. Lawrence made them.
There were eight yds. of lining used at 3, 3, 3, per yd/ We hope they
are satisfactory.

The third I shall try to have made next week. Mrs. Coussey
sailed yesterday per SS Albertsville.[21] Do you know that we have
never been to see Mrs. Selby yet. We have had very bad colds on
her last At Home Day. In fact, I have never had as early or as many
colds as during our first winter; however I am very much better now
I am thankful to relate.

Lottie Roper invited us to go to see her at Ecttio but Nettie was
indisposed by ... ourselves of the kind of invitation only the usual,
my dear, but being both down at ... made it very awkward and
indeed another thing was that it was Sunday and that it is an
extremely awkward day for getting about.

We are busy preparing the chicks' wardrobe for school. Kathleen is to blossom out in a brand new crimson frock, to keep its
glory fresh, she will wear an overall .... O.... called yesterday, took
the chicks to the British Museum. We have a very nice servant who
rejoices in the name of Violet Hoare, but as the first name is rather
too poetic, we call her 'Jane'. She is a strong girl and not afraid to
work. In fact we are inwardly churlish with pleasure but don't say so
much. She has only been with us a week and it is rather soon to pass
an opinion but if she continues as she has begun, we shall have to
congratulate ourselves. She has such a quiet manner and is so
polite and respectful, it reminds one of the old days when servants
knew their place and kept it.[22]

The report from Epsom College [a private school] came a few
days ago (Charlie is the winner of the class prize and was top in ...
subjects).[23]

There are other available family letters, five in 1904, when the
recency of Mrs. Casely Hayford's leaving England was being felt, and

one in 1905, before she returned to England with Gladys. Emm, rather than Nettie, apparently was the letter writer of the family in England. She writes in 1904, no date, reacting to Addie's description of her lovely home, and reports that Kathleen is third rather than first in her class of 22, and that Charlie has scarlet fever.

On 17 August 1904 there is a letter from Nettie who along with Emm is godmother for Baby Gladys, in which she reports on the state of the rooming house they are running and wants Casely to intercede with Mr. Bannerman to have his girls, who are dissatisfied where they are in school, to come with them.[24]

On 8 September 1904 writing from Seabrook near Hythe, Emm reports that Kathleen at age 13 is becoming "naughtier and naughtier."

On 27 October 1904, Emm writes again and makes frequent reference to purchases requested by Addie – dresses, gloves, a christening gown for Gladys. She now has servant problems as well as money problems over who owes whom what.

On 6 April 1905 Emm responds to the receipt of the photograph of the house and declares that "she hears it is the nicest house in Axim."

Returning to her *Memoirs*, Mrs. Casely Hayford described her life at this time:

> Our baby came before her time and as I was no longer young, her advent nearly killed me. Indeed it was the sound of my husband's grief that brought me back from the Borderline. As he knelt by my bedside with sobs shaking his frame to pieces, I just had sufficient strength to place my hand on his bowed head and whisper, 'Never mind, Casely dear! I'm allright.'
>
> I look back on those three supremely happy years and thank God for the rich experience of sharing my husband's life. His forethought coupled with a fine spiritual outlook, consideration, selflessness and devotion contributed in no small measure to the joy of living.
>
> Our baby was [born in] 1904 with a malformation of the hip joint, which interfered with her walking. So her father and I were both anxious that I should take her to London to see a specialist. When the time of our departure drew near, I was grief-stricken at the thought of leaving my husband, indeed so broken up was I that my sister-in-law suggested that I should not go. I had some kind of premonition that I was saying goodbye to him for the last time ... and so it turned out to be.[25]
>
> I felt, however, that because of little Gladys' disability, it would

not be right to leave anything undone which could be done to help her. I went and that was the beginning of the end.

Joseph promised to join me in a few weeks, as there was a chance of his being sent to the Colonial Office as a delegate of the Aborigines' Protection Society, which would cover the expenses. This buoyed me up considerably and I went so far as to book rooms so that we might be quite alone. I waited in vain. The winter was severe and Gladys, not three years old, contracted every conceivable bronchial ailment.

During this period of isolation in England, Mrs. Casely Hayford sent and received several extant letters from her husband which do indeed continue to show their affection for one another and the kinds of problems facing them. She writes on 31 January, no year, from 25 Conans Mansion, probably the rooms she had found to give the much anticipated privacy for her and Casely when he joined her in England.

My own darling husband,

All the evening I have been listening for the postman's knock for I knew quite well he would be the bearer of a previous missive for me so I was not the least surprised when it arrived ten minutes ago and it is still lodging in its usual resting place in my bosom until I retire for the night when it will join its predecessors in my drawer. I only wish you could get my letters with the regularity that I receive yours, but you take it all in such good spirit, darling, and I only wish I had your beautiful equanimity of mind and evenness of disposition.

The severe cold has unfortunately returned and for the last week I have been feeling quite seedy again. Indeed I am getting more than ever convinced that I am in need of a special tonic – yourself – to set me up again for strange as it may seem I am not feeling half as strong now as I did when I left the coast.

So Miss Bates will be in London soon. Has she any idea of my whereabouts? How silly of me to ask such a question. I do most sincerely hope that poor old Mr. Pinnock (?) has remembered Archie.

The stress of the present day circumstances is such as to make a little money almost a necessity to give one a proper start in life.

I wrote to Mrs. Selby to ask for Frank Manscleg's address. I asked him to come and spend an evening with us. Imagine my horror and dismay when she wrote to inform me that he died at

Aberdeen on the 26th inst. Poor Frank. I am afraid this blow will break his mother's heart.

I am quite sure that it was the extreme cold that killed him for even English people are dying in large numbers through the severity of the weather.

Whitely's funeral was witnessed by eight miles of shivering spectators indeed for many years past London has not seen such a sight for an ordinary commoner. His murderer is unfortunately for him getting stronger every day and has been committed for trial. Certainly our sins do find us out. What you say about the Kappisches fills me with astonishment. I remember at the time there was a great deal of talk about her calling herself by her maiden name for board ... and as regards the German custom the "civil marriage" is the legal one and in a very great many cases the religious ceremony is dispensed with altogether. Certainly she has made the most frightful mistake to get married again in Axim as such an action would [be] sure to be misunderstood. My only solution is that as she is now feeling the ties of motherhood, she would like to be sure of the Divine blessing resting upon her offspring and [for] this reason only she has gone through the church ceremony, but that of course she really was legally married prior to her departure for the coast. I am sending you a pamphlet which is supposed to be Dr. Renner's official report of the winding up of my father's estate. You can take it for what it is worth but for the sake of our little girl I certainly feel that some steps should be taken to recover that of which we have been so shamefully robbed, especially as he challenges us to do so.

I am longing to see your little shanty. I mean 'our' little shanty for I should come and share it with you at once if I could leave our little girl behind. I do hope the things I have already sent were received. I have in my possession a charming little [?] shawl which is unfortunately rather cumbersome unless I have someone going out.

I have slowly but surely been preparing for my return to the coast and have taken advantage of sales to lay in a stock of clothing suitable for the tropics.

Claude has not written to say whether he will take our flat or not but we shall let you know as soon as possible.

And now my love I must close. May God grant that we may be allowed to see each other very soon again.

The children send several kisses.

As ever Your devoted wife,
Addie

Letters from Casely Hayford also suggest strong affection on his part
during this period of their marriage. On 20 December 1904 he writes
"To My Own Love," on 19 May 1905 to "My Darling Wife,"

> God bless you sweetheart and make you a true blessing as a Wife
> and Mother. Think for a moment what the harvest is going to be,
> this life of love and self surrender and self perfectfulness and brush
> away the fear that would fain gather to ... the feet of sacrifice –
> again you understand and that is why I love to write to you thoughts
> that flit in my mind.

Your own loving husband,
Casely

And on 26 November 1905, he writes "To my own darling wife,"
signing "For ever your devoted husband, Casely," and on 8 January
1906 a letter to "My own darling wife" signed "with fondest love and
kisses from your own devoted husband, Casely" in which he writes,

> Then as to yourself darling [he has just spoken of Gladys' leg].
> Don't allow little things to worry you and take things cooly. It is
> wonderful how cool one can be if you make up your mind. I am
> returning to you soon, and please God, there won't be such con-
> stant separations in the future and I guarantee you will be ever so
> much better when we settle down again. We must look on the
> bright side of things and must ever trust in Him.

On 10 January 1906, from Cape Coast – "To my darling wife ... with
love and sweetened kisses from Father and your devoted Husband,
Casely." (Much about recommendations from Ernest for Gladys.)
    On 21 July, 1906, going from Tarkwa to Axim, "My own darling
wife"; promises of a holiday; inquiries concerning her health – "It's a
pity we can't do without money" – complains her letters are too short. "I
want you, darling, to think matters over. Hadn't we better keep out of the
Council for the present. Events must shape themselves out in that
direction sooner or later but in the present political situation between
the pros and cons" – discusses Sarbah[26] and continues to seek her
reactions.
    On 5 March 1906 from Tarkwa –

> To my own darling wife,
>   What a lot people miss who miss motherhood and fatherhood ...
> For I cannot help thinking that we have been ... and are happily
> mated for a purpose and God will let it forth when and if we have

prepared our souls in silence. Be brave and fearless and hopeful and ready so to ... on the side of God against the side of the powers of evil. But I know you are longing to hear how I've been getting on so I must stop this sort of moralizing.

Kisses to yourself from your loving husband,
Casely

And on 24 June 1906 – "My own sweetheart, How nice it is, darling, to have a sweet and intelligent wife who knows exactly what to do at a given moment." Also reactions to her letters of advice and a little discussion of politics. On 17 June 1906 "My own darling wife," Anxiety about her health as he was leaving. Tom and Archie met him. Post political letters quickly. "You have no need of assurance of how devotedly love is in the heart of him who will ever remain your own devoted husband, Casely."

Except for some references to political office, Casely Hayford wrote little to his wife either in the form of gossip or about his own political activities – certainly not in any detail as to the political activities. He seemed to feel considerable affection for his wife and to admire her personal qualities. However, there did seem to be some distance between them, perhaps a reflection of the comment by a maid who worked for Mrs. Casely Hayford concerning her relationship to her husband: "She was always correcting his grammar, she said." One wonders when or how the maid knew this, as it has been hard to determine just when Mr. Casely Hayford was in Freetown, if at all when his wife was there, but the letters do have a sense of fear of having one's grammar corrected.

There are only three letters extant from Adelaide to Casely during the period of this separation: 5 October 1906 and 7 and 21 February 1907. These letters are strikingly illustrative of the pain of separation, the unfulfilled promises and the problems of surviving as an African in England at that time. Her letters, of course, always provide a bit more of the social or personal experience.

Adelaide writes from 25 Conans Mansion, West Kensington, Oct. 5, 1906:

My darling husband,
    At last my patience was rewarded this morning when I saw the well known handwriting, for let me tell you it is a whole fortnight since I heard from you and I was beginning to dread and fear all sorts of things. I note however from your note that you have been a mighty traveller and I hope you are not overdoing it because my dear I would rather have you than all the money in the world. I don't

want you to kill yourself in trying to amass wealth. Archie has had a slight cold, but seems much better again. Baby has had an exceedingly heavy one and I have had to confine her to one room with a fire night and day. She is picking up and like her mother is getting as fat as butter. She has a wealth of affection for Nettie and goes to her when she will go to no one else. Emm, of course, has not got the right way with children and Baby stands a little in awe of her. So far poor little Nettie has not been successful in finding employment and it is a tremendous wrong to us all because her expenses with children's education are very high. I say that she cannot afford to keep Kathleen at school more than a year longer and that when their time is up here they must go much further out where things will be very much cheaper.

I don't know yet whether anything further has been decided upon about your coming to England, but I never cease to pray that such may be the case. I don't find England the Elysium that I thought it was by any means and am of the opinion that is only a nice place when one has heaps of money.

We have been so busy with our removal that I have not had any chance of going out so far and Baby's illness has naturally kept me very much indoors. When once we are straight I hope things will be ever so much brighter.

I have just had a letter from Tom and he seems to be very much chipper than I expected he would be under the circumstances. I have just written to tell him that Frank informed the girls that when he was in England two years ago that the authorities were so pleased with his work that he had only to apply for the fees his predecessors used to receive and that would be granted him, so I am writing to ... to that effect by this steamer.

Dr. Renner is returning to the Coast minus his wife and nothing has been done to recover the 40 pounds shortage in the ... money. I do feel awfully sick over everything as regards our Sierra Leone affairs. I have sent out by this steamer some warm things for voyage northwards and I just remember that I have not included the socks you asked for. I am most awfully sorry and I will try to redeem my character by sending them next week. Have you settled up the Jersey bootmaker's account? You promised to do so, but if you like I will send them a cheque. I have squared up Spiers and Pound. I have no coast news at all lately and am absolutely dependent upon you for anything in that line. I have sent Helen out some things and hope they will arrive in time for the confinement. I have read, learnt, and inwardly digested the Hant [?] affair and am of the opinion that there is only one course left open to an honorable man like yourself – to show him up ... May God help you carry it through.

Baby is standing by my side holding the enclosed little pink paper and tells me with her own lips that in a "letter for Papa, Mama, put it inside, Mamma." She has got a wonderful grasp of English already, but I am sorry to say is fast forgetting her Fantee. Archie too is hardly able to converse with her now and finds great difficulty in expressing himself in Fantee but I tell him he must try and talk to Baby or else you will be so dreadfully disappointed when you see them. The dear little chap has settled down wonderfully well but does not seem to like lessons very much. However, I think it will come to him.

Well, my darling, I love you but I must leave you. Send me a paper when you can. Above all try and come as soon as you are able.

Ever your loving and devoted wife, Addie

The above letter continues to express the same concerns – family (Tom, her brother, Kathleen, her niece, Archie, her stepson and, of course, Baby Gladys). Mrs. Casely Hayford apparently tries to do things to please her husband such as keeping a facility with Fantee language alive in the family with Archie and Gladys. It is most unlikely that she herself understood or spoke any Fantee. One also gets the impression that her relations with her brother-in-law, Dr. Renner, husband of her older sister, Bea, were not particularly cordial, and though she had earlier mentioned conflict over her father's estate and Renner's accounting of it, the problems mentioned in this letter may well refer to the litigation over Spilsbury's estate, over his property which should have been left to her mother Anne and to her through her mother but which was divided extensively among all his heirs, thus creating considerable family conflict. Here, too, were the concerns over money; the interest in her husband's career, but perhaps from the position of someone who might have corrected his grammar!

25 Conans Mansion
February 7, 1907

Mr darling husband,

Your letter this week was unusually late, nevertheless it has just arrived in time to be answered.

I was delighted to get the sketch of the shanty and wish I were there to superintend the furnishing of it in person. I am so glad you like the Siesta hammock and I shall send one out as soon as I can afford it for if you are not coming until early summer you must have some kind of a home till then and I only wish I knew of someone going out with whom I could entrust my few purchases.

I am still feeling very seedy and therefore keep very much to the house during this intense cold. Em and I, however, went to see Mrs. Selby two days ago and met Mrs. Riberro[27] there. She informed them that her husband was coming in June for her and that she would take the baby out but leave the older child behind.

Mrs. Muriel Clinton[28] had been at death's door with pneumonia and pleurisy and her life is not yet out of danger. Her husband has been wired to over two days ago but has sent no reply whatsoever up to date which is considered very funny by all her friends. Mrs. Riberro has also informed Em that Mrs. Kappisch had been married before the District Commissioner and not at the Catholic Church.

If this version is correct, Mrs. Kappisch has absolutely done for herself but do let me know the authentic facts. I understand too that she intends remaining in Axim to be confirmed which is very plucky of her. Baby is sitting opposite to me as I write. We had a little do here last night and ... slept here as it was too late for her to return home. She is leaving Miss Marleyn's (?) on Monday to take a temporary position at the Western hospital till it is time for her to return to Buenos Ayres. Em is busy making preparations and Lizzie has sent her wedding order. The auspicious event is fixed for April 17.

Well, my darling husband, I cannot quite grasp the situation. If I am to remain here for the early summer it will [mean] a lot of expenditure and I doubt very much whether it is justifiable. As I have already stated, my funds are fast drawing to a close and I hate the idea of your sending me remittances which would come in as nicely for us to spend *together* somewhere and which I am afraid will make it difficult for you to come at all. May God help us out of our difficulties!!

We were hoping to get an answer from Claude re this flat by this mail but we have been so far disappointed.

Em is leaving in March, at present she pays the rent and I am paying 4 pounds per month. When she goes I cannot possibly afford to pay 7 pounds a month for rent alone so that you can quite see the situation. I think in any case we had better start advertising it for the summer months.

Archie is keeping excellent health as is Baby dear, little mite.

Two or three days ago I said to her I want to teach you a new prayer, darling. Before I had time to say a word, she folded her little hands together and said, "My dear Papa, I hope you are well for Christ's sake, Amen." Wasn't that sweet, darling? She still keeps on saying, "Papa coming soon to Baby?" I allow her to say so because children have absolutely no idea of time. Any time you are able to come, Baby will consider soon.

Archie, I am proud to say, nearly always tops his form now so I am hoping great things of him. And now, my own husband, I must close and be it known that I am going straight to lie down as I am sure want of sleep has a great deal to do with my ailments.

The children sent sweet kisses. Oh, I am sincerely longing to put my arms around you dear and feel once more your loving tender embrace.

Ever your devoted wife, Addie

This is certainly a most affectionate letter, but in view of later events, it has an element of sadness about it. It is not at all clear why Adelaide cannot come home. There is no mention of Glady's continued need for medical care. And certainly Archie could have remained in England with one of Adelaide's sisters, Nettie, particularly since she had to stay there to see after the education of her children, Kathleen and Charlie. There is no indication of where Em is going, why or for how long. Em does not return to Africa, but she may be off for a short visit there. She spends most of her life in England where she dies.

The reason for the continued separation between Addie and Casely remains a mystery because, as this letter indicates, staying in England is expensive. There is never any mention of Adelaide's working. There is the familiar question of her poor health – apparently being aggravated by the English climate. The gossip networks of Africans in England at this time is also illustrated. Claude is Claude Wright, a distinguished Sierra Leone barrister who is married to Laura Davies, the daughter of Mary Smith Davies, Mrs. Casely Hayford's half sister.

The last legible letter from this period is dated 21 February 1907 – still from England.

25 Conans Mansion

My own darling husband,
   I don't know when last I felt so condemned as when I read your last lines which arrived later than any hitherto. I am more than ever convinced that I am not worthy of such a generous-minded unself-

ish husband. I deserve the scolding I got and a great deal more besides. And if I covet anything at the present moment more than most things, it is your *simple, child-like faith.* I believe that that is the great reason why you are able to face the battle of life cheerfully without undue stress, despondance or depression, under all circumstances and I am afraid this want of faith is my great stumbling block. I like to see things shaping themselves as I go along which of course is absurdly ridiculous when there is a Destiny which shapes our ends.

I am most awfully sorry you think me such a brute for entertaining the idea of leaving Gladys for two whole days. Well, darling, I didn't do so but I certainly allowed Nettie to take her for two whole nights, so that I could really have some uninterrupted slumber, according to Doctor's orders, and apart from the fact that she was very astonished to see someone else occupying my bed, she lay perfectly quiet and content as far as outward manifestations went and did not seem to miss me at all.

The money which I have duly received from your Bank has come in most acceptably. If we were not living in such an expensive flat, I should try to make 10 pds. a month do till you come but I pay one pd a week for rent, 3-shillings for board so that sum would leave nothing at all for incidental expenses. If you are coming yourself at the end of March, don't send anything else, for I have enough left to last me until then. If not, you might post me another remittance about the middle so as to meet April's expenses which will include Archie's school fees which are however not paid till towards the end of the month.

We have heard from Claude re this flat. Laura is expecting in May so they will not be coming to England at all this year. The renovations on his house have cost him no less than 300 pounds. Lizzie's marriage comes off in April and Em has been entrusted with the wedding order. She is spending a few days with Mrs. Selby. The Coleridge-Taylors were here the other evening and although I was feeling very weak, we had a delightful time. They are simply smothering us with kindness. Winter is still with us ... so is the intense cold and for the last few days there have been terrific gales causing a great loss of life. Once again African mails are detained and the steamer, *Salaga,* that was to leave England yesterday could not get out of the Jersey at all. A very poor start for a maiden trip.

Archie is keeping splendidly well and we hear nothing but football from morning till night. He has one little friend who may truly be called his satellite for he is in attendance at all hours of the day.

Baby, I am sorry to say is not well, in fact she has been in bed all day. You need not worry, darling, because she will be all right. She has a little cough on the chest and has been vomitting, etc., but I shall let the Doctor see her in the morning. I was obliged to tell you because I never keep anything from you.

Friday – The Doctor has seen kiddie dear, and thinks there is nothing much wrong with her and that she will be quite well again in a day or two. I am thankful to say that I am out of his hands, so all is going right merrily.

I am so pleased to hear that Tom is keeping up his spirit. I am sure he misses us both dreadfully.

I understand Mrs. Kappisch is still on the Coast. I have not answered her last letter because I am anxious to know first whether her marriage was celebrated at the Catholic Church or before the District Commissioner. I should be terribly grieved if this woman whom I consider my friend and who always was so nice to me, had come out simply to live with Kappisch.

Em's movements to Buenos Ayres are still very hazy. It is not yet certain that ... will be going back as she is in difficulties with the people who sent her to England. I am busy trying to evolve a native costume which will be built on original lines and yet be the essence of grace and ease and I am progressing.

Time is up, darling. Your letter had not arrived. The children send sweet kisses to darling Fadder. I wish I could report the nice things Baby says. Take care of yourself and come soon to your devoted, Addie.

The above letter unquestionably reflects an uncertainy about Casely's coming to England – now stated in terms of "if" rather than "when." Also there seems to be just a glimmer of suspicion about Casely Hayford's truthfulness to her when she says she never keeps anything from him. As in so many of her other letters and in her *Memoirs*, Mrs. Casely Hayford seems frequently to be unwell. For a person who lived to such a ripe old age, one wonders whether these frequent illnesses are physical or merely occur when she is upset over some event or another. It is curious that in all these letters her daughter, to whom she is emotionally and because of her circumstances physically tied, is only once called by her given name, Gladys. For a woman as active and independent as Mrs. Casely Hayford had always been, this confinement and without her husband must truly have been trying. Her report of Baby's illness because "he always wants to know" also has a tinge of spite or manipulation to it.

This letter also reveals two additional elements in the changing character of their marriage relationship and of Mrs. Casely Hayford as a person. One wonders whether her interest in designing an African dress "built on original lines, yet the essence of grace and ease," reflects her own preferences or is an effort to relate more meaningfully to her husband's preferences. Finally, the concern over her friend's state of morality – whether or not she is married, under whose aegis and how this behavior reflects on her, i.e. Mrs. Casely Hayford, again raises the question of whether this is her true concern or what she believes to be the concern of her husband whom she feels to be quite religious and moral.

In any case this is the last extant letter before she leaves England for Africa again ... without Mr. Casely Hayford ever having come to join her and Gladys.

In her *Memoirs* she writes:

> Distracted about [Gladys'] condition and taking the doctor's advice, I returned home ... this time to Tarkwa, the heart of the gold mining industry, whither my husband had migrated in my absence. This was a bleak, barren time in Tarkwa: no food, except mutton and coco-yam, and malnutrition made the children break our in terrible sores all over their bodies. It made me cry to dress them. There was no doctor, but the dispenser came along and prescribed plenty of milk and porridge, with a tonic for good measure. The house itself was a wretched affair, built of wood, with cement partitions inside, barbed wires at the windows to keep the thieves out. As we sat at our evening meal, the rats danced their minuets right over the table, till I was almost distracted with fright. But worst of all there was no companionship whatsoever. One civilised woman came to spend a few days in the place, but otherwise I was entirely surrounded by illiterate peasants who spoke a different language altogether. I was pregnant again, and with the memory of my first confinement in my mind, I felt I must return to my sisters in England for this second ordeal.

Tarkwa was not Axim and certainly not Accra or Freetown, for Africa during most of the colonial period had (and to some extent still has) only one key or primate city in each country, usually located on the coast. Here, one would meet such sophisticated people as were around; here one could find the conveniences which were available, here one did not feel the presence of the Jungle. Tarkwa was not a coastal city.

The added years in England had certainly not helped Mrs. Casely Hayford adjust to a world less westernized than Axim. Even the house about which she had written in such loving terms as the "shanty she wished she could supervise," now becomes a wretched affair" with rats and wiring to stop thieves. For one used to the intimate company of her family – either biologically close or most distant members, or even friends from a familiar circle of inter-connected persons – the isolation of an up-country town in an unfamiliar country must have been horrendous. Certainly, as a busy lawyer and increasingly as a political activist, Mr. Casely Hayford could not have offered the companionship she needed. Her mother-in-law, who earlier had been so kind, was, one presumes, not in Tarkwa. Quite probably, Tom "her twin in adversity and prosperity" was by that time also in Tarkwa. But as a bachelor his life style was not likely to measure up to his sister's stern Victorian standards. Her pregnancy implies some continued closeness to her husband, but there is little else to indicate that there was still a firm foundation to their marriage tie – of which both so often spoke in their earlier letters.

Also, apparently, there had been no further consideration of Casely Hayford going to Freetown to practice. It was there, in the Gold Coast, that he intended to continue to practice law or edit papers – and in a less remote part of the country at that! It must be remembered that Mr. Casely Hayford was a Brew and Fanti whose ancestral base was not Accra but Cape Coast and Axim – so for him, this was home, this was the center of his Africa. Aside from her stated reasons, therefore, Mrs. Casely Hayford must have welcomed the release going to England would provide her.

   We boarded the *Eleanorie Woermann* – a German passenger boat – and my husband was so anxious that I should get good accommodation that he booked a first class cabin on the steamer's outward trip. She remained a very short time in port, but when I caught the chief steward's Napoleonic eye, I knew I was doomed. He took me to the worst second-class cabin on the boat. There was no stewardess, no bell and no sofa for Gladys. In my condition, I could not climb up to the top bunk, and I dare not put her there; so we had to share the same narrow little lower bunk, and she kicked me all night. The adjoining cabin was a bit better, because there was a sofa which would have accommodated her. But the Chief Steward told me it was booked. So I marched right up to the Captain's private deck, and had it out with him. He was flabbergasted when I spoke to him in German, but condescended to let me

use the larger cabin, although if the ship became full I might be
turned out again.

My baby came in the afternoon. If it had been in the night, I don't
know what I would have done, because there was no bell. But God
does temper the wind to the shorn lamb. I moaned and groaned till
at last a steward heard me. Between the doctor and the barber, my
baby arrived stillborn.[29]

A lady doctor visited me as I lay there and she said, "I can't
understand why you are here at all, because when I boarded the
ship at Calabar, I was told that at Sekondi I would share my cabin
with a Mrs. Hayford and child." So the combination of a black skin
and an English name can prove a terrible handicap.

The shipboard episode must have been most traumatic for Mrs.
Casely Hayford and for little Gladys. But her strength under this and
similar crises belies an indication that she was a fragile or really sickly
person. The cabin allocation is just one of the thousands of types of
discrimination to which Africans of all classes were subjected during the
colonial period. Mrs. Casely Hayford implies that had her husband been
along the cabin change would not have been made. She was discriminated against because she was a native woman, much in the same way as
Aunt Tee was, on the ship from Washington to Hampton mentioned
above. Or put another way, the discrimination was not lessened because
she was a woman.

When Mrs. Casely Hayford arrived in England, she learned that her
sisters

> had now moved into old fashioned but very commodious rooms in
> Elgin Crescent, and as there was a four-room flat vacant at the top,
> [I] took it and frequented sales to obtain second hand furniture.
> How much easier life was in those days, I had no difficulty in
> getting tenants, but I had to cook for them, besides looking after
> our household downstairs. Emma had never had anybody to speak
> of, and Nettie had undergone such a serious operation that she
> could do nothing but light work.[30]
>
> By this time her two children were growing up splendidly.
> Charlie, a medical student at St. Mary's, passed his examinations
> without any failures, and Kathleen had developed such a talent for
> Art that she had obtained a scholarship at the Royal College of Arts,
> South Kensington. My own Gladys was attending a fine kingergar-
> ten within a stone's throw, so they were all happily placed.
>
> Mrs. Wiseman, our daily help, and I leaned on each other, and
> managed to keep things going very satisfactorily. My spare time was

taken up with charity work and church meetings, and I began to
launch out as a public speaker.[31]

I felt my grass widow position keenly, and as from the doctor's
report, Gladys looked like she was developing tuberculosis, my
husband paid our passage to return home immediately.

We settled at Cape Coast which in those days was by far the best
spot for an educated woman on the Gold Coast. There were about
a dozen of us, and we formed a Social Club, meeting once a week
for music and games. Someone lent me a piano, so we were by no
means dull. My husband himself was practicing at Sekondi; so we
saw very little of him. In fact, things had come to such a climax that
we drew up a Separation Agreement and I decided to return to
Freetown.

The Casely Hayfords were never divorced, but at this point their
marriage was to all intents and purposes terminated. Why did Casely
continue to practice at Tarkwa? Why did he place Adelaide and Gladys
at Cape Coast when he moved to Sekondi only a few miles away; why she
didn't complain or at least mention this in her *Memoirs* as affecting their
relationship – all of this rather suggests that, in fact, the relationship had
gradually been eroding during the long period of absences and upon her
most recent return from England, Adelaide and Casely were two very
different and changed people trying to be husband and wife.

Naturally, rumors were rampant. Miss Graves, who seemed to feel
she understood everything about Mrs. Casely Hayford and her relation
to her husband and her daughter, had her theory:[32]

> The upbringing of Mr. and Mrs. Casely Hayford had been very
> different. In Freetown the group of people with some Negro blood
> who were called Creoles ... had no connections whatsoever with
> the Natives ... in the Gold Coast the situation is quite different.
> There has never been a colony of returned slaves. All those with
> African "blood" are "Natives" who have never been separated
> from their tribal connections ... Mr. Casely Hayford as well as his
> first wife must have belonged to those who had a great deal of
> European blood, for his son by his first wife is almost white, has
> blue eyes, looks like an Arab and is strikingly good looking. But
> notwithstanding his white blood, Mr. Casely Hayford belonged to
> his tribe. He was brilliant as a barrister and as a writer, a journalist
> and a historian; his works on the land question in West Africa are
> the most quoted by all authorities; but he was African in sympathies
> and interests, and clung to many African customs. His second wife,
> Creole by birth with an education entirely European, would have

none of these customs. Then Mr. Casely Hayford's means were limited. He wished to spend all, or almost all on Archie (whom he afterwards sent to Cambridge University) and on defending his people in their system of land tenure. Mrs. Casely Hayford felt that she and her daughter were not getting their share. The truth was probably that both were dominating characters and neither could bear the other's domination. At any rate, Mrs. Hayford felt she could not live with her husband and left. ...

Miss Graves' account is biased in favor of Mrs. Casely Hayford whom she knew and admired. However, it does provide a full statement of one side of the difficulty. Though Miss Graves described accurately the major differences in the two worlds of Africa from which Adelaide and Casely came, marriages down the Coast were not infrequent and not necessarily unsuccessful. The fact is, as outsiders, neither Miss Graves nor I can be sure just why the break occurred. For as later letters indicate, the tie between them was never really broken, at least on Mrs. Casely Hayford's side. So why did they separate? Each had strong roots in different parts of Africa, both were very unusual people, but she, for her time, more than he; the problem of finances, the question of children, not only Archie but the fact that she had no other children. Mrs. Casely Hayford did in herself and in her family and her person represent the pinnacle of an African system that was fascinatingly different from that of her husband. In her pioneering work on the Brew family, Margaret Priestly describes Mr. Casely Hayford's world:

> ... emphasis on patrilineal descent as an important determinant of family structure; the use of legal documents in oral and written form for the disposal of property, Christian marriages to literate wives, status passing from father to son, associated with education and achievement, trade, law and government service opening up ways to acquire property, a strong familial corporate sense, wide kinship network, and the acceptance along with Christian marriage, of polygamy and unions contracted by customary law, strong emphasis on Christianity especially Methodism.[33]

How much of this really affected Mrs. Casely Hayford or was different from her values or what she was prepared to make her values, we just do not know. As I have said, she kept the tie alive between them, as will be discussed later, she accepted official sympathies at his death and she expected to receive monies from his estate. The differences between them might have been, as the maid recalled, her insistence on correcting his grammar or that, as her relative recalled, "there were always other women."[34]

AVF–D*

Home to Freetown – A Dream Begins

My reception in Freetown this time was much more friendly, and as Charlie, my nephew, had qualified and obtained a government post, I kept house for him. This was in May, 1914, and the first World War broke out in August of the same year. Being something of a surgeon, he was sent down to the Cameroons to look after the soldiers. Gladys, now and then, had to mother me, which she did with a wisdom and foresight quite beyond her years. My health, however, began to fail.

About one, one night, I woke up from a sound sleep as [I] called her before lapsing into unconsciousness, which lasted till 4pm the next day. The neighbors heard Gladys' cries, and rushed in, but she felt she must call a friend – Mrs. Rice – to come to my assistance.

So, about midnight, in her thin little night-gown, she ran out, passing the giant Cotton Tree, about which there were so many weird tales but found Mrs. Rice and her household in slumber. Determinedly, she kept on throwing gravel at the bedroom windows, till at last it had the desired effect.

Eventually, I had to undergo an operation, and migrated to my brother-in-law's, Dr. William Awunor Renner's Nursing Home (now Bata's shoe shop), where I was given a new lease of life. Dr. Awunor Renner died shortly afterwards, leaving his widow Sis Bee and her two sons, one, Roland, a qualified barrister, who became a magistrate in Nigeria, and the other Dr. Teddy Awunor Renner, now Assistant Director of Medical Services in Freetown.

My next venture was to take a house, which appealed to me because of its Lilliputian dimensions and was just within the scope of my purse. We turned it into a charming little home, but alas it was already inhabited by a nightly visitant whom we never saw, but whom we unmistakenly heard.

Our bedrooms were aloft in a newly erected garrett.

I felt I must put my surplus energy to use, so I obtained a teaching job as Music Mistress at the Annie Walsh Memorial School. In

those days there were no buses, and no cars, so my mode of
transport was a little Japanese rickshaw. I always felt that my last
moment had come when I ventured on that rickshaw, but I arrived
at my destination unharmed. I had to contend with something like
120 teenagers, divided into two classes, with an immense capacity
for staring and taking in details, and very little for music. I quite
enjoyed it and my income was enriched by the sum of 2/6 an
afternoon, twice a week, for singing lessons, with a few private
pupils thrown in.

    In those days, much more stress was laid upon what we could
give, rather than what we could get, with the result that although
our pockets were light, we were much happier than the present-day
teacher. Teaching is very strenuous, because it makes heavy
demands on every part of the personality, having no mercy on brain,
heart, physique or talents. But it has its own reward, "It blesseth
him that gives and him that takes."

Very soon upon her return to Freetown, Mrs. Casely Hayford began
to be active in community affairs. The *SLWN* announced: "A Popular
Address by Mrs. Casely Hayford to be delivered at the Wesley Church
on 12 December 1915." Her subject was to be "The Rights of Women
and Christian Marriage."[1] This was undoubtedly going to be the laun-
ching of a new career, a new image for her in Freetown, not as a
daughter or a wife but as a woman in her own right.
Meanwhile,

    Dr. Charles Easmon, having returned from the Cameroons, was
    practicing at Moyamba in the Sierra Leone Protectorate, and as
    Kathleen was now a fully-fledged A.R.C.A. of the Royal College of
    Arts – the first African woman to write letters after her name, my
    widowed sister Nettie decided to return to Africa for the whole
    family to be together.

    Indeed, England was so packed with refugees and foreigners
    through those war years (1914–1918), that the authorities were
    only too glad to ship them home. It was a most hazardous journey.
    The *Burutu* headed the convoy of thirty ships. Passengers boarded
    the steamer about 7 p.m.; the only other women being a young
    Lagosian girl and the stewardess. They had barely sat down to
    dinner when a great crash made the whole boat shiver. The steward
    spoke quietly and without any panic. "We were torpedoed,
    Madam. Get back to your cabin at once for your treasured posses-
    sions, and then run up to No.3 lifeboat." The confusion that
    ensued was indescribable and the women put the men to shame.

As Mrs. Easmon got in, she dropped her bag with all her money and valuable trinkets. The West Indian cook behind her picked it up and, handing it back to her, said: "If you had belonged to the other race, you would never have seen it again, Madam." The boats were lowered, and after an interminable hour of suspense and anxiety, they were hauled up again. They had not been torpedoed, escaping as the Captain remarked "by only a hair's breadth." But the ship next to them went down. Fearless, courageous Kathleen followed by her equally fearless mother, calmly returned to the dining saloon and finished dinner.

Meanwhile, Gladys and I, anticipating their arrival, had furnished our abode to the best of our ability, when a dear young friend, Mr. Leslie McCarthy, a practicing barrister – now Sir Leslie McCarthy, a retired Puisne Judge on the Gold Coast, rushed to tell us there was not a word of truth in the rumor. "What rumor?" I asked. "Didn't you know that the *Burutu* has gone down? I have been making exhaustive enquiries and find that it is absolutely a false alarm. So I have just come to reassure you." Real fervent friendship is a marvelous asset! My sister and daughter stayed a few days with us, then we all travelled to Moyamba together.

After the unutterable loneliness of the Gold Coast, it was like a little bit of heaven. Kathleen, with her intelligence, her spiritual type of beauty, and her charm, won all hearts, and it took my sister all her time to keep callers at bay.

Our happiness was ruthlessly shattered by the influenza epidemic of 1918. Gladys and I had returned to our eerie abode and moonlight visitant, and I began to teach English to a fine young Swiss. One afternoon in July 1918, I stood at the window to see if my young Swiss-German pupil was anywhere in sight. The whole place looked desolate and barren without a solitary individual about enveloping us all in a sinister cloud of gloom. I put on my hat to go to see for myself what had happened to the youngster. On the way I stepped into a Druggist's shop belonging to a distant relative to tell him my errand. He besought me not to go. "That," I said, "is all the more reason why I should go and for Christ's sake I am going. I am sure he has no one to attend to him." The doctors were all down, and the other residents of the house shunned him as if he were a leper. I found him in bed sick unto death with the rest of the household keeping at arm's length. He was conscious, but very wasted and worn and he looked at me so beseechingly. "I thought I was dying, so I struggled to make my will." "How splendid of you in

your terrible condition to be thinking so selflessly of others," I
remarked. I did all I could to make him comfortable, trying to put
some life into his cold limp hands by rubbing them vigorously,
when he said in a whisper, "Mrs. Hayford, please don't stay.
There's another chap much worse than I am. Please go to him
because he needs you so much more than I do." I gazed at him in
astonishment. This dear dying utterly helpless young man,
despatching me to attend someone else. Once again, I was struck
with the immeasurable divinity hidden in the depths of human
nature. Eventually, I had four young Swiss-Germans on my hands.
I interviewed the Agent and we rigged up a little ward containing
four beds. Three of the men recovered. Eventually, we were told
that there was one vacant bed in the hospital and Althaus felt he
would like to be removed. I shall never forget seeing him so utterly
feeble and helpless and his last little whispered words of gratitude
as they took him off to die.

I myself went down the very next day and I prayed as I have never
prayed before, that God would spare my life for the sake of my
fourteen year old daughter who was nursing me and who, in spite of
her years, was a tower of strength and wisdom. No doctors and
nurses were available, so she had to rely on her own God-given
intuition and common sense. She dreaded being quite alone at
night. But at last we persuaded an octogenarian just to come and
sleep. Gladys was comforted.

All this happened forty-two years ago [from 1953], it is an
episode I can never forget. My darling daughter has gone, but the
fragrant aroma of her devoted nursing and my dear Althaus's
utterly selfless sacrifice remain with me still.

After returning to Freetown, Mrs. Casely Hayford kept in touch with
her husband in a desultory way. On 18 May 1917, she wrote him coolly
of Freetown life and commented on Archie by saying, "the quicker he
gets on his feet the better; my sisters write to tell me he is wasting his
time." And again on 23 December 1917, she wrote of the appalling
conditions of Mr. Casely Hayford's father who could go to the work-
house. Apparently, Mrs. Casely Hayford and her sister Nettie visited
Dr. Easmon again, for in December 1918 she wrote Mr. Casely Hayford
from Moyamba reporting on the influenza epidemic:

Dear Casely,
    This is just a line to wish you a Happy Christmas and a bright and
joyous New Year. As far as I am concerned, I believe God has only

spared me to see little Gladys on her legs before I die. I have had a
bad time and I don't feel I shall ever be quite the same healthy
individual I was before. So many people have been ruthlessly cut
down that it is a question of deep reflection as to why me just as in
the near future awful and wicked have been permitted to live.
Evidently our work is not yet complete and my great prayer now is
to be enabled to carry through successfully not as the world counts
success but that I may some day hear the Master's 'well done.'

This letter, however, is about Gladys' future. I understand from
people in the know that the court business is very brisk and a time of
prosperity for all, I should therefore like to know definitely what
your plans about Gladys are, so that I may be able to arrange
accordingly. The little house which I am renting for 2 pounds 10
shillings a month is likely to be sold in the near future. Rents are
prohibitive in Freetown now and it will be very difficult for me to
get anything at all decent for that price. If however I were quite sure
that Gladys would be going to England next summer, I should not
keep up a house at all but just live with Nettie and share expenses.

This plan, of course, is not feasible whilst Gladys is here because
Mrs. ... is 75 miles away from Freetown. I also don't wish to make
her a boarder here because the influence of the girls is very bad
even in the best of schools, the chop [food] is so poor that in this
time of disease and stress of circumstances, I am afraid her body
would suffer which is the last thing I want ... is ... so strong and
healthy.

Would you kindly in your reply state *clearly* what your money
situations are so that I may know how I stand. If you could pay me
all *arrears* and pay her passage, I should be perfectly willing to go on
with 10 pounds a month, the balance to go towards the child's
expenses in England. Whatever your feelings to me may be, please
don't let our child suffer. She has latent talent which ought to be
cultivated. Her head mistress told me that if she had been an
English girl in England she would have been a splendid journalist.
So far she has had no chance. So far I have tried to be patient but the
time has come for her resources to be developed and it is no use
waiting until it is too late. Not only would it be hopelessly unfair but
you yourself would live to regret it.

She has had her photo taken but the man has disappointed us.
However you will probably get it in the New Year.

With love and every fond wish.

Yours very sincerely,
Adelaide Casely Hayford

The above letter and short ones to follow all suggest that Mr. Casely Hayford was not as anxious to support Gladys' education as her Mother wished. All the time one senses there was a conflict over what he was spending on Archie and what there would be left or given to Gladys. It is not surprising, of course, that Mr. Casely Hayford and she would have a different idea as to what a parent should spend for a *girl's* education. Cape Coast was not Freetown. And beyond that fact, Gladys was an unusual girl and her mother knew it. In any case, during all of 1919 there was an exchange of letters between the two parents.

On 5 January 1919, in the last extant letter from Casely Hayford to Mrs. Casely Hayford, he writes, "My dear Addie" and closes with "Yours with love from Casely Hayford." The letter was brief, concerning only Gladys and assuring her "there will be funds when she plans her materials."

The following month on 17 February, Mrs. Casely Hayford responds "Dear Casely." Concludes with "Yours sincerely." Again she is seeking the funds for Gladys to go to England which he had promised. She felt he should pay back debts and also "if he could afford to keep Archie still in England, then he could help Gladys." She speaks of Archie passing criminal law boards.

The following month she writes again to "Dear Casely" on the same matter signing "Yours most sincerely." On 19 December 1919 she writes a bit more:

> Dear Casely,
> This is just a line to wish you a Happy New Year. As the years will ..., may you have an ever increasing sense of God's presence and may your own light shine more and more into the perfect day. I am glad the children are so happy and well. They are having the time of their lives. God bless them abundantly.
>
> Yours with love,
> Addie

Probably the fact that Gladys was apparently visiting her father in Ghana, even more than the Christmas season, prompted the above letter. And by the following January (19, 1920), she writes thanking Casely for the long requested money, "hoping they will agree on the accounting" and closes with "Yours with love, Adelaide Casely Hayford."

While Mrs. Casely Hayford was trying to make plans for Gladys' future, she was also becoming better known as a personage in Freetown. She made frequent public addresses. On 11 October 1919, there was an advertisement in the *SLWN*, placed by Adelaide Casely Hayford, as president of the Young Women's Christian Association, inviting its young women members of all ages from sixteen upwards to take classes. She herself was offering classes in singing; Kathleen classes in all sorts of handicraft, woodwork and stenciling; and in addition classes would be offered "by appropriate authorities" in the Bible, Domestic Service, Cooking and Nursing.

Mrs. Casely Hayford was definitely beginning to implement seriously, initially under the aegis of the Young Women's Christian Association, the ideas she had for the education of young women in Freetown. By April she was ready to announce her plans to the public. In this issue of the *SLWN*, the following item appeared:

Our Girls

Great Public Meeting at the Wilberforce
Memorial Hall – Tues. the 6th instant at 7 p.m.
Come and hear about A Great Scheme
for an Industrial and Technical Training
School for Girls. All are invited.
Mrs. W.B. Marke in the Chair
Archdeacon Wilson will preside. Speakers
Mrs. Casely Hayford, Prof. Faduma
Solos by Mrs. A. Lake and Mr. C. William.
Recitation: Miss K. Easmon
Collection In aid of the Women's Branch of
The Universal Negro Improvement Association
and African Communities League[2]

Obviously Mrs. Casely Hayford had moved from her position in the Y.M.C.A. to a position of leadership in the Sierra Leone Branch of the Garvey Movement. The reasons for this are not clear.

In any case, the press duly reported the event in its 10 April 1920 issue giving the idea its enthusiastic support, agreeing that the situation of women in Sierra Leone was deplorable. Speaking of Mrs. Casely Hayford, the press reported as follows:

Mrs. Casely Hayford, the highly gifted Sierra Leone woman who is clearly under divine impulse and inspiration respecting her country and her people but whose gifts for service are being criminally neglected by a people who are only half awake to their own best interests, declared at the meeting on Tuesday last that the purpose underlying the idea of the Technical Training School for Girls was to enable the female section of our country to get their livelihood by honourable means and independently.

Apparently, Mrs. Casely Hayford felt at the time that support for the school would come from the citizens of Freetown and the Gold Coast even more and that this would be a chance for the wealthy of the community to help the community at large. Later, in the month of April there was another editorial suggesting the need of a similar school for boys. The following month, Mrs. Casely Hayford addressed the Public Meeting of the Ladies Pastoral Aid Association, again at Wilberforce Hall. On this occasion her subject was the restless condition of affairs in the world after the peace. She mentioned particularly social troubles in the family, industrial troubles (labor vs. capital), economic war (war between producers and consumers); disease, health problems and finally racial war. Mrs. Casely Hayford implored the women to do their share in alleviating these problems.

For reasons that are not at all clear there seems to have been a tug of war arising in the community over the school, its supporters and its leadership. Even a casual perusal of Mrs. Casely Hayford's activities indicates that in her anxiety to move on with her idea in a none too progressive community she may have approached too many, or maybe, competing groups; she may have ruffled too many feathers in the name of educational progress. A 12 June 1920 item in the *SLWN* attempts to offer some clarification:

> There has been a good deal of misunderstanding as regards the proposed Technical and Industrial School for Girls, and we feel sure that all who have the interest of the womanhood of West Africa at heart will be glad to know that this very laudable scheme has not fallen through but has been reorganized as an independent effort.
>
> While the scheme was under the auspices of the U.N.I.A., the originator, Mrs. Casely Hayford was unable to select helpers other than members of this association. She has now been able to call together a very representative committee of ladies and gentlemen who elected the following among their members to form the executive:

President – Mrs. Casely Hayford
Vice-Presidents – Mrs. Leigh-Sodipe, Professor Faduma
Secretary – Miss Kathleen Easmon, A.R.C.A.
Assistant Secretary – Mr. Alex D. Yaskey
Treasurer – Mrs. Elizabeth Macfoy
Executive Members: Mrs. C. May, Mrs. Vic Barlatt, Mrs. Marie

Rollings, Mrs. Farmer; Mrs. Ernestine Knox,
Rev. J.T. Roberts, Rev. R.R. Refell and F.A.
Miller, Esq.

Advisory Committee: Mr. Amadu Taylor, Chairman, Professor
Abayomi Cole, G.T. Lewis, Esq., Rev. and Mrs.
J.S. Wright, Dr. Horace Dove, Dr. G.N.
Metzger, H. Dean, Esq., Mrs. A. Farmer, Mrs.
Lydia Johnson, Mrs. Miller

Patrons: His Excellency, the Governor and Mrs. Wilkinson, The
Honourable the Colonial Secretary and Mrs. Maxwell, His
Honor the Chief Justice, Sir Gilbert Purcell, His Honor, Sir
Justin Parodi and Mrs. Parodi; The Director of Education,
R.F. Hunter, Esq., The Acting Attorney General, Carnigie
Brown, Esq., The Acting Treasurer, G. Belmar, Esq., His
Worship the Mayor, S.J.S. Barlatt, Esq., the Ex-Mayor, J.H.
Thomas, Esq., C. May, Esq.

The dispute was covered in the press in an article on 12 June 1920
which was signed by Ma Mashodo suggesting that the money raised by
Mrs. Casely Hayford as a member of U.N.I.A., i.e., as President of the
Women's Section, had given her the needed boost, and that the delegates from the U.N.I.A. who had just returned from their conference in
Accra reported that the money was needed for *their* organizatioin. At the
same time it was alleged that Mrs. Casely Hayford without the knowledge of the U.N.I.A. had approached the Accra Conference for funds
and was rebuffed. (See letter to Casely Hayford.) Also as Mrs. Casely
Hayford had said she would visit the Gold Coast for funds, this delegate
said he would prevent her going.[3] Mrs. Casely Hayford was trying to
establish a separate identity for her school but, at a stormy session,
admitted she had 65 pounds which she believed belonged to her for the
school, not for the Association.

Several factors came to light here. Mrs. Casely Hayford clearly
believed that through her husband or her sister, Mrs. Easmon,
described as the "Accra Delegate," she might have some clout at the
Accra meeting of Congress of British West Africa. She felt they would
endorse her idea; also she believed that American ties would be
extremely helpful. She probably saw the need for some outside force
from the Gold Coast or the States to set her supporters back in motion.
There was, of course, the other possibility that the U.N.I.A. or the
National Congress of British West Africa would both feel that the idea
of this type of school was competing with a project similar to one they

wished to undertake. In any case the controversy continued in the
SLWN.

During this period, C.D. Hotobah During wrote a letter to the Editor
which appeared on 12 June 1920, stating there was no need to raise
charitable funds for a fee-paying school – indeed there was no need to
train the girls of Freetown because there would be no jobs for them. The
greater need, he felt, was "to bring the vast number of neglected women
in the Protectorate up to standard."[4]

On 19 June 1920, Mr. Alex D. Yaskey, Assistant Secretary of Mrs.
Casely Hayford's School Committee, thanked all the citizens from the
Governor down who supported the School by attending a recently-held
Oriental Concert for the benefit of the school. In the same issue, the
paper expressed the opinion that Mrs. Casely Hayford was too sensitive
to criticism and that if she planned to undertake public projects, she
should be ready to withstand public reactions. "A few words of explanation from this gifted lady might have sufficed in the present situation."
And continuing in her support the editor wrote. "From the first we have
taken interest in the project initiated by Mrs. Hayford and we sincerely
trust she will have the grace and wisdom to carry on to a successful and
victorious end." This is one of several instances which suggest that Mrs.
Casely Hayford had difficulty in her public relations in Freetown ... at
least with a few of the more literate elite.

In the same issue with the above-mentioned editorial, there is an item
which attempted, as a reply to Ma Mashoda, to give the general public
the history of the idea of the Proposed Technical Training School for
Girls. It read:

> Shortly after originating the scheme which was the outcome of
> her work with the Y.M.C.A. and previous to placing it before the
> public, Mrs. Casley Hayford was selected President of the newly-
> formed Women's branch of the U.N.I.A. She handed over the cut
> and dried scheme to them at the first meeting after her election,
> and it was warmly received by both sections of the U.N.I.A.
>
> The idea of a house to house collection originated with Miss
> Easmon, the Secretary, who herself prepared the way for the
> collections by notice to the various churches in town.
>
> Subscription lists were prepared and issued to any members with
> the exception of the Vice President, Mrs. Rollings, who expressed
> the desire for a collecting book and Miss Evelyn Carew who kindly
> undertook to collect monies already forwarded to Mrs. Casely
> Hayford. Mrs. Easmon, the Accra Delegate referred to, informed

Mrs. Casely Hayford of a fact she had overlooked – that the U.N.I.A. had a lien on all monies collected in their name. This started controversy and wrangle with the U.N.I.A.

On three occasions, Mrs. Casely Hayford tried to get the U.N.I.A. to see the school as a separate organization but they were difficult so Mrs. Casely Hayford severed all connection with U.N.I.A. and was no longer Principal of the Women's Section.

At the last meeting of the women's group, which she attended, Miss Easmon handed over to the Treasurer the sum of 16 pds, 4 shillings, 8 p., the exact amount collected, not 15 pds. as stated in the Mashado item.

The 60 pounds deposited in the Foundation Fund of the Girl's Technical and Industrial Training School, Bank of British West Africa, was entirely collected by Mrs. Adelaide Casely Hayford and Miss Easmon except 3 pounds collected by Miss Evelyn Carew.

I have in my possession a paper signed by the principal donors stating that it was not their intention for their money to be used by the U.N.I.A.

There was no signature, but the sentiments seem clearly to be Mrs. Casely Hayford's version of the controversy.

In a letter to the Editor in the same 19 June issue, Kathleen Easmon undertook the task of answering C.D. Hotabah During. She implied that he just wanted to get into the act, that Mrs. Casely Hayford had already said there would be scholarships for deserving girls, and there would be jobs available for girls who had better training; for the Governor himself on 10 June, speaking at the Annie Walsh Memorial School graduation, announced that the civil service examinations would be open to girls. Finally, she agreed that there should be room for other schemes to educate women. And if, she asked, Mr. During wanted to help the Protectorate girls, he was free to do so.

As promised, on 26 June 1920 the *SLWN* carried a list of names submitted by Mrs. Casely Hayford of contributions to the school and the amount of their contribution:

His Excellency and Mrs. R.J. Wilkinson, Mr. and Mrs. Maxwell, the Colonial Secretary, The Chief Justice Sir Gilbert Purcell, Mr. and Mrs. E.V. Perodi, His Honor Mr. Justice, The Honorable J.H. Thomas, Messrs. Elder Dempter and Co., C. Carnigie Brown, Claude Wright, Dr. Ernest Wright, R. Golley Rich and Brs. Morrison Bakery, J. Francis Knox, C.W. Betts, J. Abayomi Cole, F.C. Bull, O. Benjamin, V. George, J.M. Vacaral, J.A. John,

Amadou Taylor, Samuel Brown, J.C. Smith-Whitfield, J.R.
Macaulay, Mrs. Butcher, O. Depuchaffery Barlatt, T.E.W.
Wakers, S. Davies, Boston Bungie.

In the 3 July 1920 issue of the *SLWN*, in an item by "Critic" The
Oriental Concert was enthusiastically applauded, "in spite of herself,"
says the writer. Especially praised were the dances of Kathleen Easmon
and the theatrical effects. Mrs. Casely Hayford joined by Dr. Metzger
and Mr. C. William sang "Good night beloved" at the end.

This same issue of the press noted on p.9 the departure of Mrs.
Casely Hayford and Miss Kathleen under the authority of the Executive
of the Girl's Technical and Industrial School for the United States with
strong recommendations from His Excellency Governor Wilkinson and
distinguished patrons to solicit money for the school. Again, the paper
stated its support of the project and wished both of the ladies bon
voyage.

Having a good idea, even a brilliant idea, is not always the right thing
and timing is often crucial in getting any project moving. As has been
stated many times, Mrs. Casely Hayford could easily have stimulated
envy or even hostility – just by being herself. In addition, her conflict and
competition with the Women's Section of U.N.I.A. and with the Sierra
Leone delegates to the Accra Conference could only have weakened her
basis for support. Groups wanting to control money raised in their name
and the need to raise private funds from a community not particularly
used to such activities can be seen in an extremely selfish way. After all,
the Sierra Leone delegates to the Accra Conferences were most anxious
that their country do well in the fund raising they had all agreed to do to
promote the Congress. No other activity, no matter how worthy, would
at that time have been seen favorably by them.

But in spite of all the hue and cry around the project as the many news
items reflected, it is interesting to note that Mrs. Casely Hayford in her
article, "A Girls' School in West Africa" published in *The Southern
Workman*, albeit for an American reading public, seemed to have risen
above the conflict or perhaps merely wanted to stress positive actions
leading to the birth of the school.[5] For she wrote as her version of the
school's origin

> Kathleen and I were concerned about the girlhood of Freetown.
> For beyond their rather sparse book knowledge there was nothing
> to occupy their time or to fit them for the battles of life – absolutely
> no practical training whatsoever. We felt we must do something to
> better the conditions.

At the back of my mind, too, was the remark of one of my own countrymen who had quite recently visited our home, and who, I felt, was voicing the opinions of thousands of others. Upon observing some draperies and curtains of native art work decorating the room, he had exclaimed, "Well, I never thought much of those things but they look quite beautiful in this room." "But, of course, they are beautiful," I responded. "Whatever did you think?" "I never thought anything at all about them in that way. I did not think that anything made by black people was beautiful. I thought all beauty came from Europe."

Instantly my eyes were opened to the fact that the education meted out to us had, either consciously or unconsciously, taught us to despise ourselves, and that our immediate need was an education which would instill into us a love of country, a pride of race, an enthusiasm for a black man's capabilities, and a genuine admiration for Africa's wonderful art work. We needed an education more adapted to our requirements, which while assimilating all that was good in European education, would help us to maintain our natural heritage of African individuality, and to become the best type African we could be.

In my mind's eye I could see a school in which girls, instead of blindly copying European fashions, would be dressed in attractive native garments which would enhance their personal charms. I could see them sitting in homes which combined European order, method and cleanliness with the beauty of native basket furniture, art work and draperies. I could see the young mothers teaching the little children on their knees that to be black was not a curse nor a disgrace, that the color scheme of the races was part of God's divine plan, and that just as it was impossible to make a world without the primary colors, so it was impossible to make a world without the Negro. I could hear the young mothers teaching their sons the glory of black citizenship, rather than encouraging them to bewail the fact that they were not white. I could hear the native musical instruments, developed on scientific European lines discoursing sweet music in the place of wheezy harmoniums. I could imagine the artistic youth of the hereafter painting pictures depicting black faces rather than white ones. I could visualize the listless, lethargic, educated town girl of today, through the medium of equipped gymnasiums and trained physical cultures enjoying the energy and vitality of her grandmother who thought nothing of spending days hoeing fields or of carrying a load as weighty as any man's. And then I could picture the sons and daughters of Africa's race 'looking the

whole world in the face,' without any apology whatsoever for the
color of their skin, and with such self-respect as to command the
respect of all nations. ...

To realize this dream,

Kathleen and I decided to go to America for the purpose of visiting
schools and, if possible, to raise enough funds to return home and
start a vocational school along these lines.[6] We therefore formed a
Committee of sympathetic Africans to foster our project of visiting
America, to investigate what was being done for the Afro-
Americans to give them opportunities of standing on their feet
through industrial education, with a view of returning home to start
a school on similar lines. ... A loan of one hundred pounds from ...
Mr. Amadou Taylor, a member of the Advisory Committee, reinforced our private resources and made it possible for us to undertake the trip.

It is difficult to know the image of the Universal Negro Improvement
Association in Freetown and why Mrs. Casely Hayford accepted the
presidency of its Women's Section. She may have seen it as a more
direct means of funding her school than, say, the Y.W.C.A. which most
certainly was under some type of white influence and control. In any
case, after she left for America the battle continued. In the 7 August
1920 issue of the *SLWN*, a letter appears addressing the importance of
the Universal Negro Association – and what it stands for. Its author, who
signs himself as "A New Negro," says the Association

stands for all things to make nations great – for Race, Unity,
Organization, Self-Help, Race Manhood, etc., bringing all Blacks
together so that they can qualify in industry, commerce, education,
cease being fools, be men, encourages aspirations towards political
freedom hence the Black Star Line Steamship Corporation and
Negro Factories Corporation.

The following week the Vice President and Assistant Secretary of the
School's Advisory Committee gave the public the final fiscal accounting
of the Oriental Concert at Wilberforce Hall, in the columns of the
SLWN. The amount raised was £92 16s 6d.

"Two and a Half-Years' Sojourn in America"

When Mrs. Casely Hayford at age 52 left Freetown with her niece Kathleen Easmon on 8 July 1920 for the United States, she was in mid-life embarking on a journey that was to be even more important to her life and more unusual, in fact, than her voyage to Germany so many years earlier. Her goal was clear: to learn how Afro-Americans, especially girls, were educated and to raise money for her school in Freetown. America, therefore, was to become an educational venture and a possible source of independence.

Fortunately, Mrs. Casely Hayford has written two different accounts of her experiences in America – one in an article, "Report of My Two and a Half Years' Sojourn in America," which appeared in the 31 March 1923 issue of the *SLWN* and the other as a part of her published *Memoirs* written many years later. While the latter version gives more of the flavor of the visit, both as to people and events, it is somewhat rambling in style and, as might be expected after so many years, often confuses the experiences she had on the first visit with those she had on her second visit. Nevertheless, the account in the *Memoirs* is extremely valuable because in it she provides the fascinating details of names and activities. The earlier account sent to the *SLWN* was for the edification of the Freetown community – a barebone report – to live up to the expectations of her supporters and to answer the skepticism of her detractors.

On the basis of other documentation, it has been possible to trace here and there her steps – when she was given hospitality and publicity "as the first African woman to come to the United States." This assertion made by Mrs. Casely Hayford was, as has been suggested, inaccurate but it is definitely true that she was the first African woman of education and status to come to the United States and also that she was probably among the first persons from her circle, man or woman (other than Coleridge-Taylor) to come.

The barest outline of this momentous trip is given in the newspaper account:

... Left on July 8, 1920 – for England and sailed from Southampton for America after flying visits to Liverpool and Manchester, arrived in the United States in New York on August 10th.

Got in touch with Dr. Jourdan, Secretary to the Negro Baptist Foreign Mission Board who lived in Philadelphia, arranged speaking engagements – went to Annual Baptist Convention in Indianapolis – met Nannie Burroughs – 'Greatest Negro woman of the day' – invited me and Kathleen to her school.

In two years, visited 36 towns – some more than once, always with two-fold object in view:

1. to learn all we could to enable us to cope more efficiently with the work in hand.
2. to raise funds, not only to keep ourselves but to advance the project near to our heart.

New York was our headquarters – visited Philadelphia, Washington, Baltimore, Richmond, Hampton, Atlanta (3 times), Birmingham, Buffalo (3 times), New Haven, Saratoga, Hartford, York, Reading, Charleston, Rome, Indianapolis, Shelton, Brooklyn, Newark, Chicago.

Visited schools galore – were invited to speak at Radcliffe and Bryn Mawr (couldn't arrange). Visited Columbia. Delightful day at Howard University and Dunbar High School – Undoubtedly, the finest day school I have ever seen, as regards modern improvements and first class equipment.

A week at Hampton (Principal J.E. Gregg agreed to become a member of the American Advisory Board).

Spelman and Tuskegee especially noted – appeared before over 50 different colored congregations besides many white ones.

Formed an American Advisory Board – Dr. J.E. Gregg, Dr. R. Moton of Tuskegee, Mrs. Booker T. Washington, Miss Nannie Burroughs and Dr. J. Jones of the Phelps Stokes Fund, Chairman of Education Commission who has deputed Mr. J.E.K. Aggrey to act as our American Treasurer.

In all, we raised about 1,800 pounds ($8,500 of which we sent back – 354 pounds 5 shillings as far back as November 1921). When preparing to leave for home our Treasurer had in hand about $1,300 (258 pounds) out of which he gave me 150 pounds for journey and expenses home and paid an unfortunate debt of 60 pound which we had incurred in a pageant – leaving a balance of 48 pounds.

Thus we spent for board, lodging, travelling expenses and sundries in two and a half years something like 1,192 pounds.

In both the beginning and ending of this Report, Mrs. Casely Hayford was concerned with the problems and disputes she had with Freetown citizens over the school. She began the report, "I dare not write a report to be published in the *SLWN* without incurring the justifiable wrath of its Editor." And in her conclusion she is even more scathing: "All I now ask is that the Sierra Leone public instead of trying to pull us down by their untruthful and damaging statements would endeavor to hold up my hands in the strenuous task which I have undertaken for the benefit of the future generations of our race."

By the time she wrote her *Memoirs* fifty years later, all the hurt and frustration she had experienced at the hands of her fellow citizens was behind her and did not cloud her recollection of this exciting venture.

The first view of the Statue of Liberty, one hand extended in welcome and the other raised to heaven as an emblem of freedom, aroused great enthusiasm. But landing was a formidable procedure with its array of officials waiting to investigate our passports, our pockets, and every detail of our proposed visit. Luckily, before leaving Freetown, we had obtained such splendid testimonials from the Governor, the Chief justice, the Bishop, etc., that we experienced no difficulty whatsoever.

There was just one fly in the ointment. Kathleen had acquired a very beautiful African country cloth with which to cover her feet on deck. I believe she had surreptitiously smuggled it out of her brother's splendid collection in Sierra Leone. Anyhow, in spite of frequent warnings that there were plenty of envious eyes on board, she would insist on leaving it about. Belonging to the tribe of Didymus, Kathleen had one definite characteristic – she didn't believe in thieves unless she beheld them, which, of course, rarely happens; but after the miraculous disappearance of her country cloth she came to the conclusion that when things are out of sight you had better put them out of mind also.[1]

The Custom House officials, never having seen any African woman before, were full of curiosity and expressed deep admiration for our collection of African exhibits, which we proposed to use at our public meetings.

But where were we to stay? Most of the hotel accommodation we found was absolutely debarred. So these kindhearted officials handed us over to two Swedish women who had boarded the steamer from the Travellers Aid Association, and having found out that as Methodists we would like to get into touch with the Methodist Foreign Missionary Society, they bundled us into a taxi and directed the chauffeur there. Thus was our first introduction to America and Harlem, the Negro quarter, where we found accommodation in a very comfortable hotel. That night, to our amazement, we saw the announcement in spectacular headlines that two African Princesses had arrived that morning in New York.

Soon after our arrival a film producer called with the request that he might be allowed to film us. So, on the front steps of our boarding house, a projectoscope was installed, attracting a throng of Negro spectators, who also wished to be in the picture. We didn't do anything much, Kathleen sat on a chair whilst I handed her our beautiful exhibits in turn. Subsequently, some Africans came up to be introduced in proper native style, which was really the hit of the performance. We never saw anything but the producer and his projectoscope, which we consider rather hard lines. That the picture was produced, however, was subsequently proved when we visited some other American towns and were greeted thus: "Oh, we know you already! We saw you on the films."

We met our friends, Mr. and Mrs. Downing, and had a few joy rides for a day or two, after having found rooms within our means. Subsequently we put up with the Rev. Norman Wilson and his wife (Pastor of Church of the Messiah, 206 East 95th Street). He was the son of our dearly beloved pastor, Archdeacon Wilson. Knowing that New York rents were prohibitive, they very generously placed a room near their Episcopal Church at our disposal, which we occupied for months on end.

When we awoke to the fact that our assets had dwindled almost to zero, we realized we must be up and doing. So Kathleen left me for a day while she went to Philadelphia to interview Dr. Jourdan, the Secretary for the Baptist Foreign Missionary Society, whom we had met in Sierra Leone. He arranged for us to speak on the following Sunday at a very large Baptist Church, where the minister would take up an offering on our behalf. Having expected to see two semi-civilized, illiterate uncouth women, the Negroes were overwhelmed with enthusiasm, especially after they had listened to an address portraying the good points of our downtrodden race, instead of the usual fetish barbaric practices, and devil worshipping rites to which they were accustomed.

One by one, although the normal collection had been taken, these cooks, scavengers, porters and stokers, etc., came up to the altar and deposited their dollar bills with such unstinted generosity that we received the handsome sum of 300 dollars – 60 pounds – for our first venture. The cash never came our way because Dr.

Jourdan took it to defray our Philadelphia expenses and to book Pullman accommodation for our lengthy journey to Indianapolis, where the National Convention of Colored Women was to be held, thus giving us an opportunity of meeting delegates from all over the country whom he knew would be ready to open their churches to us.[2] So, in our picturesque native costumes, we arrived and saw, and conquered.[3] We entered an enormous hall thronged with well dressed intelligent Negro women of all shades and complexions; and as we walked up the aisle the President, Miss Naomi Burroughs, Principal of a flourishing Girls School at Lincoln Heights, Washington, D.C., came down the steps of the platform, with both hands extended, in cordial greeting.[4] As we were not expected there was no opportunity for speaking, but Miss Burroughs suggested our immediate visit to a photographer to get some picture postcards which, from the impression we had made, would sell like hot loaves. Before the evening session we were reinforced with a hugh pile of photos, etc., 3d each, from which again we amassed a considerable sum.

We spent an unforgettable week in Indianapolis.[5] Being late August, there was a superabundance of fruit. I have never seen such delicious melons, with which we always started our principal meals; the taste still lingers in my mouth today. Our hostess suggested that we should separate, Kathleen visiting one church and I another. In this way we reinforced our Exchequer in half the time, with very beneficial results. We had made so many contacts that our itinerary increased in magnitude, with which our purse could not always cope. So through the kindness of friends, we succeeded in getting tickets which reduced our fares by half. This was indeed a boon and a blessing.

Miss Burroughs invited us to spend a week at her school at Lincoln Heights, one of the suburbs of Washington, which we thoroughly enjoyed.[6] This was our first introduction to America's seat of administration – the White House, the Capitol, Lincoln's Memorial, the world-famous buildings abounded on every side. Union Station simply took our breath away. I was expecting a great big barn-like structure, black with smoke, dirt and grime, instead of which there arose before our astonished gaze an amazing building of pure white marble and granite, with no connection whatever with belching engines and tons of smoke. It looked like a museum – a miracle of cleanliness, in its glaring white purity, with a team of coloured red caps, whose smiling faces and willingness to obey our slightest behest, added to our enjoyment in no small degree. On our second visit to Washington, later in the year, I witnessed the inauguration of the Republic President Harding, and mingled with the excited throngs.

On our return to New York, we encountered an East African student at Columbia University, Simango by name, who having heard us speak, or rather having seen Kathleen, boarded the platform, with the request that he might act as a porter by carrying our bags containing our fine exhibits of African curios.[7] This was the first, but by no means the last time. As a graduate of Hampton University, the first outstanding College for Negroes to be started, he wrote to the President requesting that we might be allowed to visit his Alma Mater. The railway fare was rather prohibitive so we had to travel by steamer; and although in former years I had experienced three freezing winters in Germany, I never felt so cold in my life.

Kamba Simango was a most valuable assistant, not only relieving me of the burden of looking after Kathleen, a Gargantuan load, entirely out of proportion to my diminutive frame, but he was also the means of introducing us to Paul Robeson, the famous baritone. At the time, Robeson was only just beginning his musical career, giving up his practice as a lawyer to concentrate on his outstanding artistic talents, becoming later one of the greatest Negro actors of his day. He was exceedingly kind to us not only assisting us at some of our meetings, but placing his flat at our disposal for a short time. His wife was sick in hospital and he was going on to London to act with Mrs. Patrick Campbell, a very distinguished actress. ...

This was really our first introduction to White America. Hampton is sponsored by multi-millionaires and some of the members of New York's exclusive Four Hundred. We were entertained at Holly House, a kind of restaurant for visitors, and stood by the President as he took the salute from a throng of Negro students looking like soldiers in their khaki uniforms.

It was a gorgeous campus, every available industry being taught, by which students could earn their living in after life. The faculty was mixed, the white race predominating.[8] We held a meeting specially for them, and following the usual procedure, I spoke and Kathleen showed our exhibits, to the accompaniment of her inspiring explanatory notes. The enthusiasm was unbounded. We had arrived. From then on our protracted stay of two years evolved into one long triumphant processional extending from Buffalo in the North, with its overwhelming majestic Niagara Falls, to New Orleans in the South, still redolent of the old French customs, manners and tradition. Our lives were so full that it would be impossible to narrate all the events which followed. ...

While at Hampton, we met a Syrian Professor from the University of Beirut, and the Principal invited us all to lunch in the Students Hall, where we partook of a very well cooked, well served two course meal, after which we were taken into the kitchen to watch the expeditious manner in which dirty plates and dishes were disposed of.

The plates were all scraped by the students and then placed in a huge machine, coming out on the other side clear, rinsed and dry, ready to be stacked up for the next meal.

I could not help wondering whether a similar invention on a very small scale for ordinary household use could not be put on the market to do away with the drudgery of washing up, which everyone detests, and which could be a veritable boon and blessing to mankind. ...

Our travels in America were wide and varied, for the most part amongst Negro Schools which we were anxious to study for the help they could give us in Africa. Starting from Miss Sarah Washington's little private school in Alabama, where we spent a most enjoyable day, we went on to Calhoun, run by a Board of Trustees from Boston, under the principalship of a most delightful cultured New England lady, who was no more than a semi-invalid, but who nevertheless kept her flag unfurled to the breeze. Atlanta, Georgia, which is quite an educational center, was our next port of call. Dr. and Mrs. John Hope entertained us right royally at Morehouse College for boys only. But in those days a boys' school was practically a man's school because as a rule education started so late that there were crowds of scholars who had left their teens behind them. The same thing applied to the girls, so that at Spelman Institute, sponsored by Mrs. John D. Rockefeller, we were surrounded by a host of grown-up young women, at a non-co-educational school – a most refreshing experience.[9]

Atlanta University where Dr. Burghardt DuBois, the eminent educationalist and Editor of the "Crisis" figured so prominently, was highly interesting, but perhaps not quite so up-to-date as some of the newer Institutions.

My weekend at Lincoln deserves honourable mention. It is one of the smaller universities. Incidentally, Lincoln sheltered Azikwe, the famous Nigerian political agitator as well as many of his race, and it is most inspiring to note that since he became affiliated with the Moral Rearmament Movement, Zik's domination proclivity has fallen off like a mantle, so that he is now out to work on terms of brotherhood, as the only basis of ever achieving nationhood.[10] I was very much impressed by the atmosphere which literally breathed out the spirits of friendliness, kindliness and goodwill irrespective of colour. Most of the staff were white Americans, and this spirit shows clearly their attitude towards their work – the students."

Naturally Tuskegee, the famous Industrial School, came in for our close scrutiny. Our first visit was in company with our dear Miss Burroughs, who spent so much time shepherding us two simpletons in the land of hope and glory.

We travelled in a Jim Crow car, which, of course, could have been easily avoided, had we only proclaimed our nationality to the Railway officials, as only American Negroes were barred from the other carriages. Such a procedure was entirely out of the question, because we could not possibly wound the feelings of all the kind, generous, coloured folk who had opened their homes and hearts to us.

Tuskegee was another remarkable episode in our career. We landed at a little station three miles from the Institution, where we saw a lot of khaki-clad specimens of magnificent Negro manhood, whom I mistook for soldiers. One immediately boarded our carriage. "Anyone here for Tuskegee?" he inquired. Responding in the affirmative, he took charge of our baggage and tickets and escorted us to his waiting car – an extremely ramshackle vehicle, but one which served its purpose very well. After bumping along for three miles we arrived at the great pile, known as Tuskegee Institute.

I cannot possibly record all the incidents that took place subsequently, but on the Sunday evening Dr. Moton intimated his desire for us to speak at the meeting in the huge Chapel. We took our places on the platform with the faculty, 300 strong, directly behind us, and a magnificent orchestra behind that. In addition, the platform was thronged with visitors from all parts of the world. We sat there and my eyes filled with tears as we watched the students, 2000 of them, take their places; the men all in khaki on the right, and the women in dark blue skirts and white blouses on the left. Everyone stood to attention till Dr. Moton bowed his request for us to be seated. He assigned me the place of honour next to him, and hurriedly whispered "We generally allow a speaker only 15 minutes, but you can go on as long as you like." The Negro

Spiritual "Deep River," to Coleridge Taylor's immortal setting, rang through the Chapel, and almost reduced me to tears at the memory of his loving personality and genial friendship.

It took me all my time to regain my composure before I stood up. As for poor little Kathleen, she was almost in a state of collapse. The whole proceedings were too overwhelming for her. The tears streamed down her cheeks, and her hands became so numb that two white women in each side had to rub them to restore the circulation. So I faced that congregation – the largest I had ever encountered. I had to pray hard for grace and strength to go through such an ordeal. God heard my prayers as he always does and I stood up absolutely fearless – forgetful of self and rose to the occasion.

I spoke for 30 minutes, dealing lengthily with the fine side of African life which had hitherto been a closed book by my hearers, since speakers (no doubt in order to arouse sympathy) were prone to narrate only the barbarities, fetish rites and devil worship which made them ashamed of their forbears. For me, it was a great inspiration because they listened with such rapt attention. ...

The next day Dr. Moton asked us to see him in his office, a massive handsome room redolent with the odour of spring violets. He then told us that the faculty had been so impressed that they had suggested a donation of 500 pounds. We never received a penny and were at our wits end to understand such behavior from a man with such a high social position and heavy financial backing. It was only on my return to Sierra Leone that I was able to sift the problem to its foundation but I am afraid the solution must remain a closed secret. ...

Some months later, I visited Tuskegee again, but this time alone, as my niece was feeling so tired and worn out that she gladly accepted an invitation from Rev. Fred Bunker and his wife, returned missionaries from East Africa, and who were responsible for Kombe's [sic] entry into Hampton University.[11] He very naturally wanted to introduce his lovely fiancee to his foster parents. So they took her in, whilst I enjoyed a similar rest at Tuskegee for two weeks. I lunched with Mrs. Booker Washington, the widow of the great founder, who spent most of her time sitting near his grave, amongst the trees of the beloved campus. She, too, has since passed away. She was in charge of the Domestic Science Department to which was attached a model house for brides-to-be. This was over thirty years ago. When will Africa see such practical schemes for the uplift of our womanhood? There was a splendid hospital, beautifully equipped, where the girls received an intensive training with which they could always face life.

Another very interesting event was our visit to Dr. Carver's Laboratory. Dr. Carver gained a world-wide reputation for discovering by-products of the ground nut from face powder to milk downwards, or perhaps upwards. He was also an extraordinarily reticent man, and it was difficult to get him to talk, but he has made for himself a niche in Afro-American history, his memory will never die.

They did know how to dignify labour at Tuskegee. On that enormous campus I never beheld one servant, every bit of work was done by the students. You could walk anywhere about the 200 acres without seeing one little bit of rubbish or paper. The school had a six day session and was divided into two schedules, work and study alternating every week. By this means every student received a two-fold training and many impecunious pupils were able to earn their fees and board by overtime work.

The only time when the students were allowed to mingle was at meals. I stood and watched them from the little gallery in the huge Dining Hall and after a volume of melody as the grace was sung, they set to work enjoying this little social hour to the full.

I witnessed the unveiling of a beautiful bronze statue of the founder, in the act of lifting a veil off the face of a poor illiterate Negro, and was once again called upon to speak. Today Tuskegee still lives in my memory.

I liked Chicago least of all the many cities we visited. For the first time we sensed an inferiority complex from the well-to-do, off-white Negroes, who abounded on every side. But our visit to Hull House, a Community Center amidst all the famous abattoirs still remains a delightful memory. Its founder, the late Jane Addams, one of the twelve most outstanding women in America, told us all about it as she sat between us at luncheon. This was in 1921, three years after the cessation of the First World War, when so many homeless families from Czechoslovakia and Balkan States particularly, invaded America in need of help. Her heart was so moved to compassion by the sight of these starved waifs and strays that she determined to do something about it. She succeeded in interesting a number of wealthy white people who supported her scheme with the generous donations for which American patrons are famous. Hull House was the result. Its scope was very varied, ranging from small children to very mature adults. What struck me most were the cultural opportunities which prevailed. Without any cost whatsoever, these children's inherent artistic ability was being fostered. No wonder they became absolutely new creatures. After attending the usual free schools for the ordinary academic subjects, their time was directed to the spiritual and ethical values of life.

It was an inspiration to watch those youngsters, their little faces radiant with joy of participating in a string orchestra, which was very immature, but as seed sown on good ground, would yield abundant fruit hereafter. Budding painters stood at their easels, brush in hand, learning the fundamentals under splendid teachers.

We had an invitation to attend the Annual Convention of the U.B.C. Mission, whose magnificent work in Sierra Leone and the Protectorate stands out as a monument of genuine enthusiasm and whole hearted endeavor, but unfortunately we could not avail ourselves of it.[12]

Perhaps my favorite city is Boston; it reminded me so much of England, and in fact that section of the United States is called New England. There we made some friends, whose real interest, and generous contributions were of incalculable help after the school materialized.

Whilst there, we staged a Pageant.

It was at Boston that we spent a memorable day in the home of Mrs. Meta Warwick Fuller, the eminent sculptor.

Married to a distinguished consulting physician, one could discern the ever present conflict between the duties of home life, and the artistic urge for expression. Dr. Fuller, was a most understanding husband and put no obstacles in his wife's path.[13]

She herself was a pupil of Rodin, who greatly admired her ability. Her model of the head of John the Baptist must rank as one of the world's great sculptures.

In her studio, I noticed a fine head of a full-blooded Negro. Just then some of the younger members of the family came rushing in. One of them said to me "I simply cannot understand how Auntie can choose an ugly head like that for a model!" Mrs. Fuller turned to me with a smile. "They can't see the beauty, but I do and it gave me a great deal of pleasure to model that head!" Of course they could not see the beauty, but with the eyes of a visionary, she could discern the depths of a fine soul, and this she had depicted very successfully.

The next city in order of preference was Philadelphia, in which we experienced the realities of brotherhood. Our friends rallied round us, especially Rev. Lloyd Imes and his wife of the Coloured

Presbyterian Church in New York.[14] They shepherded us and introduced us to their flock, who with keen enthusiasm helped us to stage our Pageant "The Answer" again, with infinitely better results than on the previous occasion at Boston. Here again, irrespective of consequences, we hired the Academy of Music, one of Philadelphia's largest buildings. The audience was loud in its applause.

One extremely interesting event was our visit to a large white Congregational Church in Brooklyn. It was the Church of Mrs. Harriet Beecher Stowe, the famous author of *Uncle Tom's Cabin.* To commemorate her outstanding work for the Negro race, her pew was occupied by any prominent Negroes from other parts of the world one Sunday every year. We thought it a very great privilege to be allowed to sit in it.

There were two ministers, white and Negro, and two choirs, white and Negro, who all participated in the service, and although I lost a beautiful little gold pendant and chain, it fades into utter insignificance at the memory of the beautiful rendering of some of the Spirituals. Once again, I was struck, with this spontaneous, unaffected Negro singing.

Thanks to Professor Mabel Carney of Teachers College, Columbia, I had a chance of speaking at the Horace Mann School – a Junior Branch of the University, and amongst the assembly was a daughter of the Rev. Harry Emerson Fosdick, one of the most eminent pastors in New York. She immediately told of my visit to her mother, who forthwith sent me an invitation to visit her.[15] It was just at the time when my Home Committee and I were at loggerheads, and her practical interest, coupled with her words of encouragement, cheered me up wonderfully.

On another occasion I addressed the members of the Church Periodical Club of St. Thomas' Church Fifth Avenue. This resulted in a yearly supply of textbooks and Teachers books also – a most welcome addition to our poor little library. ...

I also gave an address at the Central Headquarters of the white Y.W.C.A. in Lexington Avenue, the first Negro to speak from that platform, where my message left its mark.

Another episode which lingers in my memory was my visit to a very large white Presbyterian Church in New York, getting the opportunity through Miss Ethel Wakeman, a friend of Miss Carney. I understood afterwards that there had been great opposition to my appearance, by two members of the Committee, who, however, were over-ruled by the others. After my address, these very two women were the first to approach the platform to shake hands with me.

Mrs. Casely Hayford recalled a number of other persons and events which were a part of this first trip to the United States. Clearly she was most impressive and was able to influence by her person and her ideas a wide range of people.

We visited Trinity, the Episcopal Church, in the heart of Wall Street, and the richest in the world, there, instead of being plenti-fully helped to cold shoulder, which had been our experience at other minor white churches, some of the congregation shook hands most cordially with us.

Mrs. Willard Straight, now Mrs. Elmhurst, generously spon-sored our little school up to the very last. Without her annual grant of 200 pounds we would have had to close down. In fact, in those bitter days when all men forsook me my rich white friends just carried me on their shoulders with their magnificent gifts.

The late Mrs. Arthur Curtis James, who combined a lovely personality with a magnanimous heart presented me with a wonderful Projectoscope – quite an event at the time – for the development of visual education in the school, and sent me a cheque, with which to enlarge our garret, so as to accommodate boarders.

The late Mrs. Sarah Hallowell, of Boston – the widow of the Colonel who had distinguished himself in the American Civil War – stands out pre-eminently, as a lady of amazing personality. With her wealth, she could have surrounded herself and family with everything money could buy; but her purse was so consecrated, that she contented herself with a comfortable home, and the ordinary amenities of life, so as to help the needy with her generous bounty. She was an absolute saint, impregnating the very walls of her beautiful home with an atmosphere of love, goodwill, and unforgettable unselfishness. She simply radiated kindliness, so that anyone meeting her could not fail to be all the better for the contact. Her mantle has fallen on the shoulders of her daughter, Mrs. Arthur Morse of Weston, Massachusetts, who is carrying out her lovely mother's traditions, and showing the same magnanimous generosity.

The late Mr. George Foster Peabody, a Southern multi-millionaire, not only sponsored Kamba Simango's education, but took us under his wing, by inviting us to his magnificent residence at Saratoga Springs – the Epsom of America – and placing his Cadillac at our disposal. Through his instrumentality we obtained access to many places debarred to American Negroes. For instance, we addressed the Societé des Beaux Arts at the exclusive Waldorf Astoria in the interest of the School.

Columbia University enfolded us in its embrace with its amazing variety of educational facilities. We were asked to the Annual Dinner of British Empire Subjects residing in New York at the time. After a sumptuous banquet and without any preparation whatever, I was called upon to address this very distinguished company of professors and students from all over the world, and as a result we received some very welcome cheques to promote our work.

Miss Carney, on the Staff of Teachers College, Columbia, cannot possibly be left out of these *Memoirs*. She spent a lot of her time, talents and energy in helping this poor old lame dog over stiles, and having visited Africa and seen our need with her own eyes, left no stone unturned to lend me a helping hand, by arranging speaking appointments, which did not mean a small fortune, but which were very welcome in paying my immediate expenses, in that prohibitively expensive country.

The Negro churches, on the whole, most generously opened their doors and their purses, and we would have fared very badly if their help had not been forthcoming. So many of them opened their homes also, and to their lavish entertainment on our behalf.

While Mrs. Casely Hayford was diligently pursuing her goals, it is obvious that Kathleen was being diligently pursued by Kamba Simango, a fact that could not have escaped her eyes. In any case, she offers the personal reactions to the budding romance. Writing in a most matter of fact way, she said,

Leaving Tuskegee on our first visit, I spent some weeks at Pittsburgh, whilst Kathleen was quietly preparing for her wedding to Kamba Simango. She had arranged a final meeting in New York prior to the event. So when I arrived, everything was set for the occasion, and once again Paul Robeson came to our assistance as entertainer. Through the kindness of the late Dr. Jesse Jones of the Phelps-Stokes Fund, who had kept an eye on us during our numerous peregrinations, a splendid hall was placed at our disposal rent free. There for the second time we came into personal contact with some of New York's exclusive Four Hundred. The first time was at a reception in the later Mrs. Arthur Curtis James' palatial residence, when the Hampton choir sang Negro Spirituals, and Kamba Simango related his life story, which lack of space prevents met from repeating here. I remember one gentleman saying to me after this meeting, whether you have achieved your goal or not, one thing is certain. You have made an exceedingly good impression on the very best people in America.

So my little niece was married at a little Church in Connecticut, of which Rev. Fred Bunker, Kamba's foster father, was the Pastor. His congregation had converted the building into a bower of roses, besides defraying all the expenses of the wedding breakfast, in the usual magnanimous American fashion, out of sheer love for the bride.

Kathleen looked lovely. Her spiritual beauty was greatly enhanced by the white silk embroidered Susu costume her mother had made for her.

As I gave her away, the lump in my throat almost choked me, because quite suddenly I had the intuition that she would not be with us much longer. "Auntie," she would say, "I don't want to live to be very old. I would very much rather wear out than rot out."

The 19 August 1922 issue of the *SLWN* reported the event to the Freetown community.

Miss Kathleen Easmon who in company with Mrs. Casely Hayford has been away for about two years in America in the interest to raise funds for an Industrial School for Girls here was united in holy wedlock on 1st June in the Congregational Church at Wilton, Conn. to Mr. Columbus Kamba Simango, an Educationalist of Mashonga, East Africa. Rev. Fred Bunker performed the ceremony and Mr. Nicholas B. Taylor of Sierra Leone presided at the organ.

A week later on 26 August 1922, p.2, the *SLWN* carried an account provided by Mrs. Casely Hayford which gave more details:

She was attired in an African costume embroidered for the occasion by her mother. Mr. Simango was also in native costume. She was given away by her aunt becomingly gowned in Fanti costume of the Gold Coast.[16]

To return to the *Memoirs:*

As she said goodbye to me on board the "Paris," a palatial steamer entirely beyond my means but a delightful experience, she said, "Auntie, I shall hold up my handkerchief four square, and as the steamer recedes, you will know it is Kathleen behind it!" I watched all the little white penants fluttering in the breeze, with the four square handkerchief standing out in bold relief, and was over come with grief till Mrs. Norton, with whom I was travelling, came up and said, "My dear woman, don't give way like this! You will soon see her again!" But I never did. It was our final goodbye. She lived for just two years longer, spending most of her time in Portugal, learning the language so as to be of tangible assistance to her husband, on their return to East Africa; then she succumbed to an attack of peritonitis.

The following account of Kathleen's death appeared in the *SLWN* of 20 August 1924:

Death in London in early hours of Sunday July 27 at Charing Cross Hospital of Mrs. Kamba Simango – was only 32 years of age and one of the most promising women of her generation. She was a gifted speaker, like her aunt Mrs. Casely Hayford, with whom she went to America during the war on a mission to raise funds for the establishment of a school for girls in Sierra Leone. She was the first African to broadcast from Savoy Hill in London.

She died after a serious operation. Her husband and mother were in Lisbon. Funeral at Kensington Cemetery, Hanwell. Mourners were Mr. Kamba Simango, Mrs. Easmon, Miss Edmonia Smith, Miss Gladys Hayford, Dr. Easmon and Mrs. Renner, Miss McCarthy, Mrs. Pitt, Mrs. Charles Easmon and Miss I. Campbell.

Flowers from Mr. and Mrs. Casely Hayford, Miss Ira Aldridge, Mr. and Mrs. Coleridge-Taylor.

Death was from appendicitis, she was in Portugal learning the language. She was educated at Notting Hill High School and gained her ARCA at South Kensington where she was an art student.

While Mrs. Casely Hayford was to return to America within the next five years, this first trip was the major one both in her education and in her activities in securing funds and the initiation of contacts for her school. There is no doubt that the presence of the young and talented Kathleen contributed immeasurably to the success of the first trip. Kathleen's marriage may have been a disappointment, but then at that time Mrs. Casely Hayford did not know she would return to America. In a sense, her mission had been accomplished. She could return to Freetown in triumph.

Aside from these accounts by Mrs. Casely Hayford, there are other documents giving a more complete picture of the trip – her self-image as she was being introduced to Americans, into whose hands she really placed herself and bits and pieces revealing how she was being viewed by Americans. Although she had never been to America before and aside from Coleridge-Taylor no one in her intimate circle knew America personally, Mrs. Casely Hayford clearly had some image of America, especially of Afro-Americans, from her husband and his associates. Casely Hayford, as a writer and activist, was well known to a small group of important blacks prior to Mrs. Casely Hayford's coming to the States.

The press was an important vehicle for blacks in Africa and abroad as a means of knowing one another and influencing one another. Undoubtedly, his reading of Garvey's *Negro World* and agreeing with its principles brought Casely Hayford, editor of *The Gold Coast Leader*, into close contact with Garvey himself. In 1922 Garvey knighted Casely Hayford who earlier in 1920 had welcomed the emergence of the United Negro Improvement Association in his inaugural address on the founding of the National Congress of British West Africa.[17] And even though Garvey's paper was banned in West Africa, Casely Hayford continued to seek copies. In 1923 he wrote John E. Bruce, a well known Garveyite, asking him please to send him a weekly copy to his Seccondee (sic) address. And in 1928 Casely Hayford in his *Gold Coast Leader* praised Garvey's *Negro World*.[18]

During this period of Garvey's importance, his conflict with DuBois and his Pan-African Congresses are well known. Africans, like Casely Hayford, at the time, seemed to side with Garvey; therefore it is somewhat surprising that on coming to the States, Mrs. Casely Hayford sought the aegis of the National Association for the Advancement of Colored People (N.A.A.C.P.) and accepted its introduction to the important blacks in the States. John Bruce in 1923 had written Casely Hayford particularly cautioning him not to make any commitments to DuBois on his forthcoming trip to Africa because Bruce believed DuBois was "bent on mischief, due to the failure of his Pan-African scheme."[19] Of course as Mrs. Casely Hayford was not living with her husband at that time, she might well have been unaware of these currents. So while she mentions the Methodist church in her*Memoirs*, it is to the N.A.A.C.P., which she does not mention, that she had her mail delivered and from which she sought assistance through introductory letters.[20] No doubt because of early correspondence from Mrs. Casely Hayford, it is the *Crisis*, the official organ of the National Association for the Advancement of Colored People (N.A.A.C.P.), which announces to the public her arrival:

Mrs. Casely Hayford, wife of the Hon. Casely Hayford, is expected to arrive in New York from Sierra Leone during July. Mrs. Hayford is being sent by the Educational Committee of the Women of West Africa, to promote the interest of an Industrial Technical Training School for Girls – the first of its kind to be established on the West Coast. She will be accompanied by her niece, Miss Katherine Easmon, daughter of the late Dr. M.C. Farrell Easmon, principal medical officer of the Gold Coast. Miss Easmon is an associate of the Royal College of Art, London. Mrs. Hayford and Miss Easmon are well known on London platforms. They will appear in native costume and are the first West African women to lecture in America.[21]

Later in August, using the *Crisis* as a return address, Mrs. Casely Hayford wrote her husband that she did intend to have correspondence with him on this trip, because as she later admits, the American public were not aware of their estrangement and she did nothing to apprise them of it.

Addressing him as "Dear Casely" and signing it "Yours with love, Addie," she speaks of hoping against hope to meet in London but

> Providence shaped things otherwise ... Rightly or wrongly we are in America – left by the *New York* on August 7th and as things are expensive – I need money. I am confident that once we begin our campaign our effort will be crowned by success; nevertheless it takes some time to study conditions and organize a wise foundation. Then most of the influential people are out of town and will not be returning until the middle of Sept., which means a long wait for us ... so money is needed. I am sure you will see your way clear to do this.

Now settled in the room provided by Rev. Norman Wilson she wrote her husband again on 18 November 1920, informing him that Gladys was returning to Freetown and reminding him that Gladys had not seen him for seven years.

> We are really in the public eye. We are received with the utmost kindness wherever we go and even if we do not succeed in raising the amount we desire, we have certainly succeeded in giving the American Negro a new vision of Africa and her people.
>
> I never miss an opportunity of rubbing in who you are. I understand that *Gold Coast Native Institutions* is now in Yale University but I should like you please to send me a copy as soon as possible to give to a West Indian clergyman who is not only a book lover but a

great library expert. He is particularly interested in all literature pertaining to Africa.

Mrs Casely Hayford again writes for money so that she can help Tom get on his legs, wants to send for him – to give him another chance by settling on the land with enough capital to make a fresh start.

I believe that I am my brother's keeper and that it behooves me to do all I can to lend a helping hand to my own kith and kin in dire distress.

I am so pleased to hear that you are anxious for Sleop to specialize in 'Literature' and Languages. I should also like him to start shorthand at once, because it takes years to become efficient and he can always command a handsome salary from a commercial standpoint.

I do hope you are meeting with great success in your work and that you three are having a lovely time together.

Yours affectionately
Addie

Apparently Mr. Casely Hayford responded to these letters, though his answers are not available. Mrs. Casely Hayford is maintaining a feeling of affection and warmth but the strain over differing family obligations and the scarcity of funds still affect the relation between the two. One cannot help wondering whether Mrs. Casely Hayford had been foresighted enough to have among her "African Exhibits" copies of her husband's book or whether, as I am inclined to believe, some knowledgeable people, black, in particular, asked for them and perhaps embarrassed her when she realized she did not have them with her.

She wrote Mr. Casely Hayford on 20 October 1920:

My dear Casely,
Thanks for the money. [She discussed the education of the children.] I must close with much love. Kathleen joins me in love.

Yours affectionately, Addie.

Writing the following month from the same address, she said:

206 East 95th Street
c/o Rev. N. Wilson
December 17, 1920

My dear Casely,
This is just a line to wish you 'Bon Voyage' in small speed. I have

just had a letter from you stating that you were leaving soon after Christmas so I hope this will just catch you.

The *Crisis* have written to me to supply them with data concerning your book, education activities, etc. as they want to make you their character sketch at an early date. Also your photo.

Could you let me have them by return mail or as soon as possible. People out here think that we are a very united couple, and I want them still to continue to think so. That is why they have applied to me for these facts.

I asked the children to ask you for a native cloth as I am appearing so constantly in Fantee costume and now my cloth is dreadfully the worse for wear. Could you oblige me in a matter like this? We are doing such fine work and our costume opens doors which would otherwise be closed to us. Gladys is to go to Brighton – Well, of course, I known nothing of the school and I have not seen it either Miss Hutton Mills or the principal to judge what their education is like. I have only a horror of private finishing schools because they generally turn out girls with a mere smattering and superficial knowledge of anything.

I think I ought to let you know also that Charlie and Nettie are contemplating coming to England next year as the former wants to sit for an examination. In this case, I shall no longer be able to share their home and if I have to start keeping my own house open, I cannot possibly do so at the present rate of living – the 200 pounds a year agreed upon. I have tried very hard to meet you at every point but this is just an impossibility and entirely out of the question. I am so glad you have had such a happy time with the children. It is a pity there is no likelihood of the home life being continued to judge from the tone of your last letter.

Please excuse this blot. It is Kathleen's work. She joins me in love and best wishes for the yule-tide season.

Yours affectionately,
Addie

Increasingly appreciating how important her husband is to blacks in the United States, Mrs. Casely Hayford writes him again on 23 Feb. 1921 still from 95th Street.

Dear Casely,

I have just returned from Richmond Va., where I met a Mr. Mitchell who is running a very successful colored bank and who

seems to be in close with Duse Mohammed to try to establish a
bank on the West Coast. He knows you already through your
books. I suggested that he should write to you, take you into his
confidence as you are a Fantee and much more cognisant with
affairs than Duse Mohammed.[22] Of course no one here has any
idea of the relationship between us. I act as if everything is all right.

In any case both of these deals ought to mean something very
substantial to you. I am sorry you could not spare me a cloth. It
seems such a shame when I am trying to do my bit for Africa.

Addie

From the first days of her arrival, Mrs. Casely Hayford lost no time in
acquiring proper letters of introduction to reinforce or supplant those
she brought from Sierra Leone. From August to September 1920, she
was busy securing the proper introductory letters from the N.A.A.C.P.
The first letter on 23 August from Walter White is illustrative.[23]

Mrs. Casely Hayford
217 West 139 Street
New York City, N.Y.

Dear Mrs. Hayford,

I am sending you enclosed letters of introduction which I promised to write for you when you were in the office this morning. I
sincerely trust that they may be of assistance to you in placing your
cause before the colored people of New York City. And I hope you
will succeed in interesting a number of them in the very laudable
work which you and Miss Easmon are doing in Serrie [sic] Leone.

If we can be of any further assistance to you, please do not
hesitate to call upon us.

Very truly yours,
Assistant Secretary

The following was the letter sent to Rev. W. Brooks, Rev. W.P. Hays,
Rev. A. Clayton Powell, Rev. W. Spencer Carpenter, Rev. Henry H.
Proctor, Mrs. A.W. Hunton, Rev. F.A. Cullen, Rev. Everard W. Daniel,
and Rev. W.W. Brown:

This letter will introduce to you Mrs. Casely Hayford and Miss
Easmon of Gloucester House, Freetown in Africa who are
interested in the establishment of a school for girls in Sierra [sic]
Leone.

These ladies bring with them excellent credentials which they will show you. We will appreciate greatly any assistance which you may give to them in presenting the cause which they represent to the colored people of New York City.

The following day Walter White again wrote a brief note to Mrs. Casely Hayford sending additional letters and saying mail had come to the *Crisis* for her which he was forwarding under separate cover. The N.A.A.C.P. introductory letter was now being sent also to Mr. Fred Moore, Editor, *New York Age;* Mr. William A. White, Editor, *Chicago Defender;* Mr. J.H. Anderson, Editor, *Amsterdam News;* Mr. George W. Harris, Editor *New York News;* and Mr. William S. McKinney, Editor, *Brooklyn and Long Island Informer.*

Mrs. Casely Hayford was again in the *Crisis* office on 3 September 1920 and as a result Mr. White wrote the same form letter to Rev. Shelton Bishop, Mr. John T. Clark, Mrs. William Fox, and Mrs. Daisy Lampkin, all of Pittsburgh, and Miss. Nannie Burroughs of the National Training School at Lincoln Heights, Washington, D.C., and Mrs. Mary E. Cable, Miss Ella M. Clay, Mr. A.T. Long, Mr. F.E. DeFrantz, and Dr. C.R. Atkins, all of Indianapolis.

By May 1921, Mrs. Casely Hayford is once more in touch with the N.A.A.C.P. offices:[24]

> c/o Mrs. Bryant
> 6 Wellington Street
> Boston, Mass.
>
> May 28, 1921
>
> Dear Mr. Weldon Johnson,
> I do hope you will pardon us troubling you further, but your assistance has been so valuable in the past that we are taking the liberty of applying to you again for help.
> We are leaving Boston in about 10 days' time and after one or two days in New York, we intend taking the following trip and we would be so grateful if you would kindly forward us letters of introduction to the secretaries in your Association in undermentioned places, or anyone whom you think would be helpful to us in our work. Philadelphia, Atlantic City, Columbus, Springfield, Dayton, Cincinnati, St. Louis, Chicago, Detroit, Toledo, Cleveland, Buffalo.
> I do hope we are not trespassing on your good nature by giving you so much extra work, but we do feel that both you and Mrs.

Weldon Johnson are genuinely interested in us, and we are deeply grateful for the splendid backing you have given us hitherto.

With kind remembrances to you both

Believe me.

Adelaide Casely Hayford

Mrs. Adelaide Casely Hayford   June 3, 1921
c/o Mrs. Bryant
6 Wellington Street
Boston, Mass.

My dear Mrs. Casely Hayford,

In response to your letter of the 28th I am sending you letters of introduction to the secretaries of our branches in the various cities which I mentioned. I hope that these letters will be of real service to you.

I hope also that you are meeting with added success in your work. If there is anything else that I can do that will be of assistance to you, I shall be only too glad to do it.

Mrs. Johnson is quite well and sends her kindest regards,

Very sincerely,
Secretary

6 Wellington Street
Boston

June 15, 1921

Dear Mr. Weldon Johnson,

I am ever so much obliged to you for your quick response to my appeal for introductions. If our mission does not succeed, it will certainly not be your fault.

With our united kind regards to both Mrs. Weldon Johnson and yourself.

Believe me.

Yours sincerely,
Adelaide Casely Hayford

206 East 195th Street

June 24, 1921

Dear Mr. Weldon Johnson,

We are leaving tomorrow for Philadelphia and would be ever so

much obliged, if you would kindly forward us a letter of introduction to your people there. Our address will be Hotel Dale [?]
With our heartfelt thanks and the best of good wishes.

Yours sincerely,
Adelaide Casely Hayford

Mrs. Casely Hayford became well known to the N.A.A.C.P. and to
Dr. Du Bois for on 21 October 1921, at the second Pan-African
Congress, of which Du Bois was a key organizer, Miss Jessie Fawcett of
the N.A.A.C.P. mentioned in her talk the work being done by blacks in
the United States and that Mrs. Casely Hayford and Miss Easmon were
then on a mission seeking their help in the United States.
Earlier in August, 9 August 1921 from the 95th Street address Mrs.
Casely had written her husband, addressing him as usual as "Dear
Casely," ending in "Yours with love," and the formal Adelaide Casely
Hayford rather than Addie. In this letter she asks for apologies because
she did not know his financial condition and she could accept a drop in
her allowance because things have improved for her.

This proves so clearly that your attitude towards me is entirely
unjust – from a monetary standpoint, that you make me out to be a
vampire when you know perfectly well that in spite of your financial
status, I have had to work over and over again during my married
life to keep the wolf from the door. Now the time has come for me
to consider myself. I have never once said a word to Archie about
your conduct to me but now he is a man and a married man, I am
going to ask him to see to it that we get fair play according to the
terms of our separation agreement. I *intend to have a home* that is the
right of every civilized woman on this planet. It will not be luxurious
but at any rate I shall have the necessaries of life which have been
denied me for so long.
I have tried to help myself but you put every spoke in my wheel to
prevent me from building my school and to this day I have never
had the money to complete it.[25]
Gladys is a wonderful child, with an ethereal development of an
exceedingly "high" order. I am grateful for the opportunities she is
getting now which I hope will be extended for at least another three
years. Money spent on her is an investment which will be repaid
one hundred fold. If I were relying upon the present conditions of
things on the Coast, it might be unfair to ask for 200 pounds now,
but I know you are going to receive a very considerable sum and I
am asking for that sum out of it ... about half of what you owe me to

enable me to buy my furniture etc., now that I am in America and can choose my things myself. Would you therefore kindly see that this amount is paid into the Bank of British West Africa in London vis by the end of October or beginning of November at the latest so I shall make inquiries there about it. As regards the monthly allowance I shall be prepared to go on with what you are giving me as long as Gladys is in Copeland and to let the balance accumulate with the outstanding debt. For the sake of our children I want to be on fond terms with you, but I do ask for fair play and justice. If you will grant me this, we shall be able to get on better than hitherto – and I do wish Archie and his bride every happiness, although I would have much preferred him to choose one of our own. I do hope you have received the different business communications about which I have written which I thought might profit you and which you have never acknowledged.

Yours with love,
Adelaide Casely Hayford

The above letter might well have been included in the section on the marriage itself – the issues are the same – the need for money, the effort to reach out to help, the concern about the children; the only difference here is a lack of mention of health and a strong assertion of self. Being in America, in quite a new environment, probably forced Mrs. Casely Hayford to think differently about some things, yet in spite of their apparently permanent estrangement she was forced to think more of Mr. Casely Hayford as her husband than she had done for some time ... at the same time much that she was experiencing in their relationship was diametrically opposed to what she was telling her many audiences about life in Africa and the role and behavior of men.

It would certainly be fascinating to trace Mrs. Casely Hayford's footsteps through her two and a half years' sojourn in the United States. This, however, has been impossible and unnecessary. As her stops were often quite brief and to cities some distance apart, it it quite likely that her "act," if you will, was generally the same except for those occasions when she attempted the more ambitious pageant – *Asheeko* or *The Answer*. Moreover, it has been quite impossible to track down after fifty-odd years persons who would have remembered her.

There have, however, been some exciting bits of information in correspondence which are only illustrative of what might have been found, if saved, or which at some future time may still surface. In her *Memoirs*, Mrs. Casely Hayford mentions Rev. and Mrs. Imes as having

been in New York and helpful to her. Having the good fortune of
knowing these two well-known persons, I wrote Reverend Imes and
received the following answer to my queries:

> 16 Bigelow Avenue
> Dundee, N.Y.
>
> November 10, 1971
>
> ....
>
> Now as to our recollections of Mrs. Adelaide Casely-Hayford of
> Sierra Leone, West Africa. We were in our second parish, The
> Lombard Street Central Presbyterian Church of Philadelphia, and
> it was in the early 1920s. She visited that city, and spoke before a
> women's group of our congregation; one of the tangible results of
> that visit was the gift, from the women's group (in which Mrs. Imes
> took a leading part), of a kitchen range for the Girls's School which
> Mrs. Casely Hayford had founded in Sierra Leone. I believe there
> were other donations also, and am sure of a most interesting
> correspondence with her about the progress of that school. Unfor-
> tunately, we do not have any items or letters preserved from that
> experience. But we did keep in touch with her, and her educational
> labors were well-known both in England and America.
>
> Wm. Lloyd and Grace V.
> Imes

Through such face to face contact in the churches throughout the
country, Mrs. Casely Hayford met some of the most outstanding Afro-
Americans of the day, and as she tried to attend all the important
conferences occurring at the time she was in the country she must have
had, at least, a brief encounter with several more. For example, at the
meeting of the National Council of Negro Women in Richmond in
August, 1922, she met Hallie Q. Brown, Jesse Fawcett, Maggie Lena
Walker, Charlotte Hawkins Brown, and Mary McLeod Bethune, and
she herself also addressed the conference probably stressing her usual
themes. The report of her address was noted in the program.[26]

> The next speaker was Madam Casely Hayford, of Siere [sic]
> Leone, West Africa, Madam Hayford, dressed in attractive native
> costume, held the audience spell bound, as she pleaded the cause
> of African womanhood. She stressed in a very forceful way that we
> should be proud of our ancestry – that we had nothing to be
> ashamed of.

The maternity instinct, Mrs. Hayford said, was one of the most pronounced characteristics of the African woman; whose home life and devoted motherhood are worthy of emulation by any race. Madam Hayford feels that community life had its real birth in Africa, and she gave examples of how they shared each others' sorrows as well as joys. She herself was a fine illustration. Madam Hayford also mentioned the fine spirit of chivalry exhibited by the African men.

Madam Hayford came to this country two years ago to study industrial institutions with a view of establishing the first industrial training school for girls on the West Coast of Africa. The appeal of this highly cultured, charming African woman for our sisters in dark Africa was so strong and touching, that at the close of her address, when the President called for a collection to help with her work there, in less than fifteen minutes, the audience had gladly laid on the table a donation of $142.52.

Two other examples, though dated later and one which definitely resulted from her second visit to the States, nevertheless are perhaps typical of the many contacts Mrs. Casely Hayford made which are now impossible to document.

For example, on 6 January 1927 in the Minutes of the League of Women for Community Service, a still existing organization of prominent civic-minded Afro-American women in Boston which started around World War I, the following is recorded.[27]

At the conclusion of the meeting opportunity was given Mrs. Casely Hayford of South [sic] Africa to present her work of the Girls' Vocational School at Freetown. She proved a most interesting speaker and promised to be present the following Thursday at a get-together meeting where she would have an opportunity to speak at greater length.

And according to the minutes of 20 January 1927:[28]

Mrs. Bernard reported on the Get Together Meeting held on January 13th and told of the interesting talk by Mrs. Casely Hayford from the West Coast of Africa who spoke of the Vocational School in Sierra Leone: Customs and Habits in Africa.

Matching to some extent the reminiscence of Rev. and Mrs. Imes is the extant letter to Mrs. Casely Hayford from Maude Cuney Hare. The letter was sent to Sekondi and was probably never seen by Mrs. Casely Hayford. Maude Cuney Hare was a talented and creative person who belonged to the League of Women for Community Service and was Director of one of their divisions, The Allied Arts Center:

> 43 Sheridan Street
> Jamaica Plain
>
> Sept. 25, 1927

Dear Mrs. Hayford,

I suppose you are again at home and busy with school activities. I am home after a very short vacation and have been at work daily on new plans towards the establishment of the Allied Arts Center. The effort has outgrown our quarters at the League of Women for Community Service so for weeks I have been hunting a suitable and desirable place. (The financial consideration has made it difficult).

At last I have found a small house tucked in between larger ones right in the artist section of Boston proper. It is near the downtown section in a rapidly growing quarter for fine hotels, theaters, etc., with this artist colony of attractive shops, interior decorators, student studios, etc., tucked between, all are white, and if I am fortunate in securing this place, it will mean that I can put our young folks' talent and wares in a section that will be in the regular stream irrespective of race. I abhor the segregated districts.

Now I have an idea! I have thought often of your school and wished that I could help in some simple way. Why can't you send me some articles and attractively dyed clothes – native work like small pieces of wood carving, bead work, basketry and materials (size suitable for hangings for studios, table covers, etc.). Mark them at a price as reasonable as you can so that we can attract the market. I will have an exhibit of them and then keep permanently a small collection always on hand to sell. A percentage on sales to go to someone that I will have to do this.

Do you care for the idea? I have prominent white friends who think my Allied Arts Center plan an admirable one – These are the people who will come to our exhibits, etc., and it may bring in something to the school and be all around advantageous. Let me hear from you as soon as possible as I hope to have an art exhibit before many weeks.

Meanwhile, I must get these attractive plans in shape as concert work begins seriously November 1 with a concert for the Women's City Club. I hope you are well so let me hear from you soon.

> Sincerely,
> Maude Cuney Hare

Reports on the pageants appear in publications in the United States and Africa. In the 7 January 1922 issue of the *SLWN*, the following item appeared:

> Mrs. Adelaide Casely Hayford and Miss Easmon arranged with the assistance of Afro-Americans and others for the performance of a great symbolic pageant, illustrative of the contributions of the Negro to the growth and greatness of America – called "The Answer".
>
> The Overture was written especially for the pageant by Mr. Nicholas Taylor of Sierra Leone who also arranged the music for African songs and all the dances.
>
> The Voice – David S. Klug; Spirit of Africa – Gertrude Allston; The Chief – Madakare Olele; The Witch Doctor – Kamba Simango; Mother of the Chief – Adelaide Casely Hayford; Wife of the Chief – Ada L. Gaines; The Widow – Katherien Pipes; Chief's Attendant – Nellie Crichlow; The Dancer – Acca Akusha (Katherine Easmon) – Warriors, Dancers, and Buccaneers.
>
> The Play was presented under the auspices of the Women's Service Club (464 Mass. Ave.) at Symphony Hall and reviewed in *The Boston Globe*.[29]

The *SLWN* of 13 May 1922 also reported that:

> Mrs. Casely Hayford and Kathleen played in "Asheeko" at the Regent Theater in Baltimore on March 24th before an audience of 1,000.

Remembering how persistent Mrs. Casely Hayford was in getting the necessary introductions from the officals of the N.A.A.C.P., and other examples of her determination and drive and sense of public relations, it seems obvious that this rather close coverage of their activities in the Freetown press was probably submitted by her.

The *Crisis* gives an even more complete description of the pageant:[30]

> An African pageant, *Asheeko*, has been successfully presented at the Academy of Music, Philadelphia by Mrs. Casely Hayford, Miss Kathleen Easmon, Madakare Olele, C. Kamba Simango, and G.L. Taylor, native Africans. They were assisted by a generous number of Philadelphia musicians and dramatic people. The music of *Asheeko* was written by Mr. Taylor. Chorus singers, from the choir of Central Presbyterian Church [see above, p.129] and others rendered Chemalebu, native song and chant in the Chindau dialect. The men sang the Betrothal Song, "Gogogo" in the Zulu

tongue. Admirable talent was shown by Miss Hattie Savay, contralto in "The Chililio" (Chindau) and Clarence L.E. Monroe, baritone on the Invocation to the Chief.

Whether anthropologically accurate or not, this cultural program, conceived and presented by Mrs. Casely Hayford, was not only a testimony to her talent and that of Kathleen Easmon, but a most graphic way of introducing Africa to American audiences. I have no idea how many times the pageant was attempted – probably only in selected cities – but it undoubtedly highlighted the kind of impact her trip had as reflected in a summary account of their activities again in the *Crisis* in the "Horizon" section.[31]

> We have had with us in America for over a year two splendid specimens of African womanhood, Mrs. Casely Hayford of Sierra Leone and her niece, Miss Kathleen Easmon. Both of these ladies were born in West Africa and educated in England and are raising funds for a school for young African women. Their culture and unselfish devotion to their work have won them hosts of friends. Recently they have been interested in pageantry and have taken part in pageants in Boston and New York.

Of course Mrs. Casely Hayford had her very own impression of America and in her *Memoirs* she tended to blend them:

> America is not only a country of Adventure, of enormous opportunities, and of costly experiments of a lien on human nature, but it is also a country of freaks, especially in the line of religious sects. What other country could have given birth to the 'Holy Rollers,' or 'Burning Bush'. Their titles speak for themselves. But the 'Bahais,' of whom I had never heard till I crossed the Atlantic, are wonderful people. Their founder, Abdul Bahai, was a Persian – a 'miracle worker' who attracted a large following, who hailed him as their promised Redeemer. Never have I been so lavishly entertained. The Bahai repasts could rightly be designated 'Love-feast,' because of the atmosphere which prevailed. On one occasion, in spite of, or possibly because of my black skin, I was given the seat of honour next to the late founder's nephew. Certainly racial discrimination was absolutely taboo. One devoted adherent gave me a beautiful sketch she had drawn of Abdul Bahai, which was of so much greater value to her than to me, that I subsequently returned it. But to my everlasting regret it never reached her, because of change of address.

The Reverend Charles Martin, who sponsored the Moravian Church Beth-Tpillah in New York, was remembered:

> ... not only as a pastor, but a friend in need. A West Indian by birth, his significant voice, commanding appearance and distinguished personality opened doors that were often closed against coloured people.
>
> An intellectual, he possessed a library second to none among coloured folk. His Church consisted of two houses thrown into one and there was always a struggle to keep going, since it was a church mostly of hard-working daily-breaders, with very little money at their disposal. Distinguished visitors to New York used to find their way to Beth-Tpillah because of the very happy atmosphere which prevailed. I could always count on Charles Martin for good sound advice, and when I was in difficulties with my Home Committee it was he who unravelled the tangled skein, and smoothed out differences.
>
> I do not know whether this little Moravian Church is still going, but I do know it would be very difficult to replace the late Pastor, whose life of self renouncing love was truly a life of liberty.

It would be easy to assess the impact of Mrs. Casely Hayford on those she met either directly, face to face, or less directly from the platform on her first and second trips to the United States. To everyone, she would have appeared either as a fascinating curiosity debunking the familiar stereotypes about Africans or as a dynamic, impressive, and unusual woman. Also, as was true throughout her life, even travelling, Mrs. Casely Hayford was always ready to align herself with a good cause, particularly one related to peace and Africa. As late as March, 1927, for example, the letterhead of "The Circle for Peace and Foreign Relations," located in New York City, of which Addie W. Hunton was president, lists Mrs. Casely Hayford (the only African) as a member of this group which is sponsoring and soliciting funds for the forthcoming "Pan-African Congress" to be held, and which indeed was held, the following summer in New York City. This interest on Mrs. Casely Hayford's part would, I think, have been genuine, though it is not without import that her husband, whose interests and ties she was still trying to promote, was still alive at the time.

It is perhaps a bit more difficult to know what lasting effects the American trips, especially the first and longer one, had on Mrs. Casely Hayford. Of course, there were the useful contacts, the financial support, promised and received, but I suspect that the most important effect – certainly of a permanent or long lasting character – was psychological.

The underlying purpose of the trip forced her to accept and to be proud that she was an African. It permitted her to observe the aspirations and accomplishments of other blacks beyond the boundaries of Empire. She never forgot that she was a visitor, talking to people unlike herself, both black and white, but in presenting her story as forcefully as she undoubtedly did, she was, at long last, becoming an African – in the sense perhaps that her husband had always been. She would never have an African name, speak an African language, or consider an African dress other than a costume; but through this experience, what it required of her, and what it gave her, she was at last a person comfortable with her color, her origins – no longer "a real Sambo" as she had described herself so many years earlier.

The Girls' Vocational and Industrial Training School, Freetown – First Steps

Shortly after her return from America, Mrs. Casely Hayford submitted the above mentioned report of her trip to the *SLWN*, and it appeared in full in the 31 March issue of the paper. Three months later, the *SLWN* carried a detailed prospectus for the proposed school as well as some statements to establish a positive community feeling towards the school and towards Mrs. Casely Hayford, in particular:[1]

> We emphatically deplore the bunking rumors and statements which have been circulating freely respecting a woman who has won our whole-hearted admiration and respect by the indomitable grit, high courage, real selfishlessness [sic], large faith and patriotic zeal and love which have enslaved her to undertake such a strenuous difficult task, at this late period of her life's history.
>
> The proposed school is in no way a *private enterprise*. The Governing Board will consist of a Board of Trustees, an Executive Committee, a Board of Management, a Social Committee.
>
> There will also be a list of distinguished Patrons, including well-known influential Africans, together with ladies and gentlemen of repute both in America and England.
>
> The Curriculum: we are specializing in Home Making and Vocational Training. There will be classes in Domestic Science including laundry, cooking, housekeeping, hygiene, sanitation, child welfare. There will also be a special course for Prospective Brides to thoroughly fit them for duties as wives and mothers.
>
> Dressmaking will be taught by an expert. Physical culture and Games will figure prominently.
>
> Vocal and Instrumental music will be included. If space permits, we shall have a small poultry farm and market garden. If there is any demand, stenography and Native Arts and Crafts will also be taught (deplorable that all lovely art work of Africa is done by illiterates).

Training will be both literary and vocational and above all and underneath all, will be the principles of character building as laid down by the Great Master Builder, Jesus Christ himself.

The Teachers' Training Course is especially for those who having gone through existing schools are anxious for still further training either for their own use or to enable them to qualify as *Trained Teachers* and will embrace practical courses in teaching. It is in the hands of an expert with wide experience. Fees will not be higher than those of existing schools, except perhaps where special tuition is given – and after the pupils shall have reached proficiency. Any work done by them will be paid for but not in cash but will be deducted from school fees.

This is quite a new venture, and on that account may be misunderstood.

Funds are greatly needed.

Signed.S. Leigh-Sodipe
M.E. Johnson
A. Farmer
L. Price
Abayomi Cole
O. Faduma
F.A. Miller
Clariel May, Hon. Secretary
August 25, 1923.

A new venture it certainly was – a gigantic dream beyond the experience and, to some extent, at variance with the values of the post-World War I élite of Creole society. Its popularity would definitely not be enhanced, at that time, by its bearing a stamp "Made in America."

Aside from the possible prejudice against the educational philosophy on which the school was to be built and a less than unanimous warmth towards Mrs. Casely Hayford as a person, there was the additional problem of her readiness or ability to carry out or to implement such an ambitious project alone. For all her seeming independence, Mrs. Casely Hayford had never undertaken an educational project of her own. Even her classroom teaching experience was minimal. Her first endeavor in the original school she started in Freetown had been with her sister Bea at her side, and during the planning stages for this school in Freetown and fund raising in America, Kathleen had been her constant companion and support. After Kathleen's marriage, there was no hope that she would ever return to Freetown – even had she lived. And Gladys was not in Freetown. So left on her own to embark on this long anticipated project, it is not surprising that Mrs. Casely Hayford sought and needed a partner. For this important position, she chose Mrs. Ejesa Osora, the Scottish wife of the Reverend E.A. Osora (Headmaster of the Cathedral Model School), whom he courted two years as a "jealous enthusiast in promoting the welfare of our people and brought to Freetown in 1920."[2]

Mrs. Osora was apparently available because she had been released from her teaching position at the Annie Walsh Memorial School. According to a "letter from a Patriot" the difficulties were "problems over agreement – forcing her [Mrs. Osora] to work longer hours than is the case with Europeans – as well as other problems over the education for girls." Annie Walsh apparently was declining in popularity because, according to this same "Letter," there had been no candidates from the School the previous year for the Cambridge Exams.[3]

In March there is a sympathetic note concerning Mrs. Osora's release and suggesting that the school update its ways.[4] Therefore, it is quite possible that in her search for local available teaching talent, Mrs. Casely Hayford saw in Mrs. Osora another being victimized by the narrowmindedness of the Creole community – and also by the Europeans, but she probably knew very little of Mrs. Osora as a person. In any case, in 1923 Mrs. Casely Hayford and Mrs. Osora together opened the school on Gloucester Street. The attendance rose from 21 to 81 pupils, but after nine months Mrs. Osora left and founded the Osora Girl's School which later became the Freetown Secondary School for Girls under Mrs. Hannah Benka-Coker MBE.[5] Mrs. Osora's leaving was understandably very upsetting to Mrs. Casely Hayford who noticing the decline in pupils and other problems, fell into ill health and was forced the following year (1924) to close the school for a while.

Gladys came to her Mother's assistance in 1926 and they reopened the school, concentrating this time on younger children. In June of 1926, Mrs. Casely Hayford once again went to America to collect funds for the school and probably to withdraw awhile from the Freetown scene. She returned in 1927 and continued to operate the school until 1940. Such is the barest outline as provided by Mr. Sumner. But far more was happening to Mrs. Casely Hayford and her school than his account would indicate.

Our first evidence comes from Mrs. Casely Hayford herself in her *Memoirs*:

> From its inception the school was never a paying proposition. That, of course, was not my motive in starting it.
>
> It was so stunted at birth, that its chances of reaching maturity were very remote, but I will say this however, – in spite of poor organization and administration, in spite of the malignant attitude

of the community, in spite of hopelessly inadequate funds, this little school made itself felt. It stimulated the other flourising schools to extend their borders. They did so, and were able to carry out all the schemes we had planned. But we were the heralds, who trumpeted our larger opportunities for employment and service and greater vision of usefulness for the girlhood of Freetown!

We intended to make it a Vocational School but only forty little children presented themselves at the opening, so that was knocked on the head. After a European lady joined us we got forty older girls and the eighty crammed to its utmost capacity our old family house, opposite the Post Office, which I had placed rent free at the disposal of the Committee.

My colleague's stay was brief and bitter. My brother Tom always designated me as a fat head and never was the term more appropriate than when I asked the lady to join me. I might have known that as a white woman, even married to a black man, she would never condescend to work under me. She left me, without a moment's notice, taking most of the girls with her and as I had a serious breakdown, the school's collapse was imminent. But God tempers the wind to the shorn lamb. My daughter Gladys, who had been doing literary work with her father on the Gold Coast, came to my assistance.

As the new release below indicates, there is some confusion as to whether Gladys was with her father in the Gold Coast or still in England.

Mrs. Constance Cummings-John, a relative of Mrs. Casely Hayford, remembered this early period of the school's history. Mrs. Cummings-John first attended Annie Walsh and then, probably because of the decline mentioned above or perhaps some community factionalism, was placed in Mrs. Osora's school. Mrs. Osora, she said, was a strict disciplinarian who lived only for her teaching – participating in community affairs only when it was necessary as, for example, at ceremonial occasions such as presenting awards. Mrs. Cummings-John felt these two educators did not get along because they were both strong women. She herself did not attend the Girls' Vocational School "because her Mother was against her changing schools again," but she did participate in the plays Gladys wrote. One imagines that only the naive or thoroughly committed were initially anxious to follow Mrs. Casely Hayford. Her behavior and her health were just so unpredictable. It is important to remember that this was a culture where education was highly prized and important, and innovators were not welcomed.

The school's opening was announced by Mrs. Adelaide Casely Hayford as Principal in the *SLWN*:[6]

> The Girls' Vocational Training Center will be opened at Gloucester House opposite the Post Office at 9 A.M. on September 27.
>
> Pupils may be enrolled from Monday 17th to Friday 21st or from Monday 24th to Wednesday 26th from 8 am to 12 am at Bee Hive, Charlotte Street, the residence of the late Dr. Renner.
>
> School will be divided into 3 departments: (1) Kindergarten, (2) Junior, and (3) Senior.
>
> The Kindergarten section for children of both sexes between 4 and 7 aims at developing the children mentally, morally and physically by the use of the most up-to-date apparatus and methods of teaching.
>
> The curriculum includes work with brush, plastics and cardboard, physical exercises, games, and moral training as well as use of modern apparatus for teaching of numbers, reading, writing, form, colours, etc.
>
> Modern methods of Kindergarten Dept. are continued in the Junior Dept. where the curriculum includes as well as all usual subjects, special training in Geography, Literature, Drawing, and Practical Hygiene.
>
> The Senior Department aims at attaining to the standard of Cambridge Junior Examination – included all subjects necessary. Pupils are eligible to be Seniors who have attained to the standard of the Government Elementary Certificate. In connection with Senior Department when candidates show necessary ability, to form a special class for those requiring further training or to enable them to qualify as Trained Teachers.
>
> Space is limited. Parents and Guardians will be interviewed if desired at the school.

For the next several months numerous articles on the school appeared in the press. Clearly the community was being hesitant and Mrs. Casely Hayford and her committee wished to inform and assure them.

On 16 February 1925, the *SLWN* carried the following announcement:

> Girls' Vocational School and Teachers' Training Centre was honored by a visit from Lady Slater on Thursday, the 7th inst. Her Ladyship congratulated the staff on the tangible progress the school has made since its inauguration. October 3, 1923, a com-

pany of Girl Guides will be formed under the captaincy of Mrs.
Ejesa Osora.

A 26 April 1924 entry read:

> Next term of Girls' Vocational School and Teachers' Training
> College begins Monday May 5th at 8:30. The Vocational Depart-
> ment will also be opened. Mrs. Ejesa Osora will be at the school on
> Friday, May 2 from 10 to 11:30 for the Entrance Examination for
> pupils and senior division.

It is hard to know whether Mrs. Casely Hayford courted publicity or
was just always newsworthy; it is clear she was not publicity-shy.[7] So it is
not surprising to read an account in *West Africa* giving a first year's
progress report of the school.[8] I am inclined to believe that she always
saw her greatest strength in Freetown coming from the pressures she
could put on persons there from persons outside of the colony. The *West
Africa* report reads:

> Mrs. Casely Hayford's report on the first year's work of her
> school shows that despite financial struggle the school, aided by a
> timely gift from a rich American lady, had made progress. Starting
> with 14 scholars all under 10 years, it now possessed 20 to 30 in the
> senior division, with a Guide company and Brownies, and even a
> boarding department containing 2 girls. The school took 5 prizes at
> the last schools' exhibition and the Guides are now studying
> gardening ... English is taught from the earliest stages, while the
> senior girls are taking cooking, dressmaking and laundry work.
>
> This year Miss Gladys Casely Hayford is expected from Eng-
> land and will specialize in African folklore and literature, while
> later on the study of African music will be introduced, if it can be
> arranged. The balance sheet for the year shows an income of 210
> pds from school fees, 323 pounds from donations with expenses
> practically all salaries. Of 327 and a balance on hand of 200.
> Although the financial outlook is still somewhat precarious, the
> experience of the first year encourages every hope that the school
> so pluckily started is destined to continue its useful work.

Later in the year *West Africa* carried several photographs of the
students and facilities in Mrs. Casely Hayford's school.[9]

In the meanwhile, the turmoil around Mrs. Casely Hayford shifted
from "misunderstandings" around the kind of school that she was trying
to develop to a far more sensitive unrelated event which, nevertheless,
became quite a tempest in a teapot. In April 1925, the Prince of Wales

visited Africa, beginning with a stopover in Freetown. One can imagine
the excitement: a future king coming to call. Mrs. Casely Hayford was
asked by *West Africa* to cover the event and her story billed as "The first
impression of the Prince in West Africa to reach this country from the
pen of a West African," almost an entire page in length, was certain to
have been upsetting to at least one person because of the prominence
given it. Reading it now it is a simply written account with some local
reaction to the Prince himself and his visit. Of course, there were a few
remarks that might not be appropriate today such as "he made us
Africans feel very proud to be recognized as members of the great
Empire over which he will one day rule." So far as is recorded no one
took offense at that statement of perpetual affiliation. But what did
apparently cause the greatest commotion in Freetown and occasion at
least one letter to *West Africa* was the following:

> Simplicity was the characteristic feature of the whole visit. A few
> days before the Prince's arrival, frenzied women were rushing
> about trying to beg, borrow or steal gloves for the grand reception at
> Government House on that gala night. To everyone's astonish-
> ment, the Prince wore no gloves – indeed as far as clothes went,
> except for the broad yellow stripe on his trousers, he was utterly
> undistinguishable from any other officer in that gay crowd.

In the June *West Africa*, the following letter from her old "friend"
C.D. Hotabah During appears:[10]

> Sir, my attention has been drawn to the following extract from an
> article in your issue of May 2 written by Mrs. Casely Hayford.
> "A few days before the Prince's arrival frenzied women were
> rushing about trying to beg, borrow or steal gloves for the grand
> reception at Government House on that night."
> I wonder how Mrs. Casely Hayford arrived at this statement
> which I consider a libel on the respectable ladies who were invited
> by His Excellency, the Governor and Lady Slater and who
> attended the reception and ball in honor of HRH the Prince of
> Wales.
> I think an explanation is due and should be given by Mrs. Casely
> Hayford for this unwarranted and mischievous statement. At least
> she should, if she feels justified in regard to the same, make public
> the names of the frenzied women who rushed about trying to beg,
> borrow or steal gloves a few days before the Prince's arrival here.
> Freetown, May 28th.

The Editor's note, as might be expected, merely played down the statement attributing it to Mrs. Casely's "friendly humorous spirit."

But one informant remembered the entire affair quite differently:

> The article was highly criticized by many Sierra Leoneans in those days and this criticism continued for a long time. As a little girl in the thirties, I remembered many spoke against her because of this article. You see, she believed and stood firmly by her belief and early training that only the upper class should mingle together. Government House should only be open to that class and that class alone. When, however, the then Prince of Wales visited Sierra Leone people from all walks of life were selected to represent various groups at the Ball at Government House and many Sierra Leoneans who were very poor at that time strained every nerve to save their earnings to prepare themselves and their homes for this Royal Visit.

In her characteristic frankness Mrs. Casely Hayford recalled this entire episode but remembered it somewhat differently in her *Memoirs*.

> Sometime in 1923, Sierra Leone was honored by a visit from a squadron of battleships including the *Hood,* the *Repulse,* the *Renown,* etc., under the command of Admiral Sir Frederick Field. He invited us to inspect the *Hood,* later giving a magnificent reception which remains in the memory of Sierra Leoneons. This visit was the forerunner of a visit from H.R.H., the Prince of Wales, which took place the following year. That was a red-letter day for Freetown, and the Prince was very approachable and nice to us all.
>
> The inability of many of the guests to obtain gloves for the reception at Government House came to his ears, and he immediately issued a statement that he himself would go without...
>
> The Prince seemed to be bored to extinction by the ceremonial; indeed, the only time I saw him laugh was when a group of little Brownies performed before him.
>
> Prior to his arrival, I had approached the principal African ladies, whom I knew would be asked to meet him, begging them to put on native costume. I pointed out that it would be so much more picturesque, and would not only enhance our appearance but would show that we were proud of being Africans. They all turned me down. Nothing daunted, I wore for the occasion a plain black satin lappah, and a most beautifully embroidered boobah, worked by black men right up at Pujehun. The effect was, I think, altogether charming. The Prince then sent an A.D.C. to inform five or six of

us that he would like a few minutes' conversation. H.R.H. asked
me where I had been educated and what I was doing in Freetown.
To which I replied, "I am teaching."

"Teaching," said the Prince, "I would never have taken you for a
teacher." To this day, I wonder whether that was a compliment or
not.

The Prince also asked where my husband was. I was nonplussed
for the moment, but the A.D.C. came to my rescue – "Oh," he said,
"you will meet Mr. Casely Hayford when you go down to the Gold
Coast. He is a member of the Legislative Council there."

How times have changed. The outlook has altered completely.
Instead of blindly copying European fasions, which are made to suit
a white woman's personality, our women now have come to realize
that every race has its own distinctive dress, with its own appeal –
and its own suitability for particular climatic conditions.

The strain of creating so much turmoil must have taken its toll on
Mrs. Casely Hayford as well as merely the stress and strain of running
the school after Mrs. Osora's sudden departure, for on 19 September
1925 the *SLWN* carried the following item:

> Girls Vocational School was reopened after mid-rains holidays.
> Owing to the illness of the principal (Mrs. Casely Hayford) and her
> being granted sick leave until the end of the year, the duties of
> Acting Principal have on her recommendation been placed on Mrs.
> F.A. Miller who is now in charge of the school.

Mrs. Hayford recalls the events somewhat similarly:

> I visited America again to raise funds, leaving the school in
> charge of Mrs. Fred Miller, an old Annie Walsh teacher who had
> attended my Alma Mater, the Jersey Ladies college and who kept
> our little flag flying under the most adverse circumstances.

Local sentiment about the school and Mrs. Casely Hayford
apparently still needed to be assuaged because the next month, an
editorial appeared which sought to keep up community support for the
school:[11]

> The Girls' Vocational School has a splendid curriculum on the
> same lines as the Moyamba Girls' School of the UBC Mission and
> as Tuskegee in America. It would be a very great loss to the com-
> munity if some ill-disposed person should seek to hamper the
> progress of this school which is coming up so nicely and full of
> many promising young lassies of the best type. ... There is utter

need for a Girls' Vocational School in Freetown. The need is utter-most. The times demand it. Women need to be homemakers, wives, and mothers.

An editorial in the 24 October 1925 issue also asks for support for the school. In January, the paper announces the school's next term and the date for entrance examinations.[12]

In June of that year, the *SLWN* printed an article (unsolicited, by a parent):[13]

> The attitude of the public is hard to know. People in this community are so bad and inconsistent. Day to day growth progress in the school. No reason to withdraw a child simply because Lady Principal is going abroad. You don't withdraw from Wesleyan Girls' High or Annie Walsh. Help your own colour to achieve support and be patient.

At long last some community recognition came to Mrs. Casely Hayford. She was nominated by the Acting Governor to become a member of the Standing Advisory Committee for the Social Hygiene of Freetown.[14]

Mrs. Casely Hayford left for Europe and America in July, 1926 for the purpose of raising funds for the maintenance and development of the school.

It is clear from her *Memoirs* that Mrs. Casely Hayford's "peregrina-tions in America," as she called them, were on this trip far less produc-tive or exciting than on her earlier trip. Of course she was on her own this time. Perhaps she, in fact, returned too soon to America. In any case, most of her reporting of this trip really amounts to an expression of concern about the growth of the school itself. While the trip may have been consciously designed to rise funds, it served more as an escape for her from the situation in Freetown. But as her remarks indicated, the school and its problems were ever on her mind.

> On my second visit to America, I stayed at the Coloured Y.W.C.A. in 137th Street and from my window I could see all the activities going on at "Mother Zion." Some of these were pathetic – especially on weekdays. It was hard to reconcile the weekday crowd with the well-groomed, well-dressed people that flocked to Church on Sunday, and some of the funerals were pathos personi-fied. There were the poor mourners who insisted on bedecking the coffin with the choicest flowers and wreathes obtainable, – this in New York meant a small fortune – I am afraid our cousins across the sea have the same grandiloquent notions of appearing to be

what they are not, with the inevitable results of debt ... heartbreak. When are we going to learn sense?

I also gave an address at the Central Headquarters of the white Y.W.C.A. in Lexington Avenue, the first Negro to speak from that platform, where my message left its mark.

While in America I interviewed a gentleman [Rev. George Collins, pastor for students at the University of Wisconsin] telling him all about our struggles, and he said he knew a little white Southern girl, who would be perfectly willing to come out to Sierra Leone to work under me.[15] As the school could not afford the expense, once again an American millionaire lady undertook to shepherd her, during her sixteen months sojourn with us. She was a girl so absolutely devoid of superiority complex or racial prejudice that we did not even realize there was a white women on the staff. Thus she achieved what was really her primary objective in coming – to establish better racial relationships with the Colony. Lots of Europeans invited her out, and she insisted on returning the compliment by begging me to reciprocate their hospitality. A good many of them had never entered a native house before, but they were so favorably impressed that they continued their visits.

While I was in America, however, the School's fortunes were at a low ebb. To make matters worse, I got no support whatsoever from my Committee, who did not seem to realize the weight of the three-fold job I had undertaken: (1) to keep the School supplied with funds; (2) to keep myself supplied with funds, as I had no private means whatsoever, and (3) to make arrangements for the future running of the School.

With so much discouragement and lack of appreciation, and without due deliberation, I sat down and wrote them a most insulting letter, which afterwards I deeply regretted. They at once cut the ground from under my feet by cabling with an insufficient address their intention of closing the School – to which they were not contributing a penny. The authorities could not locate me, although they informed the Office at the Colored Y.W.C.A. where I was residing that if they could not locate me, there was a cable from Sierra Leone awaiting me. As I had only just received a letter from home informing me that Gladys was far from well, and had taken a holiday to visit her father in the Gold Coast, I feared the worst. It was quite a relief, after a long suspense, when I read this most inspiring cable from the House Committee "Closing the School." I was in such a quandry, realizing that it would be terribly disappointing to continue collecting for a school that did not exist.

So I immediately went to the Reverend Charles Rakin, the West Indian Pastor of the Moravian Church in New York, whose kindness I shall never forget, asking for his advice and help. He at once drafted a letter of apology, but somehow I felt that virtue had literally gone out of me.[16]

The school had literally been smashed to atoms, but not content with that, one lady had written her brother in America to put spokes in my wheel there. I was billed to address a large church on Sunday evening in New York, and having been most graciously received by the pastor, I rose to speak when one of a group of Africans in the audience also rose to interrupt me. For the moment everybody seemed nonplussed by this man's tirade, everyone, that is, except the Pastor, who promptly ordered him to sit down, much to his discomfiture, and told me to continue my speech, which required a lot of fortitude after such an experience. I felt I was being literally killed by unkindness.

Apparently this second visit to the States was far less successful than the first, for Mrs. Casely Hayford gives little detail about her experience, the people she met, etc. She does not even discuss the renewal of old friendships or what help she sought or received from the American Advisory Committee. It was probably the wrong time for her to have left Freetown and her school.

On my return for the second time from America, Sierra Leone received me not so much with open arms, but at arm's length. Truly, a prophet is without honor in his own country. I can never quite fathom why I met with such universal opposition. Had I been starting a brothel, the antagonism could not have been worse.[17]

... After keeping me waiting for months without any recognition whatsoever, the Committee resigned, and I found I could breathe freely. I substituted a small Advisory Board, consisting of the Right Rev., T.S. Bishop Johnson, my dear neighbor the Late Dr. J.F. Musselman, Chairman of the United Brethren in Christ Mission and my nephew, Dr. M.C.F. Easmon.

The Government would not sponsor my leadership, and my own people were exceedingly hostile. Hence I found myself literally hanging between two stools, with the option either of falling on the massive head of the Government to be catapulted into the air, or falling down to be mercilessly crushed under the heel of my own people. No wonder I had to invest in outsize handkerchiefs to cope with the situation.

Upon her return from the second trip to America, Mrs. Casely Hayford did not give a formal written report, but she did give a public address at the school on the occasion of Mother's Day.[18]

No doubt these comments reflected more of what visiting America had taught her:

> There is still some interest in this little depleted school ... it is meet and right to take a leaf out of America's book and dedicate one day in the year for the worship at the shrine of Motherhood.
>
> The future of Africa depends on the African Mother. I have nothing whatever to do with little gifts to be presented to Mothers – they have been made under the supervision of Mrs. Farrell Easmon and Mrs. Gladys King.
>
> ... the two great aims of our policy are (1) to build up character, and (2) to stimulate as far as possible the retention of our natural heritage of African individuality.
>
> Africa Day, viz., means at least once a quarter, the children will come to school in native dress; all the studies of the day will be centered around Africa; its history, its folklore, its habits, its customs, its natural resources, its art work; its peoples, past and present and future; we shall sing African songs, dance African dances, play African games, and we shall endeavor to instill into the hearts and minds of the children, a spirit of loyalty and patriotism for the country of our birth. This is the only way we as a people can ever give a real contribution to the world.
>
> I would like now to say a few words to these Mothers whom I so seldom see. I would ask you, firstly to give your children all the interest and encouragement you can in their school work at home. The difference in general intelligence, the conduct and the progress of the children whose parents take an interest in their work is positively appalling.
>
> Secondly, I would ask you not to be reticent if you are not satisfied. We are out to help you to the best of our ability and we welcome any constructive criticism which will enable us to do so.
>
> Thirdly, please do not grudge your children the paying of fees or school equipment. It discourages them very much, besides creating an impossible situation and retarding their progress enormously.
>
> Fourthly, do not run away with the idea that small children only come to school to play. The whole of a little child's mind is centered on one word – play. Hence all the school activities must be presented in a form which will interest and attract the child so that through his play he is learning all the time.

Fifthly, I would urge a Parent–Teachers' Meeting at least once a quarter. The child is undergoing two types of training – home training and school training – and no amount of school training will compensate for deficient home training but by getting together, we can help each other by discussing our various problems, with mutual sympathy, interest and cooperation thereby obtaining the best results from the children.

Assisted scholarships will begin Jan. 19, 1928. These scholarships are intended primarily for bright children from 5–7 whose parents will welcome any assistance with their education. They do not hold good for children who are already paying fees as in the case of sisters, unless they show exceptional promise. Children from 5–7 pay no fees whatsoever after which 10 shillings is deducted every quarter from their fees as long as they remain in school which must be up to age 12.

Every candidate must produce a Birth Certificate, a Transfer Certificate, and receipts to show that all back dues have been paid up otherwise, in fairness to other schools, she will not be accepted as a candidate. Six scholarships are also offered for children from 8–9 and all the children will be required to satisfy the Examiner in the Intelligence tests which will be held on January 19th at 9:30 a.m. on the school premises. The scholarships are open to both sexes. Boys up to 9 years only.

At the beginning of January 1928 The Girls' Vocational School published the fees for the school which were as follows:

Infants subst.	1 shilling a month
Standards 1–2	1 shilling 6d a month
3–4	2 shillings a month
5,6,7	2 shillings 6d a month

During the rest of 1928 there are one or two additional references to Mrs. Casely Hayford and/or the school in the press. In April, 1928 she is mentioned as having participated at the Celebrations of the Centenary of St. George's Cathedral and on 22 April at Wilberforce Hall she is introduced to a meeting as "one of ourselves, a treasure in an earthen vessel, a woman whose capacity for service to her country, in intellect, in heart and in social appears to keep steady pace with advancing years ... as both an orator and a teacher, and an inspiration whose students sang superb songs that had not been heard in years."

On 2 February 1929 there is a large advertisement for the school.

Girls Vocational School
Sierra Leone West Africa
Prospectus

Ch. Miss Mabel Carney, Professor of Rural Education, Col. University, New York City
Secre. Mrs. Mehea Price, Classics Teacher Wadleigh High School, New York
Treas. Mrs. Carrie Kinney, Woodward Hotel, New York
Miss Ethel Wakeman, English Teacher, Elmhurst Public School, New Jersey
Mrs. Boutte, Seventh Avenue, New York
Miss Elizabeth Martin, Secretary Social Service Work, Harlem, New York
Founder and Principal – Mrs. Adelaide Casely Hayford

Staff: Miss Elizabeth Torrey, B.A.
          Miss Gladys Casely Hayford
          Miss Davis
          Miss Vida Marke
          Miss Olla Coker

Aims and Objects:

1) to develop the spiritual, mental and physical outlook of the girls
2) to fit them to take their place as worthwhile citizens in their own communities
3) to give them the best to be derived from European culture as well as the best from our own native habits and customs so as to assist them in retaining their African nationality.

Curriculum:

Academic: Kindergarten to Cambridge; Local Examination Boys from 4 to 9
Vocational: handicrafts, spinning, weaving, basket making, cooking, dressmaking, home management
Terms: Tuition Fees, Rules [of payment]

In April, Gladys Casely Hayford addressed the Annual Meeting of the Princess Christian Mission Hospital using a Nancie story[19] as her focal point.[20] In July, the School had an all African program – Mrs. Casely Hayford introduced it and herself as stemming from Fanti, Mandingo and Maroon ancestors.[21] There were also Nancie stories with accompanying music arranged by Gladys Casely Hayford. Even Beth

Torrey was in African dress. The School had its first prize-giving at Wilberforce Hall on 20 November 1927. Mrs. Casely Hayford spoke and The Governor and Mrs. Byrne were in attendance.[22]

In the December issue of *SLWN* an even longer account of the prize-giving was presented. Mrs. Casely Hayford in her speech on the occasion had referred to the lack of backing for the school. She also gave many acknowledgements. Miss Louise Nicol, who had left during Mrs. Casely Hayford's absence, was thanked for her assistance as was Mrs. Frederick Miller who "had kept the fires during her American tour." Mrs. During, who could not leave a sinking ship, and Miss Gladys King, now Mrs. Small of the Gambia, who also stayed in spite of other offers, were also thanked. Mr. Claude Wright, Mr. S. Barlatt, Mr. T.G. Reffell, Dr. Easmon, Miss Hebron, and Miss Mabel Johnson were all thanked for being donors of the prizes. The Governor in his account said the school did not live up to rules but where there is a will there is a way. The reporter of the news story said,

> I came away very much impressed with the work that is being done by this school amidst financial difficulties and strong competition. We wish that its indefatigable Principal may be long spared to realize her ideals and to carry on successfully this useful work for the benefit and uplift of the young and our country and race. signed Yours, Fancy.[23]

Her *Memoirs* report that Mrs. Casely Hayford kept on hammering away at the Education Department

> till they offered me a munificient grant of 40 pounds, which I promptly rejected, with a rider to the effect that I considered it an insult. During the administration of the late Sir Arnold Hodson, however, I had the brainwave to send a copy of my School Report to Government House, direct, as I had an idea he did not even know of our existence. He subsequently spent a whole morning with us, inspecting our activities, particularly the weaving, which, under the able tuition of my sister Mrs. Easmon, was unrivalled in the Colony. As a result, I obtained a yearly grant of 120 pounds which, small though it was, was a veritable godsend, plus a building loan for extending the premises.
>
> The School Account Book was divided up into three headings – (1) Those who paid full fees (appreciable few); (2) Those who paid half fees – the majority; and (3) Those who paid nothing at all. So many girls have married and made their niches in the Freetown community, but alas, like the Biblical lepers of old, only one in ten

paused to say "Thank you!" That doesn't matter. I look back with
joy, because "God's whisper came to me" to be up and doing for
the neglected under-privileged girls of my race, and some day, in
the not so far future, I shall need another whisper "You have done
what you could!"

X

Adelaide Smith Casely Hayford and Gladys

Mrs Casely Hayford had only one child, Gladys, who was born in 1906 in the Gold Coast. By all accounts Gladys was an unusual person whose life for her time and place was as unique as, but more tragic than, her mother's. Parenthood in the most traditional and ordinary times can be traumatic and disappointing, but when it occurs in a changing social milieu of tension and conflict, both parent and child may suffer. In the case of Mrs. Casely Hayford and Gladys, one sees a strong woman of great talent, already thirty-eight when her only child was born, always living in an incompatible environment, alienated from her husband, the father, and the mother of an extremely creative and sensitive child who was born with an easily identifiable physical handicap. In Sierra Leone and in Africa, at that time, there was no culturally established niche for Gladys any more than there was for her mother. Consequently, the story of their relationship is one of searching, rejection, and pain.

In the *Memoirs* Mrs. Casely Hayford gives a helpful, if incomplete, recollection of her relationship with her daughter, and a few of their contemporaries have given additional comments, but the most valuable source comes from the published letters Mrs. Casely Hayford and Gladys wrote Miss Anna Melissa Graves between February 1931 and November 1942.[1]

Gladys played an important part in strengthening the Girls' Vocational School and Mrs. Casely Hayford hoped, in spite of her frequent declarations to the contrary, that Gladys would one day become principal of the school. For these reasons, therefore, it is important at this stage in Mrs. Casely Hayford's life to examine her role as mother as it affected her role as educator.

> We had quite a lot in common – my darling one gran pickin and I. We were both premature, utterly negligible, puny little infants causing our parents a lot of anxiety and trouble. We were both Wednesday's children – full of woe – Gladys need not have been,

but she took such a long time making up her mind to visit this world that she nearly killed me in the process.

At an early age we both learned to suffer, but we possessed such iron constitutions that we survived. When my daughter was only three, she contracted bronchitis, then pneumonia and ended up with whooping cough, without any cessation whatsoever. We both had a keen sense of humor. Even when she was about to be stricken down with her short fatal illness, she wrote us a letter which was full of jokes and fun, radiating her joyous personality, which I received a few hours after the cable announcing her death.

She was a lonely little girl and I fully realized how inadequate I was to act as a playmate. When we played "Follow my leader," she was disgusted with my leadership and would ask whether she might not take my place. Sometimes, with her spade and bucket, we would go down to the seashore together, and she would watch with envious eyes some practically naked little boys with whom she was longing to play. I allowed her to do so, keeping an eye on them all the time, and it did make her so happy. In her childhood days in England she found great solace in her little imaginary friend, Peggy, whom we were admonished to treat with utmost respect. When riding on a bus, we were cautioned not to sit on Peggy and to allow her plenty of breathing space, much to the amazement of the other passengers.

She didn't like text-books, and hated arithmetic; but she was a voracious little reader, devouring Kingsley's "Heroes" from cover to cover at the age of seven. I tried to teach her, but not very successfully. Some ideas stuck in her brain, however, because one evening we were watching a beautiful sunset, and she said, "Oh, mother, do look at that lovely archipelago in the sky." She soon picked up the language and acted as interpreter, so that I could participate or otherwise, mostly otherwise, in all the current events.

To a child of her temperament, loneliness may have been an asset. It gave her talents plenty of scope to develop an unlimited time for meditation. It may also have been the means of increasing her love of companionship, making her a most amazingly sociable little girl.

She was no respecter of persons, and some of her invitees were downright disreputable, but it made no difference. As long as you were a human being in need, you could count on Gladys for help. Invariably, she brought home these lame dogs, and I with my meagre income had to extend hospitality – sometimes quite grudgingly, because I was not prepared; but that was immaterial. She insisted that whatever we had must be shared. Consequently her capacity for loving swallowed up her eccentricities, and it was only at her death that I realized what a place she had made for herself in the affections of the community. I went to my bedroom window about two hours after the radio had announced her death at Accra, and saw a group of market women looking up at the house disconsolately and utterly woe-begone.

In spite of my help, she was in a chronic state of financial embarrassment, largely brought about by her marriage (without my knowledge) to a man I had never seen, and who was never able to support her and their little boy. Consequently, she suffered untold hardships.

On one occasion she had gone down to the Gold Coast for a change, and I sent a second-class fare for her to return home. She came back steerage, putting up with dreadful discomfort and inconvenience, with a joy and cheerfulness that amazed me. The steamer was in port two days, so about six of the petty seamen came to the house and told me they had done all they could to make her comfortable, and she in turn had made them so happy that they were loath to see her go, because she had left such a fragrance.

One day she was walking along the thoroughfare near the market when she saw a man lying in the middle of the road. She pulled him to the kerb and, seeing that he was still breathing, rushed into a shop for brandy and milk to revive him. By this time, quite a crowd had gathered, and one Creole woman shouted, "No make nobody tief dah little Missis purse! You no see wat e dey do?" Gladys then realized she was carrying her bag under her arm, so she looked round the crowd and spotted one man – "Oh," she said handing it to him, "please take care of it for me!" After her administrations, the man revived and an ambulance came to take him off. So the crowd dispersed and Gladys suddenly realized she had parted without her handbag. The man was still standing there and came up to her at once, "Missis," he said, "here is your bag." It transpired that this man was in and out of prison the whole time and was only discharged that very morning. But after the look of confidence and trust Gladys gave him, he admitted that he could not possibly steal from her.

My darling daughter had no sense of values, she could not discriminate in any way, either with human beings or commodities. Then too, she utterly lacked determination and perseverance. This was a great handicap throughout life. On the other hand, she could sit down, and in two minutes write a poem, which was a joy and inspiration to read.

Life did not seem quite fair to her somehow, and I must take my share of the blame. She wanted both her parents, and, had her father lived, I know she would have been his right hand. Her optimism always came to the rescue, as in this poignant little verse:

With Pa, I feel so lonesome, 'cause
    Mammy she ain't there.
With Ma, I feel like cryin', 'cause of
    Daddy's empty chair.
Then when I start a-straining at
    the leash to go away,
Ma wants a savoury omelette —— so I
    cook it —— and I stay.
Pa respects a person's feelings, and
    he up and says to me
That as an individual, I had certain
    rights you see,
An' he'd not encroach upon them.
    Thus, we struck a friendship true,
That will go on enduring, so long as
    skies are blue.
And when he says quite casual,
    'Would you like some ginger beer?'
I just unpack my box again and say,
    'Yes, Daddy dear!'

She had a wonderful national spirit which is portrayed in her writings for the different tribes, in which she brings out all their individual characteristics.

At fifteen, she left me to go to Penrhos College, Colwyn Bay, whose headmistress, Miss Rose Hovey, had been my school friend, and who was quite prepared to take her. "Ma," as she was affectionately called, wrote to tell me that Gladys' poem on "Ears" was the very finest ever written by a Penrhos girl.[2] It would have been greatly to her advantage to have remained there, but without my knowledge her father made other arrangements which were just as expensive and not nearly so effective. So, after some years in England, Gladys came back to help revive our little school, which was in a critical condition, and between her and our little white American teacher,[3] wonders were performed.

Casually, she posted some specimens of her work to Columbia

University and immediately received an invitation to migrate there without delay. She left me to go, but never reached America, because of financial difficulties. As usual, her lack of discrimination prompted her to choose to join a coloured jazz troupe with headquarters in Berlin. She bitterly regretted her decision in after-years.

Not long after, a Save the Children's Fund in connection with the League of Nations was instituted. In that year it was solely for African children, to whom I have devoted my life, so it was only natural that I should welcome the opportunity of presenting their case. Here again, lack of funds frustrated me. It is a real blot on the Freetown community that they could not contribute a penny towards the scheme for the betterment of their own children. I had been to America, why should one go anywhere else? they argued. The Lagosians did far better, but the sum they sent was too small to cover my expenses. So I suggested deputing Gladys, who, being in Germany, was close to Geneva, the seat of operations. She did remarkably well and in the end, although I was not present, the Convention did me the honour of including my recommendations in their Report.[4]

Meanwhile, Gladys' considerable literary talents were developing by leaps and bounds, expressing herself chiefly in poems. Knowing that Cambridge, a suburb of Boston, was the supreme educational centre of the States, as it sheltered Harvard University, with its Female Section, Radcliffe – the Girton of America – I took some of her poems to a lady friend, who was so impressed, that she sent them to Mr. Ellery Sedgwick, editor of the *Atlantic Monthly*. To our great surprise, three of them were accepted, and immediately appeared in this very literary American publication, resulting in an offer for her to enter Radcliffe College at once.[5] Through my dear daughter's own action, another splendid opportunity was lost.

There were times when I secretly felt that Gladys was inclined to be irreligious. I realize now how grossly I misjudged her. Whatever their appearance, she was everlastingly seeking for people's good qualities, rather than condemning them. Gladys had an outstanding capacity for love and kindness. As Carlyle often pointed out, it is this gift of tenderness and understanding sympathy that gives the measure of our intellects! Having definitely conquered fastidiousness, she was a spiritual aristocrat. I feel the least I can do is to pay this tribute to her memory:

"She knew how to talk with crowds
        or walk with Kings,
Nor lose the common touch."

In November 1939, she was lying in the very spacious and
comfortable maternity ward at Korle-Bu Hospital, Accra, expecting her baby, when a terrible earthquake shook the town. It was
about 7 o'clock in the evening and lasted only two or three minutes,
but in all that time hell seemed to be let loose. The electricity gave
out and in the pitch darkness, those poor women began to scream
and shriek for help, as the furniture careered around the ward.
Two of them gave birth at once, and above the pandemonium
Gladys' clear voice rang out as she called on the women to pray. By
the time she had finished, the frenzied shrieking and yelling had
subsided, and calm was restored; the lights went on, and peace
descended on them all. She was a patriot through and through, as
her poem "My Africa," will show.

My Africa

Oh land of tropic splendour, engirded
        by the seas
Whose forest-crested mountains lift
        heads into the breeze,
May patriotism render its praise on
        sea and shore,
Till Africa, great Africa, becomes
        renowned once more.

May God walk on her mountains, and
        in her plains be peace.
May laughter fill her valleys, and may
        her sons increase:
Restored be strength and beauty, and
        union of the past;
Till Africa comes once again into
        own at last.

Destroy race prejudices, break down
        the bars of old.
Let each man deem his brother of far
        more wealth than gold.
Till tribes be merged together to form
        one perfect whole,

With Africa its beating pulse, and
   Africa its soul.

Oh Lord! as we pass onward, through
   evolution rise,
May we retain our vision, that truth
   may light our eyes.
That joy and peace, and laughter, be
   ours instead of tears,
Till Africa gains strength and calm
   progressing through the years.

Even the most cursory reading of Mrs. Casely Hayford's *Memoirs*
prior to this section specifically devoted to Gladys suggests that Gladys
was, if not the cause, certainly a factor in the deterioration of her parents' marriage. The circumstances around Gladys' birth which Mrs.
Casely Hayford described graphically and her return to England (without her husband) because of Gladys' infirmities, the sense that perhaps
Gladys was more important than she in her husband's eyes – are vivid
memories for her. Furthermore, the *Memoirs* and Letters reveal her lack
of understanding of the quality of the relationship between Gladys and
her father – her statement that they would alter educational plans
"behind her back" seems unlikely. More likely is the fact that she did not
accept, willingly, such a change of plans.

Actually, there is much about Gladys as a person and her relationship
to her mother that Mrs. Casely does not choose to remember. Contemporaries, including her grandson, have suggested that Mrs. Casely
Hayford was jealous of Gladys – of her great talents, literary, musical,
and artistic, and her warmth and popularity as a person. Mrs. Agnes
Smythe Macaulay, a childhood friend of Gladys', recalled that Mrs.
Casely Hayford in speaking to her mother referred to Gladys as crazy
and wished so much that she were good like the Smythe children. Mrs.
Macaulay also remembered that Mrs. Casely Hayford would often not
let Gladys play the piano, so she had to come to their house to play. Also
that she threatened to sell her piano because Gladys liked it. Kobe, her
grandson, remarked that his mother was a better musician than his
grandmother. Mrs. Edmondson, her niece, said both mother and
daughter were good musicians, and that Mrs. Casely Hayford did often
try to explain Gladys' behavior or excuse it.

Mrs. Macaulay also remembered that Mr. and Mrs. Casely Hayford
often fought over Gladys (as both Kobe and Mrs. Macaulay are
reminiscing from their own childhood, it is more likely that they are

reporting what adults, of the same age as Mrs. Casely Hayford, were saying). It is, however, certainly true that Gladys left Freetown to have her baby in Accra, and that she had also gone to Accra for an extended visit when she died there. She apparently went to her father or, in the case of her son's birth and at the time when she died (though she was not sick when she left Freetown) to her father's people, when she was having difficulties with her mother and/or her husband.

According to Mrs. Macaulay, Mrs. Casely Hayford never expected Gladys to marry. And apparently, at a party at Mrs. Macaulay's home, Gladys met Arthur Hunter and married him after a very short acquaintance, while her mother was in England. Neither her family, presumably her aunt and cousins, nor her friends, approved of Hunter. As Mrs. Macaulay remembered it: "the family in Freetown did not want Gladys to marry or to have children because they feared she would go crazy if she had children."[6] The basis of this fear was apparently not known to Mrs. Macaulay, but will be explained later.

It is not clear why Gladys stayed in Accra as long as she did when she went to have her baby. Her son reports that he stayed in Accra until he was three or four years old. But Mrs. Casely Hayford speaks of the two-year-old grandson being with her. Kobe was ten when his mother died. It is quite probable that by the time she got pregnant, Gladys had been having serious difficulties with both her mother and her husband. Mrs. Casely Hayford apparently did try to make something of Hunter – she sent him to England to learn the printer's trade and, according to Kobe, even bought him a printing press. All of this was of no avail and, according to Kobe and others, Hunter began to drink. When Gladys came back from Accra, for whatever reason, according to Mrs. Macaulay, Hunter was physically abusive to her and apparently had been living with another woman by whom he had children. And, after Gladys' death, he married this woman.

One can assume that Gladys had gone again to Accra for what was to be her final visit to get away from the oppression she must have felt from both her mother and her husband. She died there of black water fever in 1950.

After Gladys' death, Mrs. Casely Hayford took over the rearing of Kobe "though" as he reports "she found me hard to manage, frequently therefore letting me stay with other people … I felt I had no home or family." Of course, Mrs. Casely Hayford was getting along in years, and beginning to lose her hearing. Kobe remembered a little bell she would ring to get his attention. He also loved sleeping in her bed with her and remembered that she was very strict – very Victorian. When he was a bit older, his mother's half-brother, Archie Casely Hayford, came through

Mrs. Casely Hayford dressed for her speaking tour in the United States

Kathleen Easmon Simango

Gladys Casely Hayford Hunter – as a young girl

Mrs. Casely Hayford and associates in the Moral Rearmament movement, in Freetown

Pupils and Faculty with Mrs. Casely Hayford

Mrs. Casely Hayford participating in a class in physical education at her school in Freetown

Gladys Casely Hayford Hunter as teacher in her mother's school

Mrs. Casely Hayford in later years

Freetown and his grandmother persuaded him "to take" Kobe. Shortly afterwards, Archie Casely Hayford did send for Kobe, paying his fare and enrolling him in the Mfantsipim School at Cape Coast from which he graduated. He later graduated from Fourah Bay and received an M.A. from Durham University. Kobe's relations with his father were so distant that when he passed him on the streets of Freetown, he called him "Sir."

Without the Graves' correspondence, one could only speculate as to the nature of the very complex relationship between Mrs. Casely Hayford and her daughter, made even more difficult because so much occurred outside of Freetown itself, and in so far as she could control it, it was kept from the whirl of Freetown gossip. There is a real pathos about a woman as distinguished and apparently as forthright as Mrs. Casely Hayford whose image is based on the denial or falsification of her true relationship with the two most important people in her life ... her husband and her daughter.

Mrs. Casely Hayford admitted that Gladys had talents, and that at times she was very helpful as a daughter, but felt that she was, in fact, a great disappointment to her and although highly sociable, she was eccentric. In her *Memoirs*, this is as far as Mrs. Casely Hayford went. And one has little else on which to draw in trying to discern the nature of their relationship when Gladys was a small child or even a young girl. The Graves' correspondence depicts their relationship when Gladys was in her mid-twenties – a most important time – as it turns out but most of the patterns had already been set. In addition to these priceless letters, Gladys left numerous poems (all written under the pen name of Aquah Laluah), none of which have been published nor had they been seen by Miss Graves. Kobe permitted me to read these poems and to select from them those specifically expressing her feelings about her mother. Five poems seem to reflect those feelings. The following seems most vividly to express her feeling about Mrs. Casely Hayford at the time of the Graves' correspondence.

Jealous

Her sweet smile is angelic
Because she's nearer heaven
Than I who am but twenty-two
Whilst Mother's fifty-seven.

I'm like some unplucked fruit
Mother is warm and mellow

Men term her charmingly discreet
But dub me a "good Fellow!"

She's like a canoe
Set in an old world frame
They call her dear Adesha
But Bobby is my name

My black hair is unruly
Her hair is silken white
Her eyes are pools of wisdom
Whils't mine are starry night
I'm vigorous strong and vital
Languorous and graceful she!

Remembering all the care, as a little girl, she gave to a frequently ailing mother, Gladys wrote:

Mother's Health

Mother's health has not been good
So of course it's understood
That she may walk a little, talk a
very little and it seems

She may think a very little, with
wrinkles on her forehead
She may sometimes nod a little!
And it is understood she dreams.

Mother's health has not been good
So of course it's understood
That a little work, or past time
for her clever little fingers,
While her convalescence lingers
Will pull her through the woods.

So Mother took to tatting, and
first she did a wee bit little
Then she did a deed bit better
Then a little every day

Then she did more than a little
and little more than treble
Of the little that she started with
And still she stays away,

> She has no time to talk to me
> but then it's understood
>
> That Mother does just what I'd like
> Until she leaves the mood.

Such a poem expresses Gladys' love and caring for an ill but obviously distant mother. This next poem is a beautiful prologue to the events covered in the Graves' correspondence and perhaps to their life-long relationship.

To My Mother

> Mother, I need you. Though a woman grown
> Mine self arbitrator mine own law,
> My need of you is deeper than I've known,
> And far more urgent than it was before
> Into your tender arms I'd love to creep
> Pour out my woes, and cry myself to sleep
>
> But even were you here, this could not be
> Convention kills the sobbing child in me
> Since soft white luster crowned
>   your smooth fair brow.
>
> 'Tis I the child, turns Mother to you now
> Then, whilst my firm hand smooths
>   your long white hair
> And my young lips press from your
>   eyes the tears,
>
> Whils't my strong arms are around
>   you, resting there in my embrace
> I loose the weight of years
> And when you smile, confiding
>   tilt your head
> To gaze into my eyes, I'm comforted.

Such love and longing on Glady's part – written probably when her mother was in America, but certainly before Gladys left Freetown – hardly fit the cool, almost insensitive, recollection of Gladys as expressed by her mother in her *Memoirs*.

Though she does not say so specifically, it is quite likely that Mrs. Casely Hayford often had Gladys on her mind when she was in the United States and that as she interceded with the *Atlantic Monthly*, she was also responsible either directly or indirectly for Gladys' interest in Columbia or Radcliffe. This was, or so it seems, an instance of the daughter's wishes following mother's plans.

The documentation provided through the twenty-nine letters Mrs. Casely Hayford wrote to Miss Graves between February, 1931 and November, 1942 is of inestimable value but also disturbing. To a large extent, the correspondence cannot be appreciated without some serious attention being given to Miss Graves herself – her assumptions about Africans, in general, and Mrs. Casely Hayford in particular, and the role she felt she could play in affecting the relationship between Mrs. Casely Hayford and Gladys.

Quite candidly, reading these letters after more than fifty years, presumably with all the persons involved now long dead, I am still horrified not only that Miss Graves intruded into their lives as she did, but that she had the audacity to publish some very personal correspondence while at least Mrs. Casely Hayford was still alive. That Miss Graves went through the motion of writing Mrs. Casely Hayford – who was, by then, quite an old lady, and even if she appreciated that her permission was being sought, she might not have known how to register a negative response – or that Miss Graves somehow felt it was her duty to illustrate or reveal "the common humanity of man, seeing something of each of us in either the mother or the daughter," in no way, in my opinion, obliterates the presumptiveness and invasion of privacy that the publication of these letters reflected. But the availability of the most soul-revealing information, if he or she is not the responsible agent, can only bring pleasure to the scholar in trying to understand the subject. For today's reader, Miss Graves is, therefore, as important a factor or actor in describing or affecting this relationship as is either Mrs. Casely Hayford or Gladys.

As a former social worker, Miss Graves came to Africa in 1930 as a missionary and to write a book – on, it is inferred, the commonality of human nature. She went first to Liberia where she substituted at a missionary school. From this school, she wrote a letter of introduction for herself to Mrs. Casely Hayford, about whom she undoubtedly had heard when Mrs. Casely Hayford was in the United States, and introduced herself as having a mutual friend, a Miss Heath of the Y.W.C.A., and a mutual interest in the cause of peace. Apparently, Miss Graves sought an invitation to visit Mrs. Casely Hayford (regrettably none of Miss Graves's letters to Mrs. Casely Hayford are reproduced in the book) who responds on 18 February 1931:

It was a joy to receive your long chatty epistle with its introduc-

tory letter, which was really not at all necessary, because kindred
spirits need no introduction ... I believe every good woman is a
Pacifist at heart ... This is just an old fasioned rather commodious
house ... If you are willing to rough it – because I have no luxuries
whatsoever – and if you can time your visit to fall in with my
holidays, I shall turn a classroom into a makeshift bedroom, and be
delighted to have you stay with us ... Your deductions are absolutely right. Human nature is the same the world over. Take
motherhood, for instance, a mother is the same *everywhere*... You
are particularly fortunate in having been able to do such extensive
travelling, which I know has been the means of widening your
outlook and broadening your vision. Otherwise you would never
think of desiring to stay with a native.[7]

Again, Mrs. Casely Hayford on 17 March 1931 extends an invitation
to Miss Graves, but postpones until she sees her any "fine arguments
about Liberia" which Miss Graves, without yet having met her, has
already introduced into their discussions. Miss Graves does not yet
know Freetown and Mrs. Casely Hayford does not know Liberia, but
Miss Graves is already willing to assess and evaluate.

From her letter of 1 May 1931, it is clear that Miss Graves has now
visited Freetown and was most warmly received by Mrs. Casely Hayford
and her family:

This is just a line to let you know how thoroughly I enjoyed your
little stay in Freetown. If you were a Briton, I should say you were
not only an enthusiastic pacifist, but an Empire builder in its
highest sense. My people are simply delighted with you, and Mrs.
Rennie was so disappointed you were not able to come to tea, but of
course she quite understood.[8]

Following this letter Miss Graves offers one of her numerous inter-
pretations, based on this very short visit. In this instance she writes:

Mrs. Casely Hayford was very pro-British (she was decorated in
the last Coronation Honors receiving, I think, an OBE) [it was an
M.B.E.]... It may have been because on account of her education,
she felt closer to the British than to even the Creoles of Sierra
Leone; or it may have been because of a sub-conscious antipathy to
her husband's anti-imperialism ... If she had had any insight she
would have known that all thinking pacifists, British as well as those
of other lands, realize that Empire building in *any* sense, means
War – not Peace.[9]

This observation by Miss Graves is one of many which indicate, I believe, that there never was a very close bond between the two women – only an operational one. They begin their letters most formally and end them equally so. And although, at times, Mrs. Casely Hayford was overwhelmingly thankful for something Miss Graves had done for Gladys, she never ceased revealing herself as the figure of greater authority and status. Miss Graves, apparently, felt this, for later she wrote: "Mrs. Casely Hayford did not take offense easily. She was absolutely convinced that she was right and others' criticism of her didn't irritate her, she heeded it so little."[10]

Miss Graves came to Freetown at a very auspicious time for Mrs. Casely Hayford. Gladys had left for America but was waylaid in Germany and Mrs. Casely Hayford did not know what to do about it. Miss Graves, therefore, was to serve as the doer, the intermediary between mother and daughter, always however, in Mrs. Casely Hayford's view, acting on her directions: "What I am asking you to do is just to mother her a little bit. She is a very difficult girl, and we do not seem to understand each other as well as we might ... I believe God sent you into my life for the special purpose of guiding my delicate erring daughter."[11]

Miss Graves, having had experience as a social worker, is perhaps as much professionally motivated as she is personally. Many of her observations seem to me to be extremely insightful, and some of her actions equally so; but as the relationship was not exclusively personal, her observations and actions were often wrong and sometimes actually harmful. Nevertheless, Miss Graves did provide perhaps the only outlet Mrs. Casely Hayford had for her impatience and frustration combined with love for Gladys. And since it is around Gladys that this correspondence evolved, Miss Graves' perception becomes important for it often determined how she acted or how she reacted to Mrs. Casely Hayford. As a background to Gladys' letters to her, Miss Graves writes:

> Her daughter Gladys became a great problem to Mrs. Casely Hayford. Gladys too was remarkably gifted, but not at all in the same way as her Mother. She was musical, making original compositions, and wrote very well, some of her poetry, when she was still quite young, appearing in "The Atlantic Monthly". She very early began having love affairs which were disconcerting to her mother, for Mrs. Casely Hayford was determined that Gladys should succeed her in the school which she had built up with such effort, and Gladys' marrying was not a part of her plan. Then too, Gladys was frail and slightly lame, and she knew how to make her physical handicaps an asset rather than a liability. Mrs. Hayford,

though determined, could sometimes be manoeuvred into over indulgence. Gladys was sent to London and was to attend school while living in her aunt's boarding house. Her father appeared and took her from her aunt's and sent her to a school in the country. Then her mother appeared and took her from that school, and finally home. She helped in her mother's school, but had no ambition to carry it on. Then she had a very serious love affair with an estimable man,[12] but her mother prevented its culmination.[13]

Gladys admired her mother more than she admired anyone in the world and she adored her, but she was torn in two ways. Sometimes the strength, which was such a support, was an unspeakable solace in her own weakness; at other times she was afraid of that will-power which seemed to fascinate her and deprive her of all will of her own, and which was making her, too, live for the school when she did not want to. At last, she decided to run. In various ways she had earned a little money and tried in various ways to make more. When she had enough to buy a typewriter, her ticket, and eighty pounds besides she left for Europe, partly with the idea of going to Columbia University in New York. But she did not have enough money to get to America, and after trying various things finally joined a troop of African entertainers who went to fairs. She made baskets and sang little songs. They led a precarious life for their entertainments were not of a very high order and they did not have many engagements. She had a very long illness in a free hospital in Berlin, and, of course, a very serious love affair with a member of the troop – a native from the Cameroons quite unedu- cated, her mother said – and she wanted to marry.[14] Her mother was in despair. Gladys absolutely refused to come home; but Mrs. Hayford wrote such an insulting letter to the fiancé that he broke off the engagement. They were still, however, in the same troop, which, when I met Mrs. Hayford in the spring of 1931, was playing in Scandinavia. Mrs. Hayford then decided to try again to get Gladys to go to a college in America. She had managed to persuade first Radcliffe and then Columbia to offer to take her without matriculation, as a special student; but Gladys, according to Mrs. Hayford, refused to go.[15]

Clearly, Mrs. Casely Hayford was always directing Gladys, who at the time she met Miss Graves was already in her mid-twenties with a mother in her mid-sixties, still describing her as "the dear child – who cannot manage her own affairs." In truth, Gladys does not seem to know how to manage her own affairs; Mrs. Casely Hayford does not know why, but, of course, Miss Graves does!

There are some discrepancies between what Mrs. Casely Hayford writes in her *Memoirs* and what Miss Graves gives in her *Notes*. Sometimes it is a difference of fact; at other times merely a difference of emphasis.

Miss Graves speaks of Gladys' very early love affairs. Mrs. Casely Hayford makes no reference to them at all in the *Memoirs*. She said she sent Gladys to Penhros at Colwyn Bay in Wales to study under an old school mate of hers and that her father removed her from this school and sent her to an equally expensive one. Miss Graves said Gladys was sent by her mother to live with her aunt in her boarding house and to attend school in London, and that her father took her from this school and sent her to school in the country. Miss Graves suggests that the idea of going to Columbia or Radcliffe somehow occurred to Gladys on her own. Mrs. Casely Hayford indicates her own role in bringing this about.

Miss Graves in her summary narrative made no reference to Gladys' mental breakdown in England though she does speak of her long illness in Berlin. We do not know whether this illness in Berlin was a physical or a mental illness. Mrs. Casely Hayford made no reference to either illness, speaking only of Gladys' eccentricity. As has been noted earlier, Mrs. Casely Hayford herself was frequently unwell and Gladys, from a small child, was her nurse; one might draw the conclusion that mother and daughter were both inclined to illness as a way of reacting to stress.

Indeed, there is much that one could write about this fascinating, talented, and sensitive daughter of Mrs. Casely Hayford. She warrants a biography of her own. Therefore, I was particularly pleased when I uncovered an unpublished manuscript which included a brief biographical sketch of Gladys as well as one or two of her poems.[16] Oxley describes Gladys as "a gracious voice from distant Africa." Perhaps because Oxley is a man, he might be forgiven the error of only mentioning her deceased father – "the late Casely-Hayford" and ignoring her very much alive, distinguished mother.[17]

Mrs. Casely Hayford began to depend on Miss Graves to help her in carrying out all her plans for Gladys after she saw how effective Miss Graves had been in assisting Gladys at the International Conference on African Children in Geneva, where she went as a substitute for her mother. Her assessment of the situation at the time Miss Graves comes on the scene is given in her letter of 7 August 1931. She writes:

> It is quite true that I wrote her *once* to tell her she was a burden and I have bitterly regretted it and expressed my contrition over and over

again, but the dear child never told you what led up to it. You do not know the unutterable anguish I have suffered, because she would go her own way, and not take any advice. The real person to blame in the whole business is her father. He never gave her a chance, and he could easily have done so, for he was a flourishing barrister. I was married for 27 years and have been a neglected widow for 23. The miserable advantages Gladys has had have come from me. Her father *never* did the right thing by us, and before I had this school I went out to teach in other schools. Things were not so bad whilst I had my own little private income, but for the last 4 or 5 years that, too, has been taken, so that I really am desperately poor, although I still have a little property which I unfortunately cannot convert into money, because of the financial depression.

No one knows better than I do, that Gladys needs further training, because her technique is not up to the mark, and because of that two years ago she left for Columbia, *at her own wish*, with money she had saved up herself, supplemented by what I could give her. She made two fatal mistakes – 1) instead of remaining in London while waiting for the extra money which the passport people demanded (and which I sent) she went off with this theatrical group to Berlin, and since *then her whole outlook has changed*. That was Christmas 1929.

In October, 1930, she wrote to say that she was ready for Columbia when I could send the money, because her uncle had visited her and got her passport through. All was plain sailing. I cabled the money and for Christmas I received the news that she was engaged, that she was going to give a Revue, instead of going to Columbia. Now dear Miss Graves, when you realize that I was depriving myself of the bare necessities of life to squeeze the amount together, just for Gladys to fling it into the sea, because she would not take advice, can you blame me if I let myself go when she proposed some other idiotic scheme?

I have quite made up my mind that she shall go to Ruskin in September. I am expecting something from my husband's estate and even if that is not forthcoming immediately, I shall be able to manage her expenses till April without it ... I shall not let her down financially, because my own needs are so few now.

...

P.S. Don't say anything about Gladys in writing to America – when she really does get to Ruskin, one can begin to talk.[18]

Miss Graves was a friend of the Principal of Ruskin, Mr. Barratt Brown, and had interceded with him on Gladys' behalf. Mrs. Casely Hayford enthusiastically endorsed the idea of Gladys going to Ruskin. For with all her talents, and even her eccentricities, Mrs. Casely Hayford wanted one thing for Gladys – to carry on in the leadership of the Girls' Vocational and Industrial School. To do this she must have proper credentials. Given the time and effort Mrs. Casely Hayford had put into the school and the success that it had become, with Gladys' ability to perform many of the skills needed in the school, this would seem to have been a normal and responsible expectation. In addition, throughout her life, Mrs. Casely Hayford was plagued by financial stringencies. She speaks about this quite frequently and there is no doubt that she saw Gladys, her talented only child, as the source of financial support in her old age. Also, although she nowhere mentions it in either her *Memoirs* or her letters, Mrs. Casely Hayford undoubtedly wanted Gladys to follow in the footsteps of her niece, Kathleen Easmon. Kathleen was all that Mrs. Casely Hayford would have wanted in a daughter – talented, trained, pretty, and committed, also probably of docile or sweet disposition – like her own mother, Nettie. It seems likely, therefore, that first the person and then the ghost of Kathleen stood between Mrs. Casely Hayford and Gladys more than the documentation supports and perhaps more than either of them consciously realized.

Also, it does seem to me that Mrs. Casely Hayford wanted Gladys to marry – not before she had prepared herself to direct the school, but certainly at some time. On several occasions, both in referring to her own desire to marry and in speaking of other persons, Mrs. Casely Hayford seemed to believe in marriage. However, in view of her own unhappiness and disappointment, and also the general family status and expectations, she would naturally want Gladys to make a good marriage ... and in Creole society that meant certain things. Discussions about this question of Gladys' romances often came up in the letters in response to questions from Miss Graves. On 11 July 1931, quite early in their relationship, she writes:

> As regards her lover, I did not know the dear child was still engaged. She wrote to tell me that they had a split and has never mentioned him since so I concluded it was all off. She is doing me a grave injustice if she thinks I disapprove of him because of his background or colour. I do not want her to marry a *man who lives by his wits*. He has no trade, no steady employment of any kind ... I am dead against her going back to Sweden.[19]

So Gladys prepares to go to Ruskin. On 24 July 1931 her mother writes:

I have just received a letter from Gladys from Stockholm, where she will remain till autumn when she hopes to go to Ruskin. She also informs me that Fraser[20] has promised her a post as soon as she gets through ... I am definitely pledging myself to help Gladys go to Ruskin in September.[21]

By 12 October, Mrs Casely Hayford writes that she has received a cable from Gladys "Proceeding Ruskin," so she continues,

My heart is at rest – Gladys has come to her senses so I can only sing a Doxology ... If Gladys is not happy there it will be entirely her own fault ... I shall manage to keep Gladys at Ruskin for 2 years, I hope, and shall feel amply rewarded if she only makes good.[22]

Two months later, 5 December 1931, Mrs. Casely gives her first and really only positive and joyful reaction about Gladys' life at Ruskin:

... I know you rejoice with me that Gladys is now at Ruskin where she has settled down very happily and seems to be making friends and getting on so well ... at a recent lecture on Schumann, for which a Chairman had to be elected by vote, her fellow students elected her, and Barret Brown [sic] writes to say she presided very well.

I am doing my best now to send her a little more money so that she can have a little electric stove in her room, and get a taxi for her lectures, because she says the steps are so trying – she is 4 flights up – so that she is completely done by the time the day is over.[23]

Later that month Mr. Barratt Brown wrote to Miss Graves and spoke of Gladys' favorable work, but also prophesied a clash between Gladys and her mother over their differing goals for Gladys.[24]

By the end of February Gladys had had a mental breakdown, which originally Mr. Brown thought was "an acute case of hysteria and placed her in a nearby private nursing home, Warneford Hospital." By the first week in March, Mr. Brown had altered his feelings and now saw Gladys' illness as being more serious. He writes Miss Graves on 9 March 1932.[25]

I have thought all along that the double strain of the conflict with her Mother and the love affair in Germany which I rather think has broken down was responsible for her collapse, rather than any strain imposed by her work here or her physical condition ... the only thing seems for her to go back to Africa as soon as she is well enough to travel.

From March to July, the major concern of Mrs. Casely Hayford was

Gladys' mental state. Her placement in Warneford Hospital was not satisfactory – there was a problem of racial discrimination and the treatment itself was inadequate. Mr. Brown recommended that Gladys be transferred to the public facility, Oxford Country Medical Hospital (Littlemore), which offered better treatment but which required, as a condition of entry, that the patient be certified as insane. This understandably presented a crisis for Mrs. Casely Hayford, but in her usual religious and pragmatic way she agreed to it – having Miss Graves and Mr. Brown as signators – but never for one minute did she believe Gladys was insane.

Miss Graves provided the psychiatrist with the facts on the family history, on the basis of which he made some of his diagnosis. I should imagine, however, that the doctor, a Dr. Goode, would have been appalled to see his words in print while both he and his patient were alive. Steadfastly, however, Miss Graves includes all: Dr. Goode said, she wrote,

> He thought that sex had something to do with Gladys' trouble, but was inclined to think it chiefly a defence mania at the beginning, and said it was of long duration ... Her mother does not love her. Neither the mother nor the child knows this consciously, but sub-consciously they do. The sub-conscious knowledge which the mother has of her feelings towards the child makes her persuade herself that she has especial affection and it shows in indulgence and, since she is autocratic by nature, in interfering "concern". Her rankling resentment against her husband, though, is so great that she does not, or so I diagnose the case, feel the love she likes to think she has for the child who is so much like him. Gladys, also sub-consciously, feels she has not her mother's real affection, craves it, and tries to win it by arousing pity, hence her having formed the habit of making the most of her affliction. She also is very much attracted by her mother, admires her greatly and feels her magnetic influence strongly; but at the same time fears doing what her mother wants her to do lest she should lose the power of being herself, knowing sub-consciously that her real self is something her mother cannot understand, since it is so much her father's; and also being conscious and also sub-conscious of her mother's tremendous will power and of her mother's influence over her, this fear has grown and grown until it has produced a defence mania.[26] There are, of course, probably sexual and other complications, but the "defence mania" is, I think, judging from her "history", the main cause.[27]

There is much in the statement that even on the basis of our understanding must be true, yet there is also much that might properly be called psychiatry of the 1930s. Further, the diagnosis was based on the understanding of one (i.e. Miss Graves') who, over such a brief period of time could be so sure about the personality and feelings of two persons, Mrs. Casely Hayford and her husband, whom the doctor had never seen. Finally, of course, there is the difference in the cultural setting ... Gladys is not an English girl – she is not even an American girl, she is a member of the Creole elite from Freetown.

It is not without interest, therefore, that Miss Graves includes a letter written about the same time by a highly qualified person who all his life knew Gladys and her mother as well as the Freetown setting. Dr. Easmon, Mrs. Casely Hayford's nephew, on 23 April 1932, wrote Miss Graves:

> the family ... have all along known that Gladys did not want to go on teaching in her Mother's school and as far as I can gather the main anxiety of her mother was not so much that Gladys would teach at the school but that she should have her gifts sufficiently developed to be able to support herself after the mother was dead ... The rest of the family consider that Mrs. Hayford has spoiled Gladys and let Gladys have her own way too much. The way Gladys used to play up the pain in the leg stunt was disgraceful. And she still continues it – did it in Germany and has been doing it at Oxford ... With regard to her love affairs: Mrs. Hayford did not oppose the only serious one I remember in Africa – the man himself, Ballanta, the musician, broke it off and married someone else in Liberia.[28]

In her letter of 22 March 1932, Mrs. Casely Hayford tried to come to terms with the reality of Gladys' illness, always, however, drawing on realistic situational factors and religion for support. But it was difficult for her because she was so far away and because she did not want to believe Gladys was insane ... or even seriously mentally ill:

> My motherhood, coupled with a steadfast faith, assures me that by now Gladys is quite herself again, but whether it will be wise for her to continue her studies is quite another thing. Her music, her literature, and her drawing all bursting to express themselves at the same time coupled with her unfortunate love affair have proved her ending. I would not be surprised if some adverse news about "Big Boy" proved the finishing touch, brought on the climax ... If she could just finish her course by concentrating on Drawing and Handwork which would not be nearly such a nerve strain as

Literature and Music – I would be so thankful because she would still have a chance of going to Achimota. I am never going to ask her to come back here unless she *does so of her own free will*. My dear, you have again stressed the point that my duty is to give Gladys the same opportunities given me. I wish I could make you realize how utterly futile the suggestion is. I had a living father *with an income*, who shouldered his responsibilities. Gladys has had an indifferent Father, who never looked after her properly, and who, after 25 years of unspeakable neglect has left me a *penniless widow*. Out of every 5 pounds I get, I give her 4 pounds – surely I am doing all I can to help her. I am so tremendously thankful that I am not only still capable of working, but *that I have work*, when so many people are unemployed, and, at present, I must just go on with the school until God opens some other door. Is it unreasonable to expect Gladys to help me if everything else fails? ... By all means write to her and give her a good scolding. I am so perfectly certain that she is quite herself again and that it would probably have a very salutatory effect.[29]

While Gladys was showing signs of improvement, she remained quite a sick girl. Dr. Goode, Miss Graves, Mr. Brown, and Dr. Easmon were all very much concerned and discussed how and when Gladys should return to Africa. It was clearly out of the question for her to return by herself and there was the problem of cost and to some extent family embarrassment in having her escorted home. All tried to keep Mrs. Casely Hayford informed of the situation. Miss Graves apparently continued to introduce subjects from Gladys' past about which she herself had curiosity or in an effort to understand more clearly what was disturbing Gladys. While Mrs. Casely Hayford did answer her queries, one can sense a feeling of annoyance or impatience in some of her replies. In her letter of 21 April, she was again forced to discuss Gladys' love life and Gladys' feeling about her. She writes:

I knew nothing whatever about Gladys' attachment to him (Humphrey Ballanta) and would have been only too pleased to welcome him as a son-in-law. I never saw or heard anything to suggest more than the ordinary boy and girl friendship and he never approached me in any way, so that I was absolutely ignorant of what was going on.

A woman cannot face life in Africa *alone* with great poverty, and a home to maintain, without acquiring a stern exterior, but no one has yet suggested I am terrifying. Gladys least of all. In fact the poor

child does just what she likes, and now we see the results. She has
gone her own way instead of following out my desires for her. So
that's that ... I have written to tell her she can follow her own
inclinations in every particular. I am going over to bring her home
myself.[30]

Two weeks later, Miss Graves received the following letter:

I have not been able to get hold of the money to go over and bring
the dear child home ... I thought it would be quite an easy thing to
raise a small loan on the school property, but no bank would
entertain the idea, and not a single friend has come to the rescue.
Hence I am positively convinced that God does not wish me to go,
otherwise he would have opened the way, but He has not done so,
because it is not necessary, *as Gladys is so much better.* I am quite
certain that by the end of the month she will be sufficiently recovered to get away to some quiet little sea-side place before returning home ... Gladys cannot stand single blessedness – and I would
never have raised a single objection if the man could have supported her. But when she returns home, clothed and in her right
mind, I dare say she will soon become engaged ... Please don't
broadcast Gladys' illness either to Beth or anyone else. You can
understand as her mother, I would like it kept as quiet as possible.[31]

Typically, Mrs. Casely Hayford and God found a way for her "to
bring darling Gladys home." Dr. Easmon came into "an unexpected
windfall," and paid Gladys' fare back to Freetown. She planned to leave
via a German steamer on the 19th of June and promised to cable Miss
Graves as soon as she arrived.

By 6 July, she writes Miss Graves that she had visited Gladys,

who behaved perfectly rationally the whole time except that she
would not talk which I put down to sheer 'cussedness' ... I have
decided to go and settle at Oxford so that I can see her every day
and put a little brightness and occupation in her life.[32]

And she does move to Oxford with a Mrs. McLaughlan and from
there, in her last letter to Miss Graves prior to taking Gladys home to
Freetown, Mrs. Casely Hayford reports on her encounter with the
doctor; characteristically she speaks of interviewing him.

Now about Gladys, after all the depressing news I received in
Africa, and the fact that she had been certified as insane, I was
picturing her as very bad – and lo! the miracle has happened – if not
altogether, almost so. I interviewed the specialist on Monday – in

one breath he told me I had spoilt Gladys and in another he told me she was afraid of me ... that Gladys had had her own way and therefore not exercized her powers of self-control, etc. Then he sent for her and put some searching questions to her. He asked her if she wished to return to Sierra Leone and she said "No," what reason she would not give. But I know why. After three years' residence in Europe, she is going back a failure, in spite of her pronounced ability, and she is ashamed. Had she followed my advice things would have been very different. A few minutes after, Dr. Goode asked her if she would like to go home with me, and she said, "Yes" – was I to book her passage? To which she acquiesced at once.

As far as I can see Gladys is just a little eccentric. At times she is absent-minded and she also has fits of depression, which I am sure will disappear as time goes on, and sometimes she is not polite as I would like her to be. But her conversation is most interesting and full of sparkling wit. She does my shopping perfectly correctly, and when we go out she is the one upon whom I lean for piloting me across the road, etc. If she shows disinclination for companionship, I just leave her. I am amazed at the marvelous progress she has made towards recovery, and all I can do is to sing a Doxology ... As far as I can see, Gladys is returning home to help me of her own free will.[33]

Of course, things did not move so smoothly, as Mrs. Casely Hayford later frankly reported from Freetown. Gladys had been troublesome on board ship and now that they had returned to Freetown she "often lacked concentration and displayed marked idiosyncracies."[34] In fact, Gladys remained a real problem for her mother for several months after their return and still accused her "of having frustrated her marriage. I have suffered quite a lot of heartbreak at her treatment of me," she wrote in August, 1933.[35] But at the same time Gladys, apparently voluntarily, returned to teach at the school.

During this period from 1933 to 1936 the school progressed nicely, due to no small extent to Gladys' talents. Its growth and problems, however, will be discussed in more detail in the next chapter. Gladys, meanwhile, seemed to have settled in. She began a correspondence course in Drawing so as to get a Diploma and qualify as a Drawing Master.

During this period there is no correspondence between Mrs. Casely Hayford and Miss Graves. But her next letter of 28 April 1936 was most informative. It is impossible to discern from this letter just how Miss

Graves learned of Gladys' marriage. She does not give this information in her *Notes* and the book, as has been said, included none of her letters to Mrs. Casely Hayford and yet, as usual, Mrs. Casely Hayford seems to be responding to initial queries from Miss Graves. Also, while Miss Graves during 1931 had kept up a lively correspondence with Gladys, Gladys wrote far less frequently, perhaps only sporadically after her return to Freetown. However, prompted by a second letter, she wrote Miss Graves in July, 1934, before she married, and not again until September, 1936 (her last letter) when she discussed her marriage, responding characteristically to Miss Graves' query, but even this was five months after Mrs. Casely Hayford's report:

> Gladys' marriage is such a financial hardship, that I have nothing left over to play with. Don't think I am grumbling, far from it. She has chosen a man of humble circumstances, indifferent education and no status whatsoever. But I am content because there seems such a perfect understanding between them. In spite of dire poverty, they are showing such splendid courage, such fine contentment, such optimism. The man is thoroughly decent, clean, honest, and devoted to his wife, and she reciprocates his affection with all her heart and soul ...
>
> The Hunters have a dear little home a few doors away from me. Gladys is back teaching as she must do her bit to bring grist to the mill, especially now the man is not working.[36]

Miss Graves sent a wedding gift to the couple on 21 September 1936, Mrs. Casely Hayford wrote to thank her for so doing, initially fearing that Gladys and her husband would procrastinate, but she learned before her letter was mailed that, in fact, they had written the appropriate thank you letter – two, in fact, one from each of them. We are not told just what the gift was, except that it was practical.

Responding to Miss Graves' response to her thank you note and probably also as a way of activating a friendly correspondence, Mrs. Casely Hayford wrote on 23 November, 1936:

> Gladys' marriage has crippled me so much financially that everything helps ... She and her man understand each other so well, and he has just got a post as a bus conductor which brings in a little and helps to keep the home fires burning. I never hear any grumbling and I think they are really learning to lean upon God as their staunch ally.[37]

The following March she wrote again to report that the couple are "inchin along" nicely. But in her last full letter, written five years later on

10 January 1942, Mrs. Casely Hayford, though older and now retired, is still her direct, frank self and gives what is her final assessment of the relationship between her and Gladys:

> She has been a source of grave anxiety to me down through the years and is not herself yet, although my faith in God remains unshaken that she will regain her normal mentality. She walked out on me 4 years ago, and married a man without education or training of any kind, penniless; and as she is no economic asset whatsoever it has been a very great strain on me to keep them going, because his wage earning capacity seems very limited. Then on account of my age – 74, I was obliged to close the school a year ago. It would have been so splendid if Gladys could have taken it over, but it was quite out of the question – indeed she is one of the individuals who should have been born with a golden spoon in her mouth, because she has never yet been able to keep herself. When the war opened she started a cafe for the forces, which would have been a great success if she had only allowed me to have a finger in the manage- ment, which was quite beyond her. So it failed, and at the present moment, I have taken a house for her at Wilberforce where she can vegetate and where the salubrious air and restful surroundings will do her a world of good. I hope you don't think I am grumbling because I have never yet had more than I can bear, and God's grace is abundantly sufficient for all my needs. She has given me a darling little grandson – just 2 years old. He is so extraordinarily intelligent and interesting that it fills my heart with joy and rejuvenates my poor, old, worn-out frame. I am afraid that is not quite true, because I am by no means worn out. My one infirmity is deafness which is really a handicap for which I get no remedy under present conditions ... I am sure Gladys would send her love if she knew I was writing.[38]

And eleven months later she writes her last letter:

> Gladys and her Babbie left us a week ago to visit her father's relatives down the coast. I expect they will be there for a little while. Signed, "Your loyal old African friend, Adelaide Casely Hayford"[39]

Gladys' seventeen letters to Miss Graves complete the picture of Mrs. Casely Hayford as mother. And there is a fascination in trying to understand this relationship between Adelaide Casely Hayford and Gladys – both were marginal women, talented, so much in need of each other but each finding it difficult to serve the other. Gladys' letters to

Miss Graves, who clearly functions as an intermediary between the two, give a poignant flavor to this complex mother/child relationship.

Gladys was already twenty-seven years old when she wrote Miss Graves – she very dependent on her mother, but pretending not to be, wanting to be free and on her own but yet clearly unable to be. Miss Graves attempted to influence this relationship – she was needed and yet not wanted – she was helpful to a point – but nothing really changed.

Gladys met Miss Graves through her mother, and through Gladys' relationship to Mrs. Casely Hayford, Miss Graves remains viable as a potential influence. We learn from these letters, written with almost weekly frequency between 31 May 1931 and 31 October 1931, that Gladys felt her mother found her a financial burden and of little help to her.

> Mother expects a quick return for the money spent on me ... I see no reason why I should be further indebted to her; since at the present moment I see no way of paying her back ... Mother will only blow me up some more for wasting her money ... I danced for three months in order to keep Mother from strain and to go on saving for Columbia. I went to the hospital and that did not cost Mother anything because I went on the Insurance System.[40]

Gladys herself recognized this and the fact that at her age she should have accomplished more. But she had her reasons – her physical condition and most of all her temperament or her desire to be a creative person:

> I can make my own way and keep myself without any further academic degrees ...[41]
> I know perfectly well my writing does leave a lot to be desired. I don't consider myself perfect by any means, but I don't think Mother is quite fair. I agree that I'd have better training but no writer has ever thrived on obligations, though a lot have starved on bread and water to stick to their ideas.[42]

There seemed to be a feeling on Gladys' part that her mother was too interfering and too demanding, yet after she herself wrote her mother about her love, Big Boy, no doubt wanting her approval, she was devastated when her mother reacted characteristically:

> Then Big Boy and another man proposed. I chose Big Boy. I knew Mother would not approve. Even if the Prince of Wales proposed it wouldn't have satisfied her ... In the meantime I got Big Boy to write to Mother. I have already told you the answers she gave him. I have not got over it, and I shall never be the same girl.

Something in me is dead now. I may get Big Boy back but I doubt it. What right has she to interfere when two people love each other?[43]

And on 21 July 1931:

Mother's letters are positive in one mail and negative in the next, besides being utterly inconsistent. One moment, I'm a brave girl, the next I'm "no use" – in one letter "you are the only joy of my life" and in the next "you are selfish and think only of yourself and are nothing but a burden and a worry. You neglect your duty to me." Under the cirumstances it is like walking on a wobbling plant and I've had enough of it.[44]

While both women were complex and, in a sense, really extraordinary, their differences in personality and the inequality in their status (mother as to daughter) kept the relationship bitter-sweet. Miss Graves made this more visible and perhaps more painful, even in her endeavor to be helpful, than it otherwise might have been.

Gladys was able to see her mother as others saw her: "I agree with you that she is an extraordinary, a wonderful woman. I know that and I admire her tremendously," yet the battle or friction between them remained, for she continued,

But at the present stage in my development she would help me more by sinking her own personality into the background, and by letting me find my own and develop it my own way instead of trying to mould me, that is my only point of contention. Nothing else ... In another two or three years, when I have got past this period, I shall be only too pleased to return home where I belong; but at present I want to be just let alone.[45]

Of course she did not really mean this, nor was it possible. Gladys was far too dependent and neither Mrs. Casely Hayford nor Miss Graves intended to let her alone. But the previous month, Gladys had, I think, expressed her dreams and the reality of her relationship with her mother:

I don't want to go to Ruskin and later to write my mother, from sheer duty: "Enclosed herewith so and so. Hope you will find it useful. Gladys." I want to write "Mother darling, I have had an awful year of it, but by George! this is the present from my FIRST Short Story in Nash's. You come first; and just as soon as I have published ten more I'm coming right home to take you in my arms and comfort you and look after you; because I shall be able to work at home now; I've got connections. I'm a writer.[46]

Here the dreaming ended and reality emerged.

> You see I must have someone to love, and if I can't love Big Boy I
> must love Mother; and at the rate we are going there won't by any
> love left by the time we have finished – only obligations on both
> sides.[47]

Within a month she left Sweden for England and Ruskin. Two brief
letters covered that period, but writing was not so necessary then,
because Miss Graves was on the scene.

On Gladys' return to Freetown, with this entire venture including her
breakdown behind her, she wrote three short letters to Miss Graves. In
the first one, 16 November 1932, two months after her return, she
mentioned the continuing struggle with her mother and her wish to go to
Achimota School in the Gold Coast rather than to continue her teaching
at her mother's school. In the second letter, written almost a year and a
half later, she mentioned life at the school and Mrs. Casely Hayford's
recurring illnesses with some resignation about it all. In her final letter,
two years later, she spoke of her marriage but without much enthusiasm:
"We have been married a year, and still find matrimony satisfactory."
And Mrs. Casely Hayford is not far away – in presence and no doubt in
influence – for Gladys continued: "We are living in a small flat quite
near mother."[48]

And on her life went until she died in the Gold Coast. We learn little
in these letters of Gladys's relation to her father or how she felt about the
estrangement of her parents. She mentioned her father only once in her
letters: "Trying to get to Columbia reduced me to nights of pain and
days of tears; and on top of that my father died. We loved each other very
dearly."[49]

XI

Adelaide Smith Casely Hayford
as Widow – The End of the Dream

Joseph Ephraim Casely Hayford died 11 August 1930. Had their marriage been different, that is either publicly acknowledged as broken, or,
in fact, still intact, however nebulous the tie, the effect of his death on
Mrs. Casely Hayford could be more easily assessed. As it was, there was
a public and a private side to Mrs. Casely Hayford's widowhood. In the
most obvious way, her widowhood was rather simple and straightforward. She was his wife at his death and she received and responded to
the appropriate expressions of sympathy.
   A letter of sympathy was sent to her by Mr. F.A. Miller, Hon.
Secretary of the National Congress of West Africa.[1]

August 15, 1930

Dear Mrs. Hayford,
   I am directed by the President and Members of the Executive
Committee of the Sierra Leone Section of the Congress to send
you and Miss Hayford the expression of their deepest sympathy for
the loss sustained by you in the death of your husband, Hon. Mr.
Casely Hayford, M.B.E., President, Founder of the Congress ...
   I am to add that it is proposed to hold a Memorial Service at
Wesley Church on Saturday 31st at 3.

Mrs. Casely Hayford responded with the following letter which
certainly maintained the fiction of the state of her marriage:

August 27, 1930

Dear Mr. Miller,
   Will you kindly convey to the members of the Congress my deep
appreciation of their heartfelt letter of condolence on the passing of
my dear husband, the Honorable Casely Hayford.
   I mourn with you all the loss of a man whose unswerving loyalty,

zealous patriotism, fine courage, indomitable grit and independent spirit have placed him in the foremost rank of African leaders for all time.

Yours sincerely,
Adelaide Casely Hayford

Apparently wishing to make her position as widow as widely known as possible, Mrs. Casely Hayford had the following announcement placed in the *SLWN*.[2]

> Mrs. Casely Hayford wishes to express her sincere gratitude for the sympathy either in the shape of cablegrams, letters or personal visits that she has received on the death of her dear husband, Casely, which took place at Accra on the 11th ulturio.

Girls Vocational School
Freetown, September 6, 1930

From this point on, publicly, Mrs. Casely Hayford is the acknowledged widow of Casely Hayford. For the first time in her already long life, she has a position of status in Freetown that is honest and unequivocal. At least psychologically, she now had a base from which to work, to go out and face the world. It is from this posture, as widow, that she spent the last creative years of her life.

Of course, in her earlier letters from America to Mr. Casely Hayford, she admitted not portraying their marriage as the failure it was, and indeed, as we have said, she apparently often wished to pick up the threads again. But in reality, during all this time – all these 24 years – she was a widow without portfolio.

In the correspondence with Miss Graves, Mrs. Casely Hayford speaks frequently of the funds she was expecting from her husband's estate – which she intended to use for Gladys' education and for her security in her old age. In her letter of 27 June 1931, she optimistically wrote Miss Graves: "I am hoping to get a little money from my husband's estate by the end of August," and again in her letter of 11 July, she writes, "I am anticipating something from my husband's estate which ought to be wound up during the next two or three months." But by 12 October 1931, she had to write, "My husband's estate is an absolute frost. He left no money and to sell the property now would be absolutely suicidal because it is almost valueless and it may be years before I can think of doing so."[3]

Mrs. Casely Hayford clearly felt, as reflected in her letters to her husband and to Miss Graves, that he had not lived up to the terms of

their Separation Agreement and that as a result both she and Gladys
were made to suffer. That the matter of her just share was never
satisfactorily (in her opinion at least) settled is illustrated by the letter of
24 August 1946, from Archie Casely Hayford to Dr. Easmon, in which
he wrote;

> My mother wrote me a very nasty letter threatening to litigate
> with me over our father's estate after 16 years of his death [sic]. I
> have not taken a penny of father's either. Can she not be reasonable
> and trusting?
>
> My love to Auntie Netty, Enid and the rest of the family,
>
> Your cousin
> Archie[4]

But to the larger society in Freetown, having publicly received and
publicly acknowledged condolences, Mrs. Casely Hayford's role as a
woman is now that of widow, mother, educator and community figure.
Aside from the events described in the earlier chapter relating to Gladys,
her life's preoccupation for the next decade, from Mr. Casely Hayford's
death in 1930 until 1940, when she was forced to close the school, was
the school. Clearly, over the years its format had been considerably
modified and simplified. She was just not able to raise the necessary
money and community support or government subsidy to carry out many
of her dreams for the school. Her inability to find an appropriate
successor – with Kathleen dead and Gladys unable or unwilling to
assume the leadership – forced her to face the fact that the school was
only going to be what she personally wanted it to be or had the strength
herself to administer.

After returning from her second trip to America and bringing Gladys
home from England, Mrs. Casely Hayford had turned her complete
attention to the school. It was a do or die endeavor. Aside from the
problem of making the school a success in itself, giving it a realistic
curriculum, securing some government subsidy sufficient, at least, to
cover some of the costs, there was also the growing problem of competition.

At the time Mrs. Casely Hayford first enunciated her ideas for a
different kind of education for girls, few persons had dared to make such
claims. And certainly no African had. What England brought and gave
to the colonies was indeed what the colonized people were supposed to
want and need in education as well as in other spheres. Gradually, of
course, more people in the colonies, including Sierra Leone, began to
question the suitability of a classical education for their children – began

to see that there were indeed other ways properly to prepare young people for life. Dislocations around World War I stimulating a broadening of local public opinion helped to introduce this questioning. Mrs. Casely Hayford herself was a source for the greatest change in attitude. After she returned from America, she was no longer speaking speculatively; she, in fact, had seen in the United States many alternative approaches to education which were not tentative but flourishing. She had met many significant and prestigious persons who saw the value in what she was trying to accomplish. Armed with this security, she became more adamant about the school, its value and the need to support it; simultaneously others increasingly saw room for alternatives and began to initiate competitive non-government schools.

Perhaps the competition that hurt the most was that of the Freetown Secondary School for Girls which was organized by Mrs. Ejisa Osora and Mrs. Hannah Benka-Coker. While Mrs. Casely Hayford was in America on her first visit, Mrs. Osora, after having been with the Girls Vocational School for only nine months, left to start a school of her own – which she called the Osora Girls School. Mrs. Casely Hayford felt Mrs. Osora's defection keenly as she herself had rescued Mrs. Osora from despair following her separation from the Annie Walsh Memorial School. One informant said Mrs. Osora had been encouraged to leave Mrs. Casely Hayford by Mrs. Hannah Benka-Coker.[5] In any case, Mrs. Osora was soon associated with Mrs. Benka-Coker in developing the Freetown Secondary School for Girls.

This school opened formally with Mrs. Osora as the first principal on 20 January 1926. Later Mrs. Osora had difficulties in the administration of the school and resigned, according to some, leaving the school in a state of ruin. Mrs. Benka-Coker then assumed the principalship in 1939. The school was more fortunate than the Girls' Vocational School in raising funds. And naturally Mrs. Casely Hayford would watch its progress. There seemed to have been an on-going rivalry among the three women and between the two schools. In November of 1928, the Freetown Secondary School for Girls won the Second Annual Prize given a school by the Governor and was apparently outgrowing its facilities, but at that time the Girls' Vocational received a better official report than did the Freetown Secondary School for Girls.[6]

By the following January the Freetown Secondary School for Girls dedicated a new building situated at the foot of Tower Hill barracks, which had been formerly used by "the Imperial Government as a Military Hospital.[7] Mrs. Casely Hayford did not attend the ceremony. By 1952, the school had moved into yet larger buildings, but two months later Mrs. Benka-Coker died. That same year, coincidentally, Mrs.

Constance Cumming-John started the Roosevelt Memorial School for Girls. But this is getting ahead of the story and beyond the time of any real concern for Mrs. Casely Hayford.

Beginning in 1929, using the occasion of the first prize–awards-ceremony of the Girls' Vocational School at Wilberforce Hall as the appropriate occasion, Mrs. Casely Hayford reminded the community of the need to support her school. And in 1930, now a widow, she seemed to begin in earnest to find ways to secure these needed funds – she began to encourage the proper contacts at home as she had done so success-fully in the United States.

While it had been necessary to revise and restrict the curriculum, Mrs. Casely Hayford was most anxious that her students perform well academically even if the numbers in relation to Freetown Girls School and Annie Walsh were small. She took pride in the fact that in 1930 when the results of the Cambridge Local Examinations were announced, Annie Walsh had nine girls sitting for the examination, but only one passed, and while it was true that Freetown School for Girls had five sitting and five passing, Girls' Vocational had only one sitting and she passed![8]

For the next two years, until she went to England, Mrs. Casely Hayford, according to news releases of the day, exerted every effort to keep the school favorably in the public light. In January Lady Rosalind addressed the school on "What Girls Can Do":

> the idea of showing what girls can do, I believe, was what prompted Mrs. Casely Hayford in establishing a Vocational School for us but the school does not do much on the vocational side, whether it is due to the want of encouragement on the side of parents, com-plained [of] by the principal or is it the financial condition of the school or both. Which is the barrier in the way of the promoter, we do not know, but we hope the day comes when something of a more concrete form is done.[9]

The following month, Lady Slater, wife of the former Governor, accompanied by Mrs. Goddard, wife of the Colonial Secretary, and Mrs. Barton, another European, visited the school. As this was placed as an announcement by Mrs. Casely Hayford, presumably the added comment reflected her concerns: "[the visit] was all the more appreci-ated because the school received no government assistance whatsoever and is entirely under native management."[10]

However, in his routine inspection of the schools later in the month, the Acting Governor did not include a visit to the Girls' Vocational School though he did visit Annie Walsh.[11] But by May, at a meeting presided over by his Lordship, the Bishop, a report of the school was read and prizes were distributed by Mrs. Goddard, the wife of the Colonial Secretary. The Report covered several changes at the school. Miss Beth Torrey was leaving; her replacement was to be Miss Etta Edwin. Two other additions were made – Miss Brown and Miss Taylor. The school enrollment was 65 students. The curriculum included Literary work in 12 classes from kindergarten to Standard VII – with a stress on character training. Mrs. Casely Hayford reported "that the greatest need in Africa is to teach honesty, truth, purity and uprightness, to be proud of their color rather than ashamed of it." The older girls, she stated, had also domestic science, care of the home, infant welfare and simple nursing. She believed, she said, "that vocational work should be the strongest component of the school but it is not because of a lack of proper accommodation and equipment and a fully trained teacher." The finances, she said, were insufficient because "very few parents are paying full fees; a hard working board of Negro women in Boston[12] gives ten pounds a year and other groups including Miss Mabel Carney in New York contribute from time to time."[13]

A very high point in the school's visibility occurred when there was a Review and Singing Competition of all Schools, Primary and Secondary, in which naturally there was considerable community interest and the Girls' Vocational School, led by Mrs. Casely Hayford, then 63 years of age, won the cup! (*SLWN*, 11/14/31). The following month Governor and Mrs. Arnold Hodson presided at a Girl Guides Program and gave out two thank you tags to members of the Council, one of whom was Mrs. Casely Hayford (*SLWN* 12/5/31). At the end of the month, the Governor presided over the Closing Exercises of the School and made fitting compliments to Mrs. Casely Hayford, to which she appropriately responded, according to the *SLWN* (12/26/31).

Another high point for the school was reached when at the Distribution of the Prizes Ceremony before a very large audience, according to the press, Olivette Stuart, whose daughter later married Mrs. Casely Hayford's grandson, Kobe, recited "The Curfew Shall Not Ring Tonight" in excellent English diction, and the singing was better than the previous year. Also the students were jubilant because they had won a prize at the Empire Day Sports for Children (Events).[14] In attendance at this ceremony were the Governor and his wife and the Director of Education as well as Miss Anna Graves.[15]

During 1932 there are rather frequent announcements in the press about the school and of Mrs. Casely Hayford's now more frequent visits to Government House. There is a brief announcement to the effect that "Mrs. Adelaide Casely Hayford, Principal of the Girls Vocational

School, embarked on the *Wahehe* for England on Monday June 20 for health reasons."[16] Mrs. Awooner Renner (her sister) and her three children also left at the same time.

This trip was, of course, made to see about Gladys and for obvious reasons no mention was made in the press of the real purpose. It is, however, interesting that when Mrs. Casely Hayford returns, there is still no mention made of Gladys.[17] Apparently, this last announcement was submitted to the paper by Mrs. Casely Hayford and included what she wanted to have said rather than being the result of how a reporter might have covered the event. Otherwise, Gladys would surely have been mentioned since she had been away for some time and as a teacher and personally in her own right was well known and well liked in the community.

Unfortunately, there is little record of Mrs. Casely Hayford's personal activities or those of the school during late 1932, 1933 and 1934. Mrs. Casely Hayford did write in May and August of 1934 to Miss Graves. From these letters we learn that Gladys is still about and "very much better than she was," but "she is not doing much school work at present"[18] and by August "Gladys is ever so much more rational than she was although she is still eccentric, she puts a great deal of useful work," presumably at the school.[19] We have no information on Gladys' participation at the school until Mrs. Casely Hayford writes Miss Graves in 1936 about Gladys' marriage and her need to work at the school in order to support herself and her husband.

Mrs. Casely Hayford definitely saw the members of her family – near and remote – as assets for her in her school. Aside from Gladys, she had the assistance of her sister, Nettie Easmon, and her niece by marriage, Mrs. Mary Hayford Edmondson. Mrs. Edmondson was the daughter of Mr. Casely Hayford's brother Mark and worked at the school from 1935 until her marriage in 1939. She remembered Mrs. Casely Hayford as being pleasant when you knew her but very strict; however, she never used the cane on the children, always using added tasks as the form of punishment. Miss Graves quotes Beth Torrey's feeling about Mrs. Casely Hayford as principal, "She felt though (and she was more explicit later in conversation than in her letters) that Mrs. Casely Hayford had made the school the expression of *her* individuality and there was no possibility of anyone else expressing theirs, except to a very limited degree."[20] Mrs. Constance Cummings-John remembered that

they prepared many girls who today are in important positions in Sierra Leone ...

Gladys and Mrs. Casely Hayford and her sister, Nettie, planned and introduced into the school the development of raw material pertaining to Africa, dyeing and weaving of native grown cotton into thread and the weaving of boobahs, mats, chair and table covers, window curtains, bed counterpanes, etc. Pottery and wood-work were also introduced, as well as brickwork, leatherwork and carvings. Girls who attended her school were regarded as having a full and all round education, for apart from the usual school sub-jects for Public Examinations, English Drama and Music were a speciality.

The height of Mrs. Casely Hayford's success came when she and her daughter Gladys converted African folk-lore-Nancie Stories into first class Plays, Songs and Dramas. Everybody in Freetown who was anybody attended the shows – Europeans, Asiatics, Americans and Africans crowded the Wilberforce hall for tickets and as Patrons. Her plays were always based on African life and belief. They were unique. The Paintings of the screens with the touch of African Village homes done by Constant and Sam Tuboku-Metzger, two Sierra Leoneans who were trained as Edu-cationalists in America, were superb.[21]

I am indebted to Olivette Stuart Caulker for some reminiscing about the school and what it was like to be a student there. Mrs. Caulker, who was reported to have performed so magnificently "in perfect English" her recitation of "The Curfew Shall Not Ring Tonight," was a pupil at the school from 1928 to 1933. Her memories were quietly fond and warm: "Naughty children were called black sheep. And to punish a talker, a red cloth cut in the form of a tongue was placed over her mouth." In addition, Mrs. Caulker tried to recall for me some of the school songs Mrs. Casely Hayford used to impress the pupils with the importance of Africa, the African way of life and the utility and beauty of Creole speech. Although not exactly sure of the wording, after so many years, Mrs. Caulker offered the following simple songs as illustrations:

The Palm Tree, The Palm Tree
What Comes Out of the Palm Tree, The Palm Tree
Don't You Love the Palm Tree, that God has made for you
Yes we do, yes we do

What Comes Out of the Palm Tree, The Palm Tree

(and each stanza answers "Thatch for Roofs," "Yeast for Bread," "Nuts to Crack," "Rings to Wear").

Creole Lullaby

'E 'old tight brown baby
Nar im back
Hush yah me borbor
Nor cry oh!

But de ojah loose
Baby fall down with a wack
Hush yah me borbor
Nor die oh![22]

There was, of course, in addition the very proper school song which
pupils proudly sang on all public occasions:

School Song

The Girls' Vocational School, may its spirit live for aye
So cheer it girls with a mighty cheer and a hip, hip, hip hurrah

And a hip, hip, hip hurrah with a clap
With a hip and a hip, and a hip, hip, hip hurrah

We stand for truth and might and courage to meet each blow
To form a part of Africa's heart that all the world may know girls

That all the world may know with a clap
With a hip and a hip and a hip, hip, hip hurrah

We stand for union and peace till joy and love abound
That our sons may share our faith and prayer and scatter sunshine
round

And scatter sunshine round. With a clap
With a hip and a hip and a hip, hip, hip hurrah

We work with body and brain that intelligence may increase
Give life the best and return the best and gain content and peace
And gain content and peace
With a clap
And a hip, hip, hip hurrah.

Mrs. Caulker remembered Mrs. Casely Hayford's religious nature
and her stress on pronunciation in school and in all the competitions in
which the school participated.

There are also the two reports mentioned earlier, on education in
Sierra Leone, which give an assessment of the role and impact of the

Girls' Vocational School.[23] The Sumner account is rather straightforward, based on documented material. There are some differences with what Mrs. Casely Hayford, at least, recorded herself and the material does not appear to be based on any discussion with Mrs. Casely Hayford. Sumner, asserts that the first school opened in 1898 at the suggestion of Rev. Charles Marke. His information on enrollments through the years is helpful and may or may not be accurate, but in the absence of other documentation must be used. His final assessment of the school was that

> although it was short-lived, it contributed to the introduction of the social aspect of education in Sierra Leone. The management of the kindergarten work was under the direction of a specialist in kindergarten methods who spent three years studying in Germany. Weaving was taught, together with Domestic Science and Housecraft. A class was conducted for brides, but this was not successful and had to be discontinued. As could be easily seen, the ideas in operation in this school were not the usual bookworm type, but they aimed at giving pupils the necessary background for a well-ordered social life. Most of the children paid no school fees and the school received no government grant. At one time the founder sent a report of her endeavors to Governor Hodson who gave a donation of 120 pounds after inspecting the school in person.[24]

The other available account of the school is perhaps more helpful, because it incorporates material Mrs. Casely Hayford herself reported. Unfortunately, it is still in manuscript form. According to this manuscript, Mrs. Casely Hayford's attempt in 1897 to start a school made it the first private enterprise in establishing Girls' Secondary Education in Sierra Leone.[25] And in discussing this endeavor with Mrs. Casely Hayford, Miss Mason said she saw it as merely a first step. "Looking back, one can hardly call it a school except that the tuition was confined more or less to the Three Rs with physical culture and music thrown in."

The Mason account is most helpful in presenting Mrs. Casely Hayford's philosophy and her recollections. She states in her interview that

> I was always convinced that secondary education for girls entailed a high standard of social and moral behavior – rather than academic attainment; my school was organized to give a broad and more cultural education ... However, I was criticized both by the government and the people, so I decided to go to America with my niece Kathleen to launch an appeal fund ... We visited many Negro

schools and were impressed by the vocational training which the
girls received ... we saw at Tuskegee a school for brides to be,
which I thought was our greatest need because it would mean a vast
improvement in home life ... upon my return home I still could get
no support from a most antagonistic government but my own
people would not look at me probably because they *were not accustomed to native leadership.* The school catered mostly to the children
of the elite and never exceeded 100 because of the lack of space. It
was housed in the old family house of the Smiths opposite the Post
Office at Gloucester Street. I foolishly joined partnership with a
European and entrusted the older girls to her care, while I took the
younger girls. It was a disastrous partnership. During a vacation in
Europe the European lady left and took most of the older girls with
her, thus reducing the enrollment from 80 to 18 ... it also left me
without funds, so I returned to the United States where I was
always more successful in reaching the wealthy, one lady gave an
annuity of 20 pounds a year.[26]

My own salary was never more than 6 pounds a month – the fees
were low and used for teachers. I was convinced that a country
cannot rise above the level of its womanhood. In the curriculum not
much stress was put on academic subjects, though some were
taught. I did not believe in burdening the pupils with homework
and examinations but encouraged and developed the teaching of
concrete and practical subjects. Some of the students sat for and
passed the Junior Cambridge Examination. We had biology, also
domestic science and handicrafts like rug and basket making.

But the school was best in music, singing and folk dancing.
Gladys was a great help. Much time was also allowed for recrea-
tion. The playing field was not big but there were many facilities.
The senior staff left because the senior classes were eliminated.
The school finally closed in 1940. My darling daughter unfortunately was not able to carry on, otherwise, the school would have
been here today. There was universal regret when the school was
closed.

During this period of her life Mrs. Casely Hayford was also busy with
other activities, some related and some not to the running of the school.
She gives some indications in her *Memoirs* of what these activities were.

In 1935 my health was so precarious that I scraped the money
together for another visit to England. So in June of that year I
boarded another German boat, the *Wahehe.* This time the whole
ship's company, from the captain downwards, vied with each other

to make us thoroughly happy.[27] There was so much attention to detail. For instance, it was rumored that my birthday was on June 27th, and to my astonishment at tea that afternoon, there appeared a splendid birthday cake lavish with currants and raisins, candied peel, covered with icing that scintillated like sparks in the sun.

On arriving in London, I went to stay at the Headquarters of the Y.W.C.A. There was a biennial conference in process, and I was utterly bewildered by the crowds of well-dressed women rushing hither and thither. At first no one took any notice of me; then I felt a gentle tap on my shoulder. Turning around, I saw a white-haired old lady, who beamed and enquired whether I had come for the conference. I told her I had only just arrived from Africa and knew nothing about it, but was looking for some place to stay. "Oh," she said, "I will take you up to the secretary at once."[28]

Thereupon we entered the lift and found ourselves in the presence of the august lady, who telephoned to the International Branch to see if they could accommodate me. The answer was in the negative. Then my white-haired old lady, who proved to be the daughter of Lord Kinnaird, founder of the movement, sat down and wrote a letter, which she handed to me. "I have my own special branch in Westbourne Park, and I have written to the Secretary to take you in." So I arrived, and found myself comfortably ensconced in a bedroom on the fourth floor. Everyone was so very considerate and nice to me, but I went down with a nasty attack of sore-throat and fever, and had it not been for the ministrations of my nephew, Charles Easmon, and his wife, I would have fared very badly.

The building appeared to have been a school, built in the days when it was sacrilege for pupils to look out of the window. Hence they are placed adjacent to the ceiling, so that in order to view the landscape, I had to climb a ladder. During my stay there, my old friend, Mrs. Warren, was a frequent visitor and she drove me about in her beautiful limousine. There were visits, too, from both Mrs. Coleridge-Taylor and Mrs. Paul Robeson, which cheered me up wonderfully.

Eventually, I migrated to the International House, off Gower Street, and there, for the first time, met Miss Lucy Deakin of Achimota College, now the University of Ghana, at Accra, who was home on furlough. She had been informed of my movements by Dr. Kenneth Todd, an English friend in Sierra Leone, who subsequently joined the Achimota staff. So she literally took me under her wing. She motored me to Cheadam, a little village near Stoke-on-Trent, where my life-long friends of the old Jersey days, the

Rev. Edward and Mrs. Charlesworth, were residing. A week with them, full of joyful reminiscences of vanished years, ended only too quickly and I returned to London to find an invitation from the Oxford Group to attend their International House party which was being held at Lady Margaret Hall, Oxford, in the very near future. I refused the invitation, not only because of my tragic experiences there a few years previously.[29]

So I declined, frankly, telling them I could not afford it. Another pressing invitation followed, stating that if I could only stay for a day or two, it would be better than nothing. Knowing that Kenneth Todd was already there and I would have at least one friend, I went. I had never before seen anything like it. We entered the magnificent dining hall to find it full of large tables, packed with laughing, merry crowds, from the four quarters of the earth. Among them I saw a young African from the Gold Coast, he and I being the only representatives of my race.

The next evening there was a large international gathering, presided over by the founder, Dr. Buchman. I noticed he had been watching me during the whole session, and on this occasion he asked me to speak. Several people came up to the platform afterwards, among them a young girl who accosted me thus: "Don't you know who I am?" "I am afraid I don't," was my reply. "Well, I am the girl who drove you home last night. I hated black people and when I saw that Kenneth Todd had asked me to drive a black woman home, I very nearly refused. However, after hearing you speak, look what I am doing"; she tucked her arm into mine with a warm little squeeze, as we walked down the aisle together.

This experience with the Oxford Group Movement in Oxford was to be Mrs. Casely Hayford's last public involvement. It served her in good stead after the closing of the school and until her death.

Quite a lot of M.R.A. people have visited me in our modest little home in Freetown, and they have always left cherished memories behind. Once Captain Ian Cape, of the Fleet Air Arm, spent half an hour with me. We didn't have much to say to each other, but he made a lasting impression on me. Captain David Sturdy, R.A.M.C., who spent 18 months in our midst, must find an honourable mention in these *Memoirs*. Not being over-burdened with work except in the mornings, he spent every available minute trying to further his movement in Sierra Leone.

It is not surprising that the Oxford Group would have had an appeal

for Mrs. Casely Hayford. Her life-long interest in world peace, the ideas
that originally brought Miss Graves into her life, her fascination with the
Bahai Movement and her generally broad but deep religious commitment which went beyond the restrictions of race and country, coupled
with the evangelical zeal in recruitment on the part of some of her
friends, like Kenneth Todd, brought her into the fold.

The Reverend E.J.Y. Harris, a retired Methodist minister in
Freetown, discussed with me these early days of the M.R.A. in
Freetown and Mrs. Casely Hayford's participation. His version, given
when he was quite advanced in years, differs from that of Mrs. Casely
Hayford to the extent that he remembered her trip to England in 1935 as
being for the purpose of attending the Oxford Group meeting in
Oxford. According to her account, however, her attendance at the
meeting was a happy coincidence of just being in the area at the time.
Reverend Harris had kindly prepared for me a very brief written
description of the history of the Moral Rearmament Movement in
Freetown in which he also gave his version:

> On the 15th of May, 1935, I met two persons. Mrs. Rosamond
> Jones on Jones Street in the morning about nine o'clock and she
> said to me "Don't you think we need a revival in the churches?"
> The same day at 4 o'clock I met Dr. Kenneth Todd at the porch of
> the Zion Church, Wesley Street and he put forth the same question
> to me. – "Don't you think we need revival in the churches?" I
> thought this must be the work of the Holy Spirit. And we said that
> no revival can take place that does not begin with the individual and
> then and there we decided to meet the next day in the morning at 5
> o'clock at the Methodist Boys' High School for a 'Quiet Time'" –
> Rev. C.L. Leopold, Dr. Kenneth Todd and Rev. E.J.K. Harris.
> That was the beginning of the Moral Rearmament in Sierra Leone.
> That same year in July we contacted Mrs. Casely Hayford who
> became very much interested in the Fellowship. It was then called
> the Oxford Group. That same year she went to England and met
> Dr. Frank Buchman, the world initiator of the Group, and they
> talked together about it and on her return her home became a
> center of the group, and for several years we were meeting there
> (Gloucester St.). Other persons who were interested were the late
> Sir Milton Margai ... also the late Dr. Teddy Renner ... and Mr.
> Fijimi Brandon, Government Printer and Mrs. Evelyn Carew-
> Coker, Matron of Fourah Bay College.

When I visited the Reverend Mr. Harris the movement was moribund

in Freetown, but I assume from his conversation that Mrs. Casely
Hayford had been an active participant as long as she lived.

While maintaining her international and religious interests through
the Moral Rearmament Movement and clearly, a leader in it, Mrs.
Casely Hayford also continued her social life with the more distinguished members of the community, now that her retirement from
teaching had given her more time to do so. Mrs. Cummings-John
describes these activities pursued by Mrs. Casely Hayford at this period
of her life:

> Aunty Ade was a highly cultured society lady and together with
> others of her kind formed an exclusive class – the Ladies' Musical
> Society – giving teas, lunches, dinners and garden parties, and were
> always friendly with the Governor's wife, helping her with the
> serving and supervision of the servants and the decorations of the
> Government House, and also serving as a medium between the
> Government and the women of Sierra Leone. There were ban-
> quets and balls, tennis and outdoor and indoor games.[30]

In her *Memoirs*, Mrs. Casely Hayford acknowledged this on-going
association with Government House:

> There is a very dramatic play called "She Stoops to Conquer"
> But there was no stooping about Lady Mountbatten. She is so high
> in the social firmament that she is quite unconscious of her atti-
> tude. Consequently, we felt no condescension, no patronage, and
> no superiority, because they simply were not there. She conquered
> by the irresistible charm of an utterly selfless spirit. The authorities
> had mapped out a dreadfully strenuous programme, and for a lady
> not accustomed to our enervating, life-sucking climate, it almost
> amounted to hard labour. At a cocktail party given in her honour at
> Government House, she shook hands with something like 650
> guests. It was a handshake – not a limp, loose affair, but a hand-
> shake whose source was the heart, so that warmth, kindliness and
> goodwill circulated right to the finger tips. In this, of course, she
> was most ably supported by His Excellency the Governor and Lady
> Beresford-Stooke, who never spared themselves along these lines.
> Lady Mountbatten had only arrived that morning, and in the
> afternoon had taken the Barracks and Red Cross Centers out of
> town in her stride.
>
> As an octogenarian, I was feeling rather tired, and someone
> kindly brought me a chair, in which I was comfortably ensconced
> when the A.D.C brought up this distinguished visitor to have a

chat. And how did she greet me? – "Don't get up," she smiled. This – from the late King's cousin to a little old African woman – shows how considerate the British nobility can be. Had I been a hundred years old, I would still have got up. And what did I say to her? "After these strenuous exertions, I hope you are going to bed." She gave a ringing little laugh – "After this, I am dining with the Brigadier, but I still look forward to seeing you again tomorrow."

The next day was equally strenuous. Lady Mountbatten went through miles of hospital wards, with a kindly word here and there for the sick patients. She visited the Government Hospital, under the charge of my nephew, Dr. M.C.F. Easmon, Director of Medical Services. Thinking of Lady Mountbatten's fatigue, he pointed to a ward and whispered, "Don't take her in there." She heard him, but went through the ward nevertheless, with a comment to my nephew, "What I do, I must do thoroughly."

Her visit was only of two days' duration, so it was quite impossible to carry out the programme planned. One thing, however, that was not planned, was a cocktail party arranged by the Indian community. She had left such a trail of affection behind her in India that the people here felt they dare not allow her to depart without some definite recognition of their love and esteem. So this party was sandwiched in with all the other engagements, and once again, this lady showed her greatness by appearing as the guest of the evening in her simple work-a-day clothes, there being neither time nor opportunity to change into anything more elaborate.

As a parting gesture, she pressed my hand in both of hers, saying, "It has been such a pleasure to meet you."

Mrs. Casely Hayford was a writer of fiction as well as non-fiction. In addition to the *Memoirs* on which this book is based, clearly an unusual endeavor for a woman of her day anywhere, references have been made to her article, "A Girl's School in West Africa," published in the *Southern Workman*, and her controversial coverage in *West Africa* of the then Prince of Wales' visit to Sierra Leone.

Less well known but equally provocative are her two pieces of fiction – both short stories – "Mista Courifer" and "Savages." "Mista Courifer" is the better known of the two, having been published in a popular anthology.[31] "Savages" appeared in the journal of the short-lived organization, The West African Society, and is mentioned only inferentially by Mrs. Casely Hayford in her *Memoirs* as "a response to the damaging article on African intelligence by Huxley."

In "Mista Courifer," in an amusing and simple way, Mrs. Casely

Hayford captures all the humor and pressure involved in Africans trying
not to be themselves but Englishmen. Mr. Courifer, a Freetown carpenter specializing in the making of coffins and sometime preacher, having
been briefly to England, is determined that his lifestyle and his son,
particularly, shall look English. His house furnishings, the clothes he
wears and those he orders for this grown son from Liverpool were
naturally all English. The son, Thomas, has a minor civil service position from which his father, naturally, expects him to rise, but Thomas
rebels. He rebels against the discriminatory practices on the job which
permit long leaves for Europeans and no vacations for Africans; he
rebels against the Liverpool clothes and the European-style house. He
appears publicly in African dress with his bride-to-be similarly garbed
and they plan to live in a simple but tastefully done mud hut.

In this story Mrs. Casely Hayford presents her basic attitude towards
social change which is very definitely a reflection of her own life experiences – the need to blend the best of both cultures – African and
European, Sierra Leonean and English. Thomas should be in African
dress and live in an African-style house but he should also speak up for
his rights against a European employer who in turn can be expected to be
reasonable. His wife should be chosen to be his companion, not a
household drudge and cook as his mother is.

In "Mista Courifer", Mrs. Casely Hayford places the responsibility
for the present situation and the needed changes in the hands of the men
in the society. The women in her story – Thomas' mother, his sister and
his future wife – are all reference points, not actors. One surmises Mrs.
Casely Hayford herself had felt the rigidity of too many women.

"Savages," an even shorter story than "Mista Courifer," is set on a
cargo boat en route to West Africa, in 1907, "which happily lacks the
snobbery of a liner." Mrs. Abiose Ilorin, obviously a European, is the
only woman passenger and therefore a kind of companion to the Captain, also a European. As the ship approaches the shores of West Africa,
the captain demurs – "this place is full of savages," he announces,
further explaining that he puts in there only because the natives supply
palm oil for the rum he delivers.

Shortly, canoes full of natives – Kroomen "magnificently strong"
including "brave, fearless and courageous women" come alongside the
cargo boat. One couple catch Mrs. Ilorin's eye as together they mount
the boat by the rope ladder, the man gently helping his wife as she
climbs. "Hardly savages," Mrs. Ilorin thinks and says.

A few days later, the Captain informs Mrs. Ilorin that "that giant
Krooman" has been badly injured – and there he lies, groaning and
looking helpless with his little wife beside him "speechless, motionless,

unconscious of the daylight and the darkness." The Captain promises soon to "find an old mattress for him and rig up some little shelter from the rain." Mrs. Ilorin shares silently their tragedy and gently touches the hand of the wife.

At the end of the voyage, Mrs. Ilorin seeks a dictionary from the Captain to find "a definition of a savage."

Mrs. Casely Hayford's fictional writings reflect more accurately than her *Memoirs* her resentment and painful observations of the cost to the colonized people of colonization – the loss of the value of traditional ways and the impossibility of being a fully accepted participant in a western culture. It is regrettable that none of her many speeches in their entirety is available for undoubtedly she spoke often and forcibly of this dilemma.

The continued activity in her old age augmented perhaps by some belated recognition in Sierra Leone as an educationalist and international figure was acknowledged by her being awarded the M.B.E. by George the Sixth on 9 June 1949 in the 13th year of his reign. Mrs. Casely Hayford was then 81 years of age.

XII

"A Close Up and a Close Down"

To the end of her life, Adelaide Smith Casely Hayford viewed herself and the events around her with remarkable objectivity. She was a person abut whom people had strong feelings but who also saw herself in relation to other people. Fortunately, she wrote her final self-assessment, which has never been published before.

And now comes the most difficult portion of these *Memoirs* to relate. To see myself as others see me, not to mention my own close observation of predominant characteristics.

One thing is glaringly patent – my tremendous conceit – not so much vanity as conceit. How I revel in nice little pats on the back and in neatly turned little compliments! How happy I feel inside ...

Then undoubtedly I am a bit of a snob. I have often looked down upon people of my own race who have been plentifully helped to an inferiority complex. Of this I am heartily ashamed and am glad to report it is definitely on the wane. It is not a bit of use grumbling at this type of European treatment, when we do exactly the same to each other.

I am also a very poor loser. I haven't the exuberant sporting spirit which takes everything smiling in its stride and I envy people who have.

"Do it at once!" should have been nailed on my back at birth because procrastination has stolen so much time ...

Then may I whisper that I am a bit of a coward. Many a time I have shunned "being in the right with two or three" and have decided somewhat reluctantly to follow the crowd.

But over and against these set-backs, and standing pre-eminently higher is my Napoleonic spirit of domination. This cannot be gainsaid, and I believe it is more or less true of very short people who want to make up in importance the inches they lack in stature.

We all have some good points, however. One which will never be annihilated is my inexhaustible fund of irrepressible bubbling humor, definitely inherited from our beloved Mother ... I am more than thankful for this God-given asset which has been my saving grace in many heart-breaking situations.

Yet another characteristic is my inordinate love of children. I see God in every little child's face, be they ever so dirty and unkempt! The freedom from guile, the exquisite purity, the unalloyed joy in the ripple of childish laughter makes me so very happy.

At Christmas 1940, I was obliged to close down my school, through the exigencies of war, old age and lack of definite pecuniary security. Is it any wonder that bidding adieu to the children, especially the little ones, contact with whom had done so much to enrich my life, became really bitter sorrow.

My niece, Camele, Teddy Renner's wife, has summed me up to a "T". She says, "Auntie's friends are divided into two air-tight compartments – those who are good and those who are not good and I come in between."

Not so very long ago, someone said to me, "Your father must have been quite an outstanding character, but what a pity he did not lay more stress on amassing money and increasing his wealth." Why, of course, he couldn't. He was not made that way. "But supposing this had been his aim in life, where would you have been?" We would probably have been puffed up with our own importance, bulging out in love of display, demanding pride of place, snobbishly patronizing those who were worse off, lavish on selfish expenditure and miserly in the interest of others ...

Quite recently one of my friends said to me, "What a pity you didn't remain in America. It would have made you!" I wondered. It certainly would have made my portrait, but would it have made me? It is patently clear that one cannot serve God and mammon. Generally speaking from my own observations, the people who are prosperous are definitely lacking in the eternal verities. This does not apply to rich folks whose wealth is sanctified to God's use.

As I look back on my long life, I know that chronic impecuniosity has been the least of all my hardships. Infinitely worse has been the hard-baked criticism, the cold-blooded indifference, the deliberate schemes to put spokes in the wheels of my progress, the abnormal jealousy, the deep animosity, and the utter lack of appreciation on the part of my own people. These coupled with the ruthless overdosing of an inferiority complex and dreadful racial discrimination on the part of the white race have often filled my soul with deep resentment.

It is quite true that there have been times when more money

would have been welcomed. But there have been so many compensations, not the least being the tried and tested friendships of my many white friends from the highest walks of life to the lowest, and if in reading these *Memoirs* they forget all I have narrated, I want them to remember that all of the tragic experiences, all the bitterness, all the anguish I have suffered because of my color, have been entirely wiped under by the weight of love, kindliness, and goodwill meted out to me on every side by members of their race.

I have lost practically all my earthly possessions either through thieves or misadventure, but thank God I retain the spontaneous hearty laughter of my girlhood especially when directed against myself. I feel that people are laughing with me rather than at me so it is quite a communal affair.

Now, I am holding out my fast diminishing torch for the younger generation to blaze afresh and carry on the trail. For the most part they have had splendid educational facilities and opportunities of training.

Shall it be Noren Renner, now a Doctor in the Air Force, the eldest son of my nephew Teddy, the Director of Medical Services in Sierra Leone, or one of his junior brothers, Louis or Archie? They have all been brought up in England, but there is still time for them to learn to know Africa. Or my grand-nephew Teddy or Charlie Renner? Or my step-son Archie Casely Hayford who of late has reached tremendous heights of patriotism, but is rather advanced in years. Or my one grandchild, Cobina Sydney Hunter – Gladys' offspring – not yet a teen-ager but who shows great promise – or young Charlie Easmon, an outstanding intelligent youngster of five summers, the only son of my nephew, Dr. M.C.F. Easmon, or one of those youngsters whose family ties are not quite so strong – a Wright, a Smith or a Reffell.

The evening shadows are falling. I am facing the setting sun, perhaps even more beautiful in its misty radiance than in the zenith of its noonday glory.

I am sorry, because I am lonely, having buried my six brothers and sisters, the last being Mrs. Farrell Easmon, who passed away painlessly and peacefully in the early hours of Christmas morning, 1951.

My final word to subsequent torch-bearers is just this: NEVER be ashamed of your color. God *never* makes mistakes, and when he gave you a black skin, I am sure He felt you could serve Him better in this way than in any other way. I want your aim in life to be the best type of black personality you can be. I found from experience that this is the only way to happiness, the only way to retain one's self-respect, the only way to win the respect of other races and the only way in which we can ever give a real contribution to the world.

Adelaide Smith Casely Hayford died in Freetown, Sierra Leone, on 24 January 1960. In spite of the reality of the world around her, in spite of her own experiences, she never ceased thinking or acting like a member of the 19th century Creole élite. Hers was a world of "noblesse oblige" – of class, education, vocation and money. In the fine points there were, it is true, some significant omissions in this final summing up. Where was the life long love of music, or even the continuous concern over her health? What of her role as Mother, as Wife? How could she not remember Gladys or even J.E. Casely Hayford? Her last statement was not at all enlightening for the uninformed. What were her real lasting satisfactions; her deepest disappointments in so long a life?

Mrs. Casely Hayford remained a very private person; she had, according to several informants, a select circle of friends, people like the Taylor Cummings, Mrs. Conton, the Hebrons, the Wrights, the Stuarts, the Markes, the Bostons; but none of these appeared in any part of her *Memoirs*. Her concern was only with persons associated with the school, not her world outside. And in her final roll call, only family, close and distant, were acknowledged.

I find some difficulty in seeing Mrs. Casely Hayford as a humorous person, though she clearly saw herself as one. But there is little evidence of humor, for the unconvinced, either in her *Memoirs* or her letters.

For me, the most interesting aspect of Mrs. Casely Hayford's personality, as a member of the 19th century Creole élite, is her continuous discussion of race and color as a basis of status. Nineteenth-century Freetown was essentially a color-blind society – status was based on education, life-style, money, religion. I have earlier made some attempts to explain why color was so important to her. Her own difference in color from the rest of the family, her identification with her mother who was very dark, her felt rejection by her white stepmother, other experiences in England, Germany, and especially the United States – for all of these reasons, Mrs. Casely Hayford understood and accepted the burden of color, but that she saw it as her mission to convey this to her compatriots is saying something very different. It is admitting the reality and importance of color in this African society where both insiders and outsiders have said it is not the case.

It is important to note that, wherever a people of one color is suppressed by the people of another color, understandably color becomes important as a symbol of status. Even in nearby Liberia where there was no visible white dominant group, there was considerable conflict in the nineteenth century over color – between the "pure Negro" and the mulattoes.

Because of her family, her experiences, her talents, her writings, and her vocational accomplishments, Adelaide Smith Casely Hayford was clearly a most unusual woman – for her time anywhere and for Africa in modern times. Her educational and personal philosophy was well ahead of her time. One must ask why she was not better known. Was it that she was almost too equal to be accepted; too advanced to be understood by European and American society?

Her personality, sharpened by a quick mind, was never afraid of challenge or even indictment but she was always too big to fear, to feel inferior or to carry grudges. Of course her friends and other contemporaries often saw her not only differently from the way she saw herself but differently depending on who they were – she was a highly cultured lady or a well accomplished musician, or a vindictive woman, or a gentle, sweet and most beautiful lady whose courtesy and genteel manners remained with her in her old age, or one always moving with the "uppits," or proud of her African origins, or a speaker of perfect English always in a soft but clearly heard voice, or pleasant when you knew her, or of high morals and very religious, but never a good mixer – one, rather, who kept within her social class and was forever reminding others of her kind not to forget where they belonged.

As strong as it appeared to be, Mrs. Casely Hayford's African identity was forged more by her experiences away from Africa than from her life in Africa – first in Germany, perhaps in England, and most certainly in America. For in America she learned to derive strength from associating with a wide variety of black people, to see and learn from their accomplishments but at the same time to feel as they did the unbridled fist of prejudice.

The absence in her life of a male – companion, protector, friend, father, brother (Tom was always in need of her help rather than the other way around), husband or son – in a society such as one finds in Africa made her more vulnerable to the stabs of community jealousy. Even men dared attack her. For example, C.D. Hotobah-During, a barrister-at-law, was a frequent public detractor. To be unusual, advanced, and unprotected is to invite community attack. Her lack of financial resources proved to be her final deprivation.

But in her life on three continents over nine decades, Mrs. Casely Hayford managed to symbolize the problems of modern women – and of modern black women. Identity (cultural and racial), marriage, motherhood, widowhood, career goals, community responsibility are all reflected in the life of this remarkable woman. Perhaps the most important conclusion, if one can evaluate in a meaningful way one life over another, that can be drawn from knowing Adelaide Smith Casely Hayford is that not only was she a survivor but she was an achiever as well!

NOTES

Introduction

1. Maude Cuney Hare, an Afro-American from Texas, married to William Hare, was very active in artistic circles in Boston. Meta Warrick Fuller was a distinguished Afro-American sculptor who lived just outside of Boston with her husband, Dr. Solomon Fuller, who was born in Liberia and became the first black psychiatrist. Mrs. Fuller studied with Rodin in Paris and she and her husband were the parents of four sons. Otelia Cromwell was an Afro-American scholar and teacher. A graduate of Smith College in 1900 and a Ph.D in English from Yale, she taught in the schools of the District of Columbia and was Professor at the Miner Teachers College in that city. Miss Cromwell was the author of several articles and three books, the last a biography of Lucretia Mott, the Quaker abolitionist.
2. John W. Cromwell, father of Otelia Cromwell, was an editor, historian, teacher, and lawyer and a member of a talented group of blacks for whom Alexander Crummell was mentor and leader and who in their personal lives as well as in their organizational affiliations (The American Negro Academy, for example) were particularly concerned about Africa, knew well or corresponded with many Africans and felt keenly the relationship between Africans and Afro-Americans.

Chapter 1

1. There is disagreement as to whether the name Casely Hayford should be hyphenated or not. As Mr. Casely Hayford did not use the hyphen, it is omitted in this book. Moreover in his will, Mr. Casely Hayford explained his position: "All the issue of my said son (Archibald Casely Hayford) lawfully begotten under the Customary Law of the Gold Coast or by the Laws of England or the Gold Coast shall bear the name of "Casely" immediately before the surname "Hayford" to the end that Casely Hayfords may be known as such from one generation to the other ..."
2. Nannie H. Burroughs, an Afro-American Baptist educator, started an Industrial Training School for Girls just outside of Washington, D.C. Her school and the woman herself became an important model for Mrs. Casley Hayford.
3. Arthur T. Porter, *Creoledom, A Study of the Development of Freetown Society* (London: Oxford University Press, 1953), pp.20-1. See also James W. St. G. Walter, *The Black Loyalists: The Search for a Promised Land: Nova Scotia and Sierra Leone* (New York: Holmes and Maiers Publishing Co., 1976).
4. *Ibid.,* p.25.
5. John Peterson, *Province of Freedom, A History of Sierra Leone 1787–1870* (London: Faber and Faber, 1969), pp.27–8.
6. Porter, *op. cit.,* p.36.
7. Leo Spitzer, *The Creoles of Sierra Leone, Responses to Colonialism, 1870–1945* (Madison: The University of Wisconsin Press, 1974), p.11.
8. Christopher Fyfe, *A History of Sierra Leone* (London: Oxford University Press, 1962), p.170.
9. Porter, *op. cit.,* p.57.
10. A.B.C. Sibthorpe, *The History of Sierra Leone,* 4th ed. (London: Frank Cass and Co.,

1970), p.14.

11. In the interest of more efficient or facile administration and in establishing the necessary public hegemony, a colonial territory was often divided into a colony per se with the usual administrative set-up of a Governor, appointed officials and clerks and so-called protected area within the sphere of European control but technically ruled by sovereign chiefs and in due time Protected areas, with the proper official Ordinances, were changed into official Protectorates.

When the Settlers were white as they were in all other parts of the British Empire in Africa, the distinction between the westernized white Colony and the traditional black Protectorate was easily seen, accepted and maintained. But when, as in Sierra Leone, the Settlers in the colony were black, or certainly not white, there was a sensitivity and tension – and still is – about this distinction. Obviously, one of the problems of creating a free and unified nation is obliterating any traces of these historical differences between the Freetown colony and the up-country Protectorate. Mrs. Casely Hayford lived at a time when these distinctions were taken for granted.

12. Porter, *op. cit.*, p.45.
13. Sibthorpe, *op. cit.*, pp. 3, 50, 57.
14. Peterson, *op. cit.*, p.284.
15. Fyfe, *op. cit.*, p.437.
16. *Ibid.*, p.437.
17. Rev. E.W. Fashole-Luke, "Religion in Freetown," p.10. Christopher Fyfe and Eldred Jones, *Freetown, A Symposium* (Freetown: Sierra University Press, 1968).
18. T.N. Goddard, *The Handbook of Sierra Leone* (New York: Negro Universities Press, 1969). The dates here are different; Fourah Bay was founded in 1828; the first Bishop, Vidal, arrived in Freetown and St. George's became a cathedral on 6 December 1852. The actual ceremony was probably in 1853.
19. Fyfe, *op. cit.*, pp. 199, 464.
20. See note, p.27.
21. Spitzer, *op. cit.*, pp. 23-5.
22. Peterson, *op. cit.*, pp.294-6.
23. Fyfe, *op. cit.*, pp.197, 406, 434-5.
24. For a partial genealogy of the Smith family, see Appendix.
25. *Ibid.*, p.438.
26. *Ibid.*, p.537.
26a. *Ibid.*, p.334-445.
27. Ronald Ross et al, *Report of the Malaria Expedition of the Liverpool School of Tropical Medicine Parasitology* (Liverpool, 1900).
28. Hollish Lynch, *Edward Wilmot Blyden, Pan-American Patriot, 1832–1919,* London: Oxford University Press, p.55, describes Blyden as "one of a few Negroes to make a significant impact on the English-speaking literary and scholastic world in the nineteenth century." Clearly, Blyden was an impressive figure whose intellectual values influenced both Liberia and Sierra Leone. For a fuller account of his life and influence see Lynch, chapter 5, pp.84-104 and Chapter 10, pp.210-47.
29. Spitzer, *op. cit.*, p.64.
30. Fyfe, *op. cit.*, p.615.
31. Spitzer, *op. cit.*, p.159.
32. "Because of its Marxist, militant and anti-colonist orientation, the government found reason during the war years (WWII) to keep in confinement with prisoners of war, Mr. Wallace Johnson who at the time was the organizing secretary of the West African Youth League." Porter, *Creoledom*, p.128.
33. Porter, *op. cit.*, p.26.
34. Graham Greene, *The Heart of the Matter: The Collected Works of Graham Greene* (London: William Heinemann Limited, 1977), p.22.

Chapter II

1. While this might have been written government policy and the dream of the founders, in fact the government did little to support the education of Africans at any level. Most of their education was provided by missionaries. Government scholarships for primary schools were not introduced until the 1920s and Fourah Bay College, started by the Church Missionary Society, did not get government support until the 1940s although there was a government-subsidized teacher training programme in the late 'twenties and early 'thirties.
2. Fyfe, *A History of Sierra Leone, op. cit.,* p.182.
3. Sibthorpe, *The History of Sierra Leone, op. cit.,* p.174.
4. *Ibid.,* p.178.
5. "Outside child" is a term to describe being born out of wedlock. It is also possible that these children were excluded for reasons of morality.
6. *Ibid.,* pp.178, 202-3.
7. Fyfe, *op. cit.,* p.425.
8. Sibthorpe, *op. cit.,* p.188.
9. See below, Chapter V, p.55.
10. Annual Report of the Education Department for the Year 1924, p.8.
11. These nine points are excerpted out of order from the twenty-four main sections and innumerable sub-sections of the Ordinance.
12. The plans for this speech are discussed later in her correspondence with Miss Graves. See also *S.L.W.N.* 5/25/32, pp.10-11. The meeting was the Conference on the Child called by Save the Children Fund, Spring 1931. Mrs. Casely Hayford was to have been the West African delegate.

Chapter III

1. Margaret Priestly's history of the Brew Family in Ghana is a major exception. See Margaret Priestly, *West African Trade and Coast Society, A Family Study* (London: Oxford University Press, 1969).
2. Fyfe, *A History of Sierra Leone, op. cit.,* p.471.
3. Capt. F.W. Butt Thompson, *First Generation of Sierra Leoneans,* p.19.
4. Fyfe, *op. cit.,* p.348.
5. *Ibid.,* p.328.
6. Butt Thompson, *op. cit.,* p.52, refers to William Smith as being "born in 1816 and repatriated when he was nine years of age, educated by the CMS, becoming a junior clerk in the Mixed Commission Court, eventually its Registrar and Police Magistrate. He died in Jersey in 1896, the father of as remarkable a family as this colony has known."
7. Licentiateship of the Faculty of Physicians and Surgeons of Glasgow.
8. The specialist qualifications of a surgeon as a Fellow of the Royal College of Surgeons of Edinburgh.
9. The above material was provided by Mrs. Charlotte Smith Pobee Wright in Freetown 5/30/70.
10. Fyfe, *op. cit.,* p.295. But according to Dr. Easmon, their relative, Davies, married a sister of Mary, Charlotte, whom Easmon calls the eldest daughter of William Smith, Jr. The family records, however, indiciate that Charlotte was the youngest daughter of William Smith, Jr., and that she died before reaching maturity. Her dates were 1851–1857.
11. Dr. M.C.F. Easmon, "Sierra Leone Doctors of the Nineteenth Century," *Sierra*

Leone Studies, p.51.
12. Fyfe, op. cit., pp.471-2.
13. Dr. M.C.F. Easmon, "A Nova Scotian Family," Sierra Leone Studies, pp.57-60a.
14. L.R.Q.C.P. is Licentiate of the Royal College of Physicians.
15. Minnie Tate was one of the Fisk Jubilee Singers – a choral group that became prominent in Europe under the direction of Frederick Loudin in the interest of raising money for Fisk University, a black college in Nashville, Tennessee.
16. The letters corroborate family litigation in general and specifically with respect to the Spilsbury estate. Mrs. Casely Hayford felt her mother's relatives had mismanaged her property while she was in England.
17. In a letter 9/5/72, Miss Elizabeth Farewell, Headmistress of Jersey College for Girls, in response to my query about Adelaide Smith, wrote "As you know the Island was occupied by the Germans during the Second World War and the College buildings were taken over for use as a Military Hospital. Almost all our records were destroyed during this period. I have no record whatsoever of this early period of the school's history."
18. Anna Melissa Graves with whom Mrs. Casely Hayford carried on an extensive correspondence. See below chapters VI and X.
19. Responding to my letter of inquiry, the Principal of Königin-Katharina-Stift Gymnasium at Stuttgart on 4/17/78 wrote the following: "During the last war most of the school's records were destroyed. We are, therefore, not able to help you in this matter (i.e. supplying the names of the two nieces and the dates of their enrollment). We controlled all the files which we still have, but could not find any dates or names you mentioned."

Chapter IV

1. This hotel is still standing and in use on Oxford Street in Freetown. It was made famous by Graham Greene in his well-known novel, The Heart of the Matter.
2. In 1900 fresh from Smith College, an honors graduate in English, Aunt Tee was asked by her favorite professor, Miss Julia Caverno, who taught Greek at Smith and came from a family of strong abolitionist leanings, to consider a position at Hampton Institute. Against her own preferences and better judgement but not wishing to displease her professor, Aunt Tee took the overnight boat trip to Hampton (being forced by the then "Jim-Crow" laws to sit up on deck all night, as all available rooms were allocated to white passengers – all of whom were men) and was duly interviewed by the president and faculty of Hampton.
   After a day and a half, the president informed her that she was not selected, probably would not do well there, and should look elsewhere. At that time there were few if any blacks, male or female, on the faculty at Hampton and surely few if any white faculty (male or female) who had Aunt Tee's credentials. But perhaps she was over-educated for the post, being neither a real white woman nor the kind of black woman many white educators of the period would have preferred. And knowing Aunt Otelia, I am sure her manner was far from subservient!
3. W.E.B. DuBois, A Recorded Autobiography, interviewed by Mosis Asch, Folkways Records, Album No. FD5511, Side 1, Band 4.

Chapter V

1. Parkes was a distinguished civil servant whose intermediary role between the Creoles

and the chiefs during the Bai Bureh Uprising was crucial, and he most certainly knew the Smith family well. He "had gone to England to study law but illness forced him in 1881 to return to Freetown where he was given a clerkship in the Commandant's office at Bonthe." Having interested himself in Sherbro affairs, writing newspaper articles, etc., he was promoted in 1884 to the Aboriginal Branch of the Secretariat. Competent and industrious, Parkes, like so many promising Creoles at his time, died young at the age of 38.

2. 6 February 1897, p.6.
3. Robinka Mason, *The Development of Girls' Secondary Education in Sierra Leone* (Fourah Bay College, 1957). (Manuscript).
4. D.L. Sumner, *Education in Sierra Leone* (Freetown: Government Printer, 1963).
5. Mason, *op. cit.,* p.9.
6. Sumner, *op. cit.,* p.194.
7. Chief Bai Bureh actually came, not from Mende country in the south but from a northern community.
8. Spitzer, *The Creoles of Sierra Leone, op. cit.,* 1974, pp.60-1.
9. Fyfe, *A History of Sierra Leone, op. cit.,* 1962, p.318.
10. *Ibid.,* p.407.
11. Philip St. Laurent, "The Negro in World History: Samuel Coleridge-Taylor," *Sunday Advertiser,* Tuesday, October n.d., 1968, p.38.
12. *Ibid.,* p.30.
13. Dr. Zachariah Keodirelang Matthews was a leading African political and academic figure in South Africa. He was in 1932 the first African graduate of Fort Hare University College and later its principal. He was also the first African graduate in law in South Africa.

   Z.K. (as he was called) was active in the Africa National Congress, becoming its President for the Cape Province in 1949. He was arrested for high treason and stood trial until 1958 when the charges against him were dropped. At the end of March 1960 he was detained under the State of Emergency and imprisoned for about 6 months without charge or trial. He was named Ambassador to the United States and Permanent Representative to the United States and Permanent Representative to the United Nations for Botswana in 1966. He held both posts until his death in 1968.

Chapter VI

1. For some time I was unable to identify this person and had assumed, from the age Mrs. Casely Hayford must have been at the time, that she had either met this earlier love during her return to Freetown when she first started her school or immediately upon her return to England.

   Fortunately, in the summer of 1979, I met Dr. Raymond Sarif Easmon who volunteered the information that his father, Dr. A. Walter Easmon, uncle of Dr. M.C.F. Easmon was, at one time, engaged to Mrs. Casely Hayford. It was quite true that Dr. A. Walter Easmon had tuberculosis, but he did not die, as her text suggests, he merely married another woman.
2. From a short biographical sketch of Mrs. Casely Hayford prepared for me by Mrs. Constance Cummings-John, a distant relative and former Mayor of Freetown.
3. Margaret Priestly, *West African Trade and Coast Society, A Family Study* (London: Oxford University Press, 1969).
4. *Ibid.,* p.183. yet earlier in his life during the latter part of the nineteenth century, Casely Hayford, along with his uncle, was a figure in a cultural renaissance in Africa which began among the Fanti. Using the column of *The Gold Coast Echo,* a paper he

then edited, he stressed the importance of indigenous customs, language and dress.

5. J.E. Casely Hayford, *Gold Coast Nature Institutions* (London: Sweet and Maxwell, Limited, 1903).

6. J.E. Casely Hayford, *The Truth About the West African Land Question,* (London: C.M. Phillips, 1913).

7. J.E. Casely Hayford, *Ethiopia Unbound* (London: C.M. Phillips, 1911).

8. W.E.B. DuBois, *The Souls of Black Folk* (Chicago: A.C.McClurg & Co., 1903).

9. Casely Hayford, *Ethiopia Unbound op. cit.,* pp.31-3, 35-7.

10. *Ibid.,* p.64.

11. "Ghana's Pioneer Pan-African." *West Africa,* 3 September 1971. p.1011.

12. Gordon MacKay Haliburton, *The Prophet Harris* (London: Longmans Group Ltd. 1971).

13. Priestly, *op. cit.,* p.187.

14. An informant gives the following accepted version of Gladys' difficulties. "Gladys was born slightly crippled – one leg shorter than the other. Doctors say this was due to the shock Aunty Ade had during this period when she was carrying Gladys. This was the end of her marriage. She never saw her husband again." This, or course, was incorrect, but is included because it was a popular version.

15. Many letters are excerpted because of the reluctance of Mr. Archie Casely Hayford to have me spend too much time in his office which admittedly was being redecorated when I was there, or to do more than read the letters. I copied verbatim as quickly as I could the letters with pertinent information but as Miss Graves noted (see below), Mrs. Casely Hayford's handwriting was not the easiest to read. Mr. Casely Hayford did permit me to have copied a few letters – but he came with me while they were being done!

16. This reluctance to have Gladys carried on someone's back, African style, is probably only one of the many indications of Mrs. Casely Hayford's westernization and elite Creole status.

17. Ernest and Mark were two brothers of J.E. Casely Hayford.

18. Mrs. Casely Hayford apparently saw that she, at least, could not live on the Gold Coast and thought that they could be happier in Sierra Leone. Circumstances proved her right.

19. Helen is a daughter of Ernest Casely Hayford.

20. Mrs. Casely Hayford continues to assert the fact that her husband is an Anglican.

21. From a distinguished Ghanaian family, whose relative, Christine Coussey, later marries Kamba Simango, the widower of Mrs. Casely Hayford's niece, Kathleen.

22. This servant is most surely either Irish or English.

23. Charlie, who grew up to be Dr. M.C.F. Easmon mentioned earlier, had a most distinguished career in medicine but ironically, as his obituary in West Africa indicated, in spite of his brilliance (he qualified at 21), because of the changing racial picture and politics in Sierra Leone, he was able to practice there only as a "native medical doctor" in the service of those among whom his own father a generation before had held one of the top positions.

24. Bannerman is another distinguished Cape Coast Family; see Priestly, 1967, p.125.

25. Since they certainly saw each other again and ostensibly kept a common home again in Africa, one must assume she meant they no longer felt as husband and wife to each other, though as the *Memoirs* indicate, she does become pregnant again.

26. John Mensah Sarbah, Barrister-At-Law in the Gold Coast and author of *Fanti Customary Law;* Sarbah's father to whom he dedicated his book was a "merchant, Cape Coast Castle, Sometime Member of the Legislative Council of the Gold Coast Colony, and Captain Commanding the Gold Coast Rifle Corps, During Ashanti Expeditions, 1873–1875."

27. Mrs. Riberro is probably the wife of M.F. Riberro, the barrister-at-law who executed

Casely Hayford's will.

28. Mrs. Clinton is undoubtedly the mother of Mrs. Lizzie Dawson mentioned in the next paragraph.

29. Although she makes no mention of any other pregnancy, an informant did say she had two pregnancies besides Gladys. One was a son. Neither child was born alive.

30. On page 71 in the letter to her husband, she makes very light of this operation, so it is very difficult to know its true seriousness.

31. There is no evidence on the subjects of her talks, or to whom she spoke, but when she spoke in public in Freetown her topics were usually Christian marriage and the education of African girls.

32. Anna Melissa Graves, *Benvenuto Cellini Had No Prejudice Against Bronze-Letters from West Africa* (Baltimore: Waverly Press, Inc., 1942), pp.32-6.

33. Priestly, *op. cit.*, pp.182-91.

34. One informant, a relative, gave a version quite different from that of Mrs. Casely Hayford yet this version seemed to have been the accepted one in Freetown.

> To her utmost surprise, shock, disgust, and despair when she arrived in Accra, the capital, about ten or more young women, well-dressed in native attire, came in individually at different times, as is the tribal custom, to welcome her, they each brought her gifts and introduced herself to her as Lawyer Hayford's wife. (Not as Mrs. Hayford for those who married according to the native fashion are just known as wives. Only Christian marriages are referred to as "Mrs." and there can only be one "Mrs."). The shock was too much for her so Mrs. Casely Hayford then booked the first available passage back home to Freetown.

> Another version is that Casely Hayford was married to the Queen of Tarkwa. The reference in his will to Princess Ambah Saah of Lower Warsaw followed by references to each of his children, Awura Abba and Awura Ambah before he mentions Mrs. Casely Hayford or Gladys gives some credence to this theory.

> There is also the theory that Mrs. Casely Hayford had had all she could accept when Mr. Casely Hayford wanted to bring another woman, probably the Princess, into their home to live!

Chapter VII

1. The *SLWN*, founded in September 1884 by the Reverend Joseph Claudius May, Principal of the Wesleyan Boys' High School, and edited by his brother, Cornelius, was strongly influenced by the ideas of Edward Blyden. According to Fyfe (p.496), the paper tended to approve anything distinctly African and to deplore slavish imitation of European ways. Its columns were open to the activities and ideas of Mrs. Casely Hayford, therefore the paper is the major source for data in this and the following chapters.

2. The Universal Negro Improvement Association and African Communities League, later separated and known more popularly as the Universal Negro Improvement Association, was organized in July 1914 in Jamaica, BWI and led by Marcus Garvey (1887–1940). Its premise was that race was the most importance value for Negroes, that Africa was for Africans and that the solution to the Negro question in the United States was to return to Africa.

3. The entire episode apparently caused considerable dissention within the Freetown community and was given much publicity in the press. Nevertheless, some points were left either unclear or unanswered. For example, the delegate to whom this action referred was never identified other than a being apparently the accredited member of

the Sierra Leone delegation to the Accra Conference. *SLWN* 6/12/20, p.8.
4. Mr. C.D. Hotobah During, a Freetown barrister, was frequently at odds with Mrs. Casely Hayford and her plans. He was later a member of the Legislative Council.
5. Adelaide Casely Hayford, "A Girls' School in West Africa," *Southern Workman*, October 1926, Vol. LV, No.10, pp.449-56.
6. Kathleen Easmon was very close to and extremely supportive of her aunt. She helped her in the starting of the school, went with her to America to raise funds for the school, and there is no telling what a different story Mrs. Casely Hayford's life would have been had not Kathleen married Simango and left with him to continue missionary work in East Africa.

Chapter VIII

1. Twin surname of the Apostle Thomas. Book of John, Chapter 11, v.16; Chapter 20, v.24; Chapter 21, v.2.
2. Actually The National Baptist Women's Convention.
3. Apparently, Mrs. Casely Hayford was unaware of the following exchange of letters which undoubtedly accounted for her warm welcome at Indianapolis:

September 3, 1920

Miss Nannie Burroughs
National Training School
Lincoln Heights, Washington, D.C.

My dear Miss Burroughs,
I am writing to you in connection with the visit to this city of Mrs. Casely Hayford and Miss Easmon who come in the interest of a proposed girls school to be established at Sierra Leone.
These ladies bear excellent credentials and their work according to all indications is one that is deserving of hearty support.
Through the kindness of Dr. Jordan of Philadelphia, they have been invited to attend the National Baptist Convention to be held in Indianapolis from September 10th to 14th – those I believe are the dates.
I am giving them a letter of introduction to you and I shall personally appreciate you seeing that they meet the right people and that they are given an opportunity to present their cause to the convention.

Very truly yours
Assistant Secretary

Before the convention there was a brief exchange of letters between Kathleen and Mr. Walter White, Assistant Secretary of the NAACP.

Foreign Mission Board
National Baptist Convention
701 S 19th St.,
Phila.,
Sept. 7, 1920

Dear Mr. White:
Thank you very much for sending us the letters of introduction as you promised.

We are leaving Philadelphia today and our address in Indianapolis will be c/o Dr. Jordan, 823 North West Street.

We should be ever so much obliged if you would kindly forward any mail that might come for us.

Thanking you in anticipation.

Yours sincerely,
Kathleen M. Easmon

Sept. 9, 1920

Miss Kathleen M. Easmon
c/o Dr. Jordan
833 North West Street
Indianapolis, Ind.

My dear Miss Easmon:

I am glad that you received the letters of introduction which I sent you and I sincerely trust that they will be of assistance to you in Indianapolis and Pittsburgh.

I am sending under separate cover, a number of letters which have been received addressed to you and Mrs. Hayford.

We are wishing you the grestest success at Indianapolis and other cities in the middle West.

Very truly yours,
Assistant Secretary

WEW. LGP
encl.

4. Nannie not Naomi.
5. Among the first impressive experiences Mrs. Casely Hayford had in the United States was attending this 20th Annual Meeting of the Women's Convention Auxiliary to the National Baptist Convention in Indianapolis, Indiana in 1920.

This group had been organized in 1901 in Richmond, Virginia. At the Indianapolis meeting Mrs. Casely Hayford met Miss Nannie Burroughs who was a founding member, at that time the Corresponding Secretary and later its second president from 1948 to 1961.

Miss Burroughs and Mrs. Casely Hayford apparently became quite attracted to one another. Mrs. Casely Hayford later visited the National Training School just outside of Washington, founded and directed by Miss Burroughs, and no doubt saw it as an exciting model for the kind of school she wished to develop in Freetown.

Like Mrs. Casely Hayford, Miss Burroughs was a very religious woman and according to one account "she often wrote and spoke about the power of Christian commitment and character to restore good to evil surroundings. In 1953 she penned a list of 13 keypoints she viewed as being essential to the pull up – of the Negro race ..." (Ethel M. Gordon, *Unfinished Business,* Detroit, Michigan, 1976, p.34.)

Miss Burroughs developed twelve principles which the Negro must do for himself, and one can see a marked similarity between them and the ideas espoused by Mrs. Casely Hayford. Miss Burroughs' principles were:

1. The Negro must learn to put first things first. The first things are: development of character traits; a trade; and home ownership.
2. The Negro must stop expecting God and white folks to do for him what he can do for himself.
3. The Negro must keep himself, his children, and his home clean and make the

surroundings in which he lives comfortable and attractive.

4. The Negro must learn to dress more appropriately for work and for leisure.
5. The Negro must make his religion an everyday practice and not a Sunday-go-to-meeting emotional affair.
6. The Negro must highly resolve to wipe out mass ignorance.
7. The Negro must stop charging his failures up to his 'color' and white peoples' attitude.
8. The Negro must overcome his bad job habits.
9. The Negro must improve his conduct in public places.
10. The Negro must learn how to operate business for people – not just for Negro people, only.
11. The average so-called educated Negro will have to come down out of the air. (He is too inflated over nothing. He needs an experience similar to the one Ezekiel had (Ezekiel 3: 14-19). And he must do what Ezekiel did.
12. The Negro must stop forgetting his friends. (Gordon, *op. cit.*, p.34.)

The Rev. Samuel J. Williams in *Gems of Rarest Rays Serene, A Running Resume of the Historical High-Lights. Characterizing the Past Sixty-Five Years of The Women's Convention, Auxiliary to the National Baptist Convention, U.S.A., Incorporated,* (Detroit: Harlq. Press, 1966), gave an impressive picture of Nannie Burroughs as a person whom Mrs. Casely Hayford would certainly want to emulate – "she was zealous in her passion for the enlightenment and uplifting of the womanhood of her race ... she was never afraid to venture ... she was not disobedient, just determined ... when she spoke, folks listened; where she led they followed" (pp.44-6).

Dr. Harrison, also quoted in Williams, described Miss Burroughs as "brilliant as a whip, as keen as a razor, as rugged as a cross saw, as stubborn as a mule, as impatient as a race horse, as steady as an ox, as wise as a serpent, but as harmless as a dove, as sweet as a rose, and as gentle as a lamb, so long as you do not rub the fur the wrong way. [She] forgives, but she never forgets" (p.46).

Little wonder that Mrs. Casely Hayford found Miss Burroughs to be the most exciting woman she met in the United States. It is ironic that even today Miss Burroughs is so little known outside Baptist circles.

6. A large collection of papers (c.135,000 items) of Nannie Helen Burroughs (1878–1961) has been donated to the Library of Congress (Manuscript Division). Unfortunately, there is no mention of Mrs. Casely Hayford or her visit to the school in any of these extant papers.

7. Kamba Simango was born around 1890 in Mashanga at the mouth of the Sabi River in Mozambique (Portuguese East Africa). When he was about thirteen he began working for Europeans in Beira. He became a student of the Missionary, Fred Bunker, for about 6 years; while at Bunker's mission school he met a Miss Julia Winter, a former Hampton Institute teacher who inspired him to come to the United States, which he did on 3 August 1914. He graduated from Hampton in 1919 and then enrolled at Columbia University.

Simango was very talented and apparently very charismatic. Tall, quite dark and very pleasant. I had the privilege of meeting him in Ghana where he spent most of his life as a contractor and as the husband of Christine Coussey by whom he had three children.

Later, on a visit to the United States, Mrs. Christine Simango and I visited Roland Hayes who remembered with much joy having heard Mr. Simango perform, as a singer.

8. The faculty had changed very little at Hampton since 1900 when Aunt Otelia made her visit there. See page 209.

9. Mrs. Casely Hayford is obviously somewhat confused about the American system of education and as is frequently the case with visitors from abroad, she does not

distinguish college from university or either from institute.

10. Mrs. Casely Hayford herself later joins the Moral Rearmament Movement, see p.194

11. Kombe is Kamba Simango.

12. This differentiating between Sierra Leone and the Protectorate was one which was common for many years among both Creoles and Protectorate citizens until independence. Sierra Leone for centuries was the name attached to the peninsula with its range of mountains like a crouching lion (Serra Lyoa in Portuguese). It was only much later that it was applied both to the peninsula and the hinterland Protectorate.

13. Dr. Solomon Fuller was born in Liberia and was the first black psychiatrist in the United States. He and Mrs. Fuller were the parents of three sons.

14. There is some confusion here as to which place – Philadelphia or New York – Mrs. Casely Hayford is actually referring to. See correspondence below with the Reverend Lloyd Imes.

15. There is little available information on Miss Mabel Carney but that supplied by Teachers College from K. Newman, Secretary to the President (8/23/72), indicates that she was at Columbia University from 1915, appointed as Instructor of Rural Education until she retired as Professor of Education in 1942. Her first degree was from the State Normal School, DeKalb, Ill., in 1903 and her subsequent degrees an A.B. in 1918 and an M.A. in 1919 from Columbia.

    The circumstances of her visit to Africa are not known. However, she did give courses to numbers of African students and missionaries including Kamba Simango.

16. Mrs. Casely Hayford apparently was trying to show her husband as well as her audience her African identity by wearing Fanti cloth. See page 123.

    An informant relative who met Simango and Kathleen in London after their marriage described him as "big tough guy in physique" and also added that her uncle, Dr. Edward Mayfield Boyle, a physician at the time in Baltimore and a relative of Mrs. Casely Hayford was "dead against the match" as he felt that

    > poor, dear, pretty, vivacious, brilliant, petite and very, very, delicate Kathleen had been sold down the river by late Aunt Hayford ... because of this match our late uncle and late Aunty Hayford ... were not on speaking terms and never did keep up correspondence up to their deaths. Strange to say late Kathleen used to remark that Uncle Boyzie and Aunty Hayford were at logger heads because Aunty Hayford was sort of heady.
    > Mrs. Edna Horton, 6/12/72

17. Tony Martin, *Race First, The Ideological and Organizational Struggles of Marcus Garvey and the Universal Negro Improvement Association* (Westport: Greenwood Press, 1976), p.116.

18. Hayford to Bruce, 23 November 1923, Bruce Papers 1–15 (Schomburg Collection, New York Public Library). Martin *op. cit.,* pp.94, 106.

19. Bruce to Florence his wife, 2 January 1924. Bruce Papers quoted in Martin, *op. cit.,* p.136.

20. Mrs. Casely Hayford may have known or heard of Dr. DuBois since both had studied in Germany at about the same time, but in any case, she not only sought his assistance in the United States but was one of the two people who introduced him to an enthusiastic audience on 27 January 1924 at Wilberforce Memorial Hall:

    > The President of the National Congress of British West Africa (Sierra Leone Section) Hon. C. May then called upon Mrs. Casely Hayford to support the remarks of Barrister Nelson Williams, and she in a brief speech engaged the audience's attention by describing Dr. DuBois and his work for the African Race, laying stress on the difficulties that the Doctor has had to contend with in different spheres.
    > *S.L.W.N.* 4/5/24, p.12.

21. Vol. 20, No.4. 8 August 1920, p.169.
22. Duse Mohammed Ali, half-black, half-Egyptian author, editor of *African Times & Orient Review*. According to Edmund David Cronon, *Black Moses, The Story of Marcus Garvey and the Universal Negro Improvement Association* (Madison: The University of Wisconsin Press, 1955, p.15), he was particularly interested in Africa but especially in the campaign for home rule in Egypt. And for a time he employed Marcus Garvey on his paper (p.43) and Garvey reciprocated later by employing him on his newspaper *The Negro World*.
23. WFW/LGP, Box 6. N.A.A.C.P. papers (Manuscript Division, Library of Congress).
24. JWJ/RR Box-C8 N.A.A.C.P. papers (Manuscript Division, Library of Congress).
25. Perhaps this is a reference to the meeting in Accra of the Congress of British West Africa.
26. The National Association of Colored Women – Thirteenth Biennial Session, Richmond, Va., 6-12 August. Sunday Afternoon 6 August 1922 (p.32).
27. Minutes of the League of Women for Community Service, Vol.III, p.221 (Radcliffe Archives).
28. *Ibid.*, p.222.
29. The Women's Service Club and the League of Women for Community Service are both old organizations of black women in Boston; the former is an outgrowth of, and to some extent competitive with, the latter. Each owns a rather impressive town house in Massachusetts Avenue in the South End of Boston, though the building owned by the League (558 Massachusetts Avenue) is architecturally and historically more outstanding, having been a station on the Underground Railroad.
30. Vol.23, No.5, p.222, 13 March 1922.
31. Vol.23, No.1, p.73, 2 May 1922.

Chapter IX

1. *SLWN*, 23 June 1923, p.9.
2. *Ibid.*, 24 January 1920, p.5.
3. *Ibid.*, 13 January 1923, p.5.
4. *Ibid.*, 10 March 1923, p.9.
5. Sumner, *Education in Sierra Leone, op. cit.*, p.194.
6. *SLWN*, 1 September 1923, p.9.
7. Her name more than that of any other one women as personage appeared in the colums of the *SLWN*. For example, on 5 April 1924, commenting on the recent activities around a meeting of the National Congress of British West Africa held in Freetown, special attention is given her in a news account as well as in an editorial.
   The news account read:

   But the speech of the day was that delivered by Mrs. Casely Hayford who appeared in native costume and warmed the audience by her peculiar eloquence as only those who have heard her know. She spoke of the duty of her *(...Microfilm illegible...)* in the development of a country and urged on the importance of training the children to self-help and the observance of Congress Day, March 28, as they do Empire Day, May 24th.

   The editorial (p.8) echoed her charge:
   a very important suggestion was made by Mrs. Casely Hayford in her inspiring speech last Friday week, when she urged that Congress Day should be a day for universal observance by every section of the African community and that it should be the Day of the people, as much precious to them as Empire Day is of importance to the Empire.

8. 28 February 1925, p.171.
9. 25 July 1925, pp.892-93.
10. 27 June 1927, p.1.
11. *SLWN*, 3 October 1925, p.11.
12. *Ibid.*, 16 January 1926, p.9.
13. *Ibid.*, 19 June 1926, p.4.
14. *Ibid.*, 3 July 1926, p.9.
15. She was Miss Elizabeth Torrey of Elberton, Georgia who later taught at Athens, Alabama.
16. There is some confusion in names here: above (p.134) she recalls Reverend Charles Martin of the Moravian Church in New York City as a friend and a West Indian; now she speaks of Reverend Charles Rakin, as the West Indian Pastor of the Moravian Church in New York. They could be two different persons or a printer's error.
17. In spite of her later feelings, Mrs. Casely Hayford initially was apparently accepted in Freetown as an authority on education. She is listed as the only African woman and one of three women on the 16-member Board of Education in 1924. See T.N. Goddard, *The Handbook of Sierra Leone:* Grant Richards Limited, London 1925. Appendix XV, p.291.
18. *SLWN*, 3 December 1927, p.6.
19. Nancie or Ananse stories are a type of African folktale, Ananse is a wise spider. Most West African folk tales refer to prehistoric times when animals and human beings lived together and had social relations within the same community.

    The most distinctive feature of these tales is that while the actors are animals, they speak and act as human beings in an animal environment or as animals in a human environment.

    The stories, almost always told by Mothers and Grandmothers in the evening around the fire, are a form of moral training. Many stories break off into song, one singing a line or two followed by a chorus. The narrative proceeds and again the solo and chorus are repeated.

    In Ghana, or the Gold Coast, the spider was a favorite actor, but in other areas the tales were woven around a variety of other animals – crabs, ants, chickens, chimpanzees, crocodiles, goats, elephants, hippopotami, snails, rats, etc.
20. *SLWN*, 13 April 1929, p.9.
21. *Ibid.*, 6 July 1929, p.12.
22. *Ibid.*, 23 November 1929, p.9.
23. *Ibid.*, 14 December 1929, p.5.

Chapter X

1. Anna Melissa Graves, *Benvenuto Cellini Had No Prejudice Against Bronze. Letters from West Africa.* Baltimore Md., Waverly Press, Inc., 1943. Little is known of Miss Graves other than that she had worked as a social worker at Sleighton Farms School for Girls, a correctional facility in Pennsylvania, from 1927 to 1928 and that to seek proof of the basic brotherhood of humanity, she went to West Africa in October 1930, where she met the several women whose letters to her she later edited.
2.   *Ears*

        When God made the world and all therein
        In a sad moment of great wistfulness
        And loneliness, He fashioned Him a man.
        "That he may cling," God said – and shaped
        his hands

"That he may laugh," God said – and made
his mouth,
Then paused debating, whether vision given
Would make the creature infinitely wise;
"That he may see," God said – and shaped
his eyes;
"That he may follow Me, until I choose that
we shall meet,"
God said – and gave the creature feet.

The finished creature, now with life imbued,
On the world's threshhold palpitating stood;
Whilst suns, stars, worlds, and moons about
him whirled,
The full creation, pulsing still being hurled
Into position by God's mighty Hand;
The cooling sea revolving the hot land.
Man started forward. "Turn to me" God
cried;
But man, who heard not, could not turn
aside,
Walked swiftly into life, bereft of fears.
God caught him back, and laughing made
him ears.

From the heart of conscience,
The path of silence,
The thunder of chaos,
The cycle of years,
The mystery of singin,
The whisper of angels,
The devil's shadow
God made the ears,
Then laughing at this modelled piece of
grace
Shaped question-wise and wondering what
use
Mortals would make of them, He kissed the
ears in place.

Graves *op. cit.*, p.45.

3. Beth Torrey.
4. The report Mrs. Casely Hayford would have given at the Geneva Conference to
which Gladys went as her substitute reflected most accurately and fully her educational philosophy. It was published in full in the 25 June (1932, pp.10-11) issue of the
Sierra Leone Weekly News. Her philosophy was based on certain basic premises, which
were in fact quite far ahead of her time – that you cannot alienate an African child
from his social and cultural environment in the process of educating him, if you wish
to have a strong and secure person and a strong and secure country. There must,
therefore, be instilled in every child "some pride of race, love of country, and pride in
their own colour." In a general way, she felt that education should receive far more
financial support than it did, that African arts and crafts should be emphasized, that
economic independence should be stressed through a more efficient use of the land
and that high priority should be given to the education of girls in Domestic Science.

To achieve the proper education, Mrs. Casely Hayford delineated 14 points for Freetown and a brief general recommendation or two for the Protectorate.

Her Recommendations for Freetown were:

1. Agriculture on a large scale (with Agricultural Banks), as well as other industries. This will give the people some economic independence, after which we might consider.

2. Trade Schools of all descriptions, for both sexes, as there would then be money to employ the artisans turned out by these schools.

3. A centre for higher literary education for both sexes, for those who are sufficiently advanced and capable of assimilating it. No race can thrive without writers, poets, artists, musicians. It is quite true that Fourah Bay College caters for an Arts Course with a degree as well as theological training. I would like to see a centre for Art as well Arts.

4. A large percentage of the Government revenue to be spent on education for the introduction of more Teachers' Training Colleges for both sexes, for every type of training. Without trained teachers we can never have good schools.

5. Better salaries for teachers, which would attract the highest class to the profession.

6. Schools for native arts and crafts staffed by specialists in every branch of African Art as a magnificent medium for fostering national outlook and pride of race.

7. More encouragement to well-educated Negroes of the right type to develop their initiative. A school entirely controlled by white people can never promote a national outlook in the mind of the African child. If a child is to retain his rightful heritage of an African individuality he must have qualified native teachers and leaders with a full understanding of our child psychology, and who would be encouraged to produce African textbooks, which would also bring about a better understanding between the races.

8. That well-educated intelligent Africans should be allowed to collaborate with Educational Advisory Board to the Colonial Office.

9. That more attention be paid to games and physical culture, and that music, singing, dancing, and acting should be encouraged rather than discouraged, as being splendid media for promoting a sense of social and communal values, which, after all, are the chief foundation of all African customs. These subjects add enormously to the health and happiness of the children. I found from experience in my little school that the children are far more ready to tackle the prosaic subjects of Reading, Writing, and Arithmetic, with the addition of these sweets. They are also far less troublesome, and respond to discipline much more easily. As a matter of fact, the severest punishment is to forbid them from participating in these subjects.

10. The breaking down of barriers which are being drawn so tightly round Government-Assisted Schools that by a few years' time the non-assisted schools will be extinct. The present system is perfectly justifiable when a school is not worthy of support, but otherwise is a death-blow to African enterprise which will eventually kill our soul.

11. The dissolution of the recent arrangements between the Government and the Missionaries, by which the latter become largely dependent, and cannot carry out their own inclinations.

12. That American Negroes of the right type should be allowed to settle in Africa, without the strict embargo that obtains at present.

13. And most important of all: that the education of the African girl should be taken seriously, for upon her depends the future of Africa.

14. That Schools for "Home Economics" which would turn out teachers for the existing schools should be instituted, so that a girl could get a thorough training

instead of the smattering she gets today. In connection with these schools, there
should be Training Homes for brides-to-be, where they would be properly
grounded into their duties as wives and mothers. A school for bridegrooms-to-be
would also be invaluable benefit.

Her Recommendations for the Protectorate were:

The greatest need is aboriginal teachers. How are they to be procured in a country
which is one vast illiteracy with the exception of the handful that have been trained in
the Mission Schools? I suggest this solution:

A great many aboriginal families now live in Freetown and some are engaged in
petty hawking and trading. Some of these children go to Mohammedan Schools,
which are not well organized. A few of the better-class daughters of chiefs go to the
Secondary School, but the great majority run wild about the town. I would like to see
some kind of Community Centre, where the girls would be taught the three R's;
simple hygiene, keeping their persons, the house, the compound clean; simple
domestic science and clean cooking; methods, tidiness, neatness; how to buy and sell
to the best advantage; how to cut their coat according to their cloth, instead of getting
into constant debt; elementary infant welfare, weaving and basketry. After a few years'
course, they could return to their own particular tribe as paid teachers. This presents
difficulties because girls get married so soon. Hence the necessity of beginning to
train them at an early age, so that from fourteen to seventeen they may do some useful
effective teaching amongst the members of their own tribe.

A travelling school would be a splendid suggestion for boys, who could learn better
methods of agriculture from an expert, as well as plain carpentry, etc.

5. The following poems by Gladys (Aquah Laluah), "West African Melodies",
appeared in *The Atlantic Monthly*, Vol.CXXXIX, January – June 1927, pp.489-90,
accompanied by this introduction on page 572:

"Aquah Laluah is a young African who studies for several years in Europe. She is a
member of an ancient African family and the granddaughter of a native king."

(Neither grandfather was a native king. De Graft Hayford was a minister and
William Smith, Jr., a civil servant.)

Nativity

Within a native hut, ere stirred the dawn,
Unto the Pure one was an Infant born;
Wrapped in blue lappah that His mother dyed,
Laid on His Father's home-tanned deerskin hide,
The Babe still slept, by all things glorified.
Spirits of black bards burst their bonds and sang
'Peace upon earth' until the heavans rang.
All the black babies who from earth had fled
Peeped through the clouds-then gathered round His head.
Telling of things a baby needs to do,
When first he opens his eyes on wonders new;
Telling Him that to sleep was sweetest rest,
All comfort came from His black mother's breast.
Their gift was Love, caught from the springing sod,
Whilst tears and laughter were the gifts of God.
Then all the Wise Men of the past stood forth,
Filling the air East, West, and South and North;
And told Him of the joy that wisdom brings
To mortals in their earthly wanderings.
The children of the past shook down each bough,

Wreathed frangipani blossoms for His brow;
They put pink lilies in His mother's hand,
And heaped for both the first fruits of the land.
His father cut some palm fronds, that the air
Be coaxed to zephyrs while He rested there.
Birds trilled their hallelujahs; all the dew
Trembled with laughter, till the Babe laughed too.
All the black women brought their love so wise,
And kissed their motherhood into His mother's eyes.

The Serving Girl

The calabash wherein she served my food
Was as smooth and polished as sandalwood;
Fish, as white as foam from the sea,
Peppered, and golden fried for me;
She brought palm wine, that carelessly slips
From the sleeping palm tree's honeyed lips.
But who can guess, or even surmise,
Of the countless things she served with her eyes?

The Souls of Black and White

The souls of black and white were made
By the selfsame God of the selfsame shade.
God made both pure, and He left one white;
God laughed o'er the other, and wrapped it in night.

Said he, "I've a flower, and none can unfold it;
I've a breath of great mystery, nothing can hold it.
Spirit so illusive the wind cannot sway it,
A force of such might even death cannot slay it."

But so that He might conceal its glow
He wrapped it in darkness, that men might not know
Oh, the wonderful souls of both black and white
Were made by one God, of one sod, on one night.

6. During the summers of 1972, 1974 and 1979 interviews were conducted with numerous persons who knew or who were related to Mrs. Casely Hayford, all of whom are mentioned in the Preface.
7. Graves, ... *Letters from West Africa, op. cit.*, 2/18/31, p.35.
8. *Ibid.*, 5/1/31, pp.37-8.
9. *Ibid.*, f.n., pp.37-8.
10. *Ibid.*, p.59.
11. *Ibid.*, 6/27/31, p.41.
12. Humphrey Ballanta, apparently a singer of some note who was in Africa at the time. While Gladys probably told Miss Graves about him, Dr. Easmon, Mrs. Casely Hayford herself and Beth Torrey ("if Gladys loved Humphrey, and he her, I cannot understand why she did not defy her mother to marry him" p.57) (3/532 to Miss Graves) did not see it as an important affair. It is more likely that Gladys carried a torch for him that was not, in fact, reciprocated.
13. Graves, *op. cit.*, p.34.
14. This romance did seem to be the crux of serious difficulty between Gladys and her mother. The man, called "Big Boy," was a member of the troop, was all that Mrs.

Casely Hayford says he was or was not and he and Gladys were in love and planned to marry. Mrs. Casely Hayford did write him "an insulting letter" which we have never seen, but probably merely included what she herself said to Miss Graves. It is quite likely that the letter was not the real reason for the break-up ... which he initiated. It was Gladys' going to Ruskin. Gladys says he encouraged her to do so, and that is probably true, but once she had left him and the troop either his ardor cooled or he reassessed the correctness of Mrs. Casely Hayford's letter.

15. Graves, *op. cit.*, pp.34-5.
16. Lloyd G. Oxley, *The Black Man in the World's Literature: Gladys May Hayford (1906–) Poet.* Starr Papers, special collections, Mugar Library, Boston University.
17. This is particularly ironic since Mrs. Casely Hayford in her 1 May 1931 letter to Miss Graves states: "Mr. Oxley called three times on Saturday and finally found me in after dinner. I thoroughly enjoyed my chat with him, but like Mr. Chorleton ever so much better." Graves, p.38.
18. Graves, *op. cit.*, 8/7/31, p.49.
19. *Ibid.*, 7/11/31, p.42.
20. A.G. Fraser, Principal of Achimota School in Accra, Gold Coast.
21. Graves, *op. cit.*, 7/24/31, p.4.
22. *Ibid.*, 10/12/31, p.52.
23. *Ibid.*, 12/5/31, p.53.
24. *Ibid.*, 12/18/31, p.54.
25. *Ibid.*, 3/9/32, p.55.
26. Defense mania, a psychiatric term, implying the building up by a patient of an extreme behavior pattern against certain perceived threats.
27. Graves, *op. cit.*, p.66.
28. *Ibid.*, 4/23/32, pp.63-4.
29. *Ibid.*, 3/22/32, pp.56-7.
30. *Ibid.*, 4/21/32 p.60.
31. *Ibid.*, 5/4/32 pp.60-1.
32. *Ibid.*, 6/6/32, p.69.
33. *Ibid.*, 6/28/32, p.71.
34. *Ibid.*, 11/16/32, p.73.
35. *Ibid.*, 8/81/33, p.75.
36. *Ibid.*, 4/28/36 p.80.
37. *Ibid.*, 11/23/36 pp.82-3.
38. *Ibid.*, 1/10/42, p.85.
39. *Ibid.*, 11/7/42, p.87.
40. *Ibid.*, 7/14/31, p.92; 7/15/31, p.94.
41. *Ibid.*, 7/10/31, p.90.
42. *Ibid.*, 7/14/31, p.93.
43. *Ibid.*, 7/15/31, pp.94-5.
44. *Ibid.*, 7/21/31, p.96.
45. *Ibid.*, 8/28/31, p.100.
46. *Ibid.*, 7/15/31, p.95.
47. *Ibid.*, 7/15/31, p.95.
48. *Ibid.*, 9/20/36, p.108.
49. *Ibid.*, 7/15/31, p.94.

Chapter XI

1. *SLWN*, 8/30/30, p.12.
2. *Ibid.*, 9/13/30, p.27.

3. Even so, she apparently did not want to admit her rejection.

Mr. Casely Hayford's will was executed at Seccondee (Sekondi) on 20 September 1913, when their marriage was ostensibly still strong but probably revealing to him, at least, the differences between the two of them. In any case, the will is a five and a half page single spaced typed document which is clearly designed to meet his responsibilities and allegiances based on both customary or native law and western or civil law.

There is no mention of Mrs. Casely Hayford until the top of page two after mention has been made of Archibald, his son by his previous marriage (by Western standards), one niece, two nephews, Princess Ambah Saah (apparently his wife by customary law), two daughters – Awura Abba and Awura Amba (probably by the Princess) – and a cousin, Awura Abba Brew.

In sum, Mrs. Casely Hayford seems to have been the beneficiary not only after other relatives, but in terms of cash and insurance after other kinds of bequests to institutions and in the form of scholarships in memory of his brother and first wife. And when Mrs. Casely Hayford is remembered, it is on a shared basis: "I direct that the surplus of the said money shall be divided into three equal parts, two of which shall be paid to said Archibald Casely Hayford absolutely and the remaining part shall go to my wife Adelaide Casely Hayford for the *maintenance of herself and my daughter Gladys Mary Casely Hayford"!* And should Gladys die, then Mrs. Casely Hayford would only get one half of that one third! He leaves a house to Gladys. But Archibald was to inherit almost all of his real property and furniture – except that going to princess Saah and his above mentioned daughters.

He also remembers by name another natural son, Danison Alfred Hayford (who interestingly does not have the Casely attached to his name). And he asks that "he be buried beside his beloved wife Beatrice Madeline Casely Hayford in the Public Cemetery at Axim."

4. A close reading of the will reveals he did not have to *take* anything from his father's estate, as most of it was, in fact, willed to him but at a time when he would have been too young to influence his father.
5. Mrs. Charlotte Wright interview, 5/30/72.
6. *SLWN,* 11/24/28.
7. *Ibid.,* 2/9/29.
8. *Ibid.,* 5/5/30, p.5.
9. *Ibid.,* 1/10/31, p.9.
10. *Ibid.,* 2/14/31, p.9.
11. *Ibid.,* 2/21/31, p.9.
12. My assumption is that the group of Negro women to whom she refers is the League of Women for Community Service, to which Mrs. Maude Cuney Hare belonged and before which Mrs. Casely Hayford spoke, but I could not find any mention of this commitment in their extant minutes.
13. *SLWN,* 5/30/31, p.12.
14. *Ibid.,* 1/9/32.
15. This is the same Miss Graves, of course, with whom Mrs. Casely Hayford had the protracted correspondence.
16. *SLWN,* 6/25/32, p.8.
17. *Ibid.,* 9/3/32, p.5.
18. *Ibid.,* 5/24/34.
19. *Ibid.,* 8/23/34.
20. Graves, ... *Letters from West Africa, op. cit.,* p.57.
21. This entire quote came from a letter to me from Mrs. Constance Cummings-John who was related to Mrs. Casely Hayford through marriage. Mrs. Casely Hayford's sister, Bea, was married to Mr. Awooner Renner, a maternal uncle of Mrs. Cummings-John.

22.   *Creole Lullaby* (translation)

> She held her brown baby tightly to her back
> (Hush my son, do not cry)

> But the wrapper (ojah) got loose
> and the baby fell down with a whack
> (Hush, my son do not die!)

23. Sumner, *Education in Sierra Leone op. cit.*
24. Sumner, *op. cit.*, pp.194-5.
25. Mason, ... *Girls' Secondary Education in Sierra Leone, op. cit.*, p.9.
26. Mrs. Casely Hayford, now well along in years, had probably forgotten just when Mrs. Osora left her. Other evidence suggests, as reported above, that it was when she was in the States that Mrs. Osora left.
27. Again, we have the problem of Mrs. Casely Hayford's memory in contrast to what actually happened. She is not reporting on the trip to England when she also went by the *Wahehe* to get Gladys. The treatment she received in 1935 by a German crew was the third time she had been on a German ship. She is obviously contrasting this latest trip with the discrimination she had suffered so many years previously. But she just chose to overlook one trip to make her point.
28. This was Mrs. Casely Hayford's introduction to the Oxford Group of Moral Rearmament as it is officially called. She became one of the many Africans attracted to it and carried the word back to Freetown.

    According to Padmore (George Padmore, *Pan Africanism or Communism*, Garden City, New York, Anchor Books, pp.343-4), Moral Re-Armament (MRA) was:

    > since the outbreak of the cold war ... the most formidable challenger to the Communists in the colonial field ... the only organization ... able to make headway against Communist infiltration in Africa ...
    > An MRA Task Force toured West Africa in 1953 to propagate the "Four Absolutes" of its American founder, Dr. Frank Buchman, "absolute honesty, absolute unselfishness, absolute purity and absolute love ..."
    > Their success was apparently phenomenal in Nigeria, less so but still effective in the then Gold Coast.

    And while Padmore notes MRA also in South Africa and Northern Rhodesia (Zambia), he makes no mention of Sierra Leone, but it is easily seen how its influence might have affected this small British West African colony with a group of sufficient education and sophistication to be receptive to ideas from abroad.

    The lure of a trip to the United States, to Makinac, Michigan, or to Caux in Switzerland was a great temptation to people from all walks of life and especially to a person like Mrs. Casely Hayford who was spiritually inclined, European oriented and well travelled.
29. Undoubtedly, she is referring to her earlier visit when she went to the hospital in Oxford to get Gladys. One wonders why she would include this reference at all, especially without more explanation.
30. See note 21 above.
31. Langston Hughes, *An African Treasury, Articles, Essays, Stories, Poems by Black Africans*, New York: Pyramid Books, pp.132-40.

APPENDIX

INCOMPLETE GENEALOGY OF ADELAIDE SMITH CASELY HAYFORD

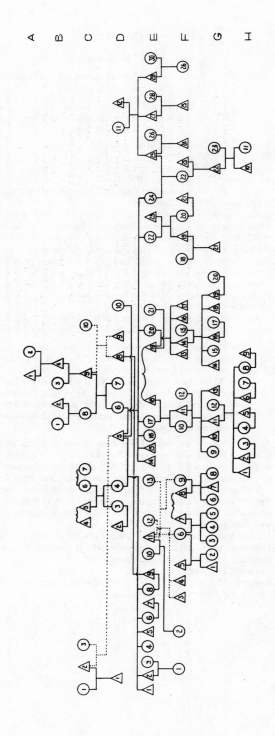

KEY

A.
1. Well-known English surgeon
2. African woman

B.
1. Betsy Carew
2. Thomas Carew
3. Elizabeth Fowler (Maroon)
4. George Spilsbury

C.
1. English woman
2. William Smith, Sr.
3. Fanti woman
4. Governor Macaulay
5. Kenneth Macaulay
6. recaptive African girl
7. recaptive African girl
8. Hannah Carew
9. Joseph Green Spilsbury
10. African woman

D.
1. Frederick Smith
2. Reverend Robert Dillon
3. Margaret Macaulay
4. Charlotte Macaulay
5. William Smith Jr.
6. Anne Spilsbury Smith
7. Elizabeth Spilsbury
8. Thomas Spilsbury
9. Henry Spilsbury
10. Elizabeth Jewell Smith – the third Mrs. Smith
11. Mary Awuraba
12. The Reverend de Graft Hayford

E.
1. William Henry Smith
2. Dr. Robert Smith
3. Daughter of Governor Chilley Pine
4. Charlotte Smith
5. John Frederick Smith
6. Mary Smith
7. Dr. William Broughton Davies
8. Philippa Smith
9. Thomas Spilsbury (also D8)
10. European lady
11. Judge Francis Smith
12. Elizabeth Blankson
13. Eva Lumpkin
14. Joseph Smith
15. Thomas Smith
16. Emma Smith
17. Elizabeth Smith Awoonor Renner
18. Dr. William Jarvis Awoonor Renner
19. Mr. Peter Awoonor Renner (Barrister)
20. Hannah Smith Awoonor Renner
21. Beatrice Franklyn Awoonor Renner
22. Annette Smith Easmon
23. Dr. John Farrell Easmon
24. Adelaide Smith Casely Hayford
25. Joseph Ephraim Casely Hayford
26. Beatrice Pynoch Casely Hayford
27. Ernest Casely Hayford
28. wife of Ernest
29. Mark Casely Hayford
30. wife of Mark

F.
1. Chilley Smith
2. unknown daughter of Francis Smith
3. Robert Smith
4. William Smith
5. Joseph Peter Brown-Pobee
6. Charlotte Smith Brown Pobee Wright
7. Dr. Jenner Wright
8. Claude Wright (Barrister)
9. Eva Smith Wright
10. A Calabar woman
11. Judge Roland Awoonor Renner
12. Theresa Smith Awoonor Renner
13. Charles Awoonor Renner (Barrister)
14. William Awoonor Renner (Barrister)
15. Ada Hebron Awoonor Renner
16. Ernest Awoonor Renner (died in infancy)
17. Walter Awoonor Renner (died in infancy)
18. Enid Sawyer Easmon
19. Dr. M.C.F. Easmon
20. Kathleen Easmon Simango
21. Kamba Simango
22. Gladys Casely Hayford Hunter
23. Arthur Hunter
24. Archibald Casely Hayford
25. Samuel Collins Hayford
26. Mary Hayford Edmondson

G.
1. ... Brown-Pobee (died in infancy)
2. Josephine Brown Pobee Karefa-Smart
3. Dr. Sophie Wright Ramanokoto
4. Margaret Wright
5. Grace Wright
6. Eva Wright
7. Dr. Claude Wright
8. Frances Wright (Barrister)
9. Lelia Ann Spilsbury Awoonor Renner Culerick
10. Dr. Culerick
11. Dr. Edward ("Teddy") Awoonor Renner
12. Carmela Pitt Awoonor Renner (West Indian)
13. Charles Awoonor Renner
14. Ernest Awoonor Renner
15. American woman
16. Raymond Awoonor Renner (Barrister)
17. Marilyn ... Awoonor Renner
18. Dr. Walter Awoonor Renner
19. Donald Awoonor Renner
20. Anne King Awoonor Renner
21. Dr. Charles Syrett Easmon
22. Kobina "Kobe" Sydney Hunter
23. Lucilda Yema Caulker Hunter

H.
1. Dr. Noren Awoonor Renner
2. Louis Awoonor Renner
3. Edna Barnes Awoonor Renner
4. Archie Awoonor Renner
5. Helen Akiwumi Awoonor Renner
6. Egerton Luke
7. Elizabeth Awoonor Renner Luke
8. Mark Hunter
9. Jessie Hunter

INDEX